book.

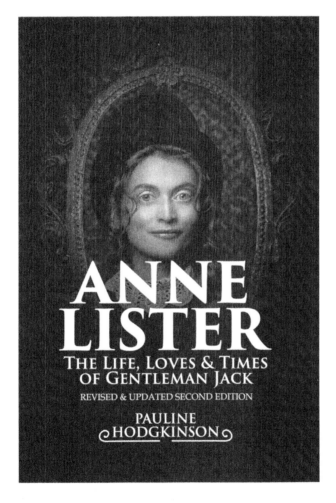

ANNE LISTER

The Life, Loves & Times of Gentleman Jack

REVISED & UPDATED SECOND EDITION

PAULINE HODGKINSON

TABLE OF CONTENTS

"I am resolved not to let my life pass without some private memorial that I may hereafter read, perhaps with a smile, when Time has frozen up the channel of these sentiments which flow so freely now."

Anne Lister, Journal entry 19th February 1819

THE LIFE, LOVES & TIMES OF MISS ANNE LISTER

Anne Lister has been described as a larger-than-life heroine, a firebrand who stubbornly defied convention, and lived her life how she wanted to live it. To some, she was a 19th-century intellectual, traveller, and diarist. To others a landed gentry entrepreneur. She has been described as the Byronic heroine, highly intelligent and perceptive, magnetic, mysterious, and charismatic, arrogant, and self-centred. To some viewers of the television drama 'Gentleman Jack', a scandalous, promiscuous lesbian.

Throughout history there have been notable people and events, which have been sadly consigned to relative obscurity. Sometimes a chance discovery can reignite interest, and in a few instances that chance encounter can excite the world to lament the faded memory of that notable person, or that event lost in time. One such person is Anne Lister a woman of substance who defied convention, prejudice and the limitations forced upon women of her age.

Anne Lister first came to the attention of the populace with the much-acclaimed BBC One and HBO production dramatization, giving us the audience an insight into her adventurous, and eventful life. The first, eight-part serial, that premiered on 22nd April 2019 in the United States, and in the United Kingdom on 19th May 2019 was created and written by the celebrated screenwriter, producer, and director, Sally Wainwright OBE. Just two years in the life of Anne Lister was revealed in all its colourful exuberance to a global audience of millions. Her life and the way in which she conducted herself has inspired a modern generation of women to be true to their self, to be the best they can be, and to have courage to do the things which pleases them.

Born in the 18th century into a landed Yorkshire family, Anne Lister lent herself to education and knowledge, something which was not possible for most women of that time. Before the dawning of the 20th century, education was limited for women in Britain, and even claimed to be dangerous to their brain. Of course, we know today that the restrictions had more to do with the control of women rather than a health issue. This situation continued even after the early 1900's, as disadvantaged women from the lower classes were, with a few exceptions, unable to access a good education. Anne's position in society enabled her to fly in the face of convention to absorb knowledge, especially subjects traditionally reserved for men with which to improve her social standing.

There have been many outstanding women throughout history who have achieved much through their dogged determination and strength of character. Though we know what they accomplished, we do not know their innermost thoughts, how they behaved, how they conducted their lives, the places, and people they met and their intimate relationships. Through a collection of journals, written by Anne Lister, parts of which were once deemed so shocking that they were considered for destruction, they allow us the privilege to know about Anne's life, her achievements, her innermost thoughts, her intimate affairs, and the times in which she lived.

What was so revealing and offensive for some who read her text, was the fact that Anne was a Lesbian, a woman who loved only women, who had several affairs and many flirtations, which she describes with the most intimate detail. There amongst the day-to-day accounts of her life she also exposed the inner self of a masculine woman, and how she coped with the pressures of being different. We are given the privilege of witnessing what she was able to achieve, not only in her private life but in her business dealings, the like of which was unheard of some two hundred years ago.

Her Journals have been a revelation; they prove that lesbianism was alive and flourishing, even though such interactions were unspoken yet not unknown. The journals represent some of the earliest and certainly the most thorough documentation of upper-class lesbian lives available to historians. Lesbian was not a word known to exist, the act was unspoken and rarely written about, it was a subject that if mentioned would be in whispers and most people would be horrified to learn if such a thing existed. Anne Lister not only consciously analysed her sexuality, but she interacted sexually and emotionally with a broad network of women drawn from both the gently and aristocracy.

Anne Lister's diaries record details of her daily life in meticulous detail, and much is still waiting to be deciphered, which surely will reveal even more astounding facts from this truly fascinating and extraordinary woman. We can learn of her rigorous program of work and study, the weather, the purchase of clothing and everyday items, days out, trips around the country, and travels abroad, meals consumed at home or when traveling, the price paid for numerous merchandise and accounts of petty disagreements between the provincial gentry are all laid out before us.

Lister devised a code that would enable her to write what she pleased without worry that her innermost thoughts could be known by anyone other than herself. The coded sections, which occupy around one-sixth of the diaries, document her most personal thoughts and experiences. Anne used a mixture of Latin and Greek letters and mathematical symbols, with each sign corresponding to equivalent ones in the Roman alphabet. It can be assumed that Lister did not intend the coded passages to be read during her lifetime. Her code hand hid the private, intimate details of her life and its inner subjectivity.

Lister chronicles, in her private code, a series of intense and overlapping lesbian relationships, sexual desire and practice, with erotic sensuality. Her code allowed her to describe in secret her liaison's and with whom she explores the act of sex, and the results of those experiences, whether they give pleasure and satisfaction to herself and/or her partners.

She records with heartfelt sorrow the hurt and pain living with the reality of personal rejection by being different, or less feminine than what was expected of her gender. Anne must have cut a curious figure striding out through the streets, and across the moors wearing black, her chosen colour to represent both her masculine disposition and the sense of loss she felt after her one true love married a man. She was considered unusual, even odd, her unconventional choices made her different, but she could not or wished not to change herself... *"It is natural not made up or put on..."* and whilst courting respectability, she refused to conform to what society expected of a woman.

THE LISTER FAMILY

Even as a young child Anne Lister appreciated her heritage and the position in society that her ancient lineage could afford her. With her eye on owning the ultimate prize, Shibden Hall her ancestral home, and the lands and properties which belonged to the estate, Anne was tireless in her efforts to reinvent herself to attain the position in life that she believed was owed to her by birth.

Captain Jeremy Lister (1752–1836)

Anne's father, Jeremy was one of eight children of Jeremiah and Ann (Hall) Lister. Jeremy was born in the ancestral home of Shibden Hall, West Yorkshire, England in 1752. Aged eighteen Jeremy was commissioned on 26th December 1770 as an ensign with the 10th Regiment of Foot, sent to Canada and later stationed at Fort Niagara he fought the American rebels in the first battle of the War of Independence in Lexington and Concord, Massachusetts, where he was wounded in the right elbow. Once in Canada he took up the flute, his elder brother James wrote to ask him to cease playing the flute and take up the violin. He was given the incredibly sad news his sister Phoebe had died and was the second member of the family to die of consumption in two years. With cold detachment young Jeremy wrote back... *'Very sorry to hear of my sister's death, but it is what we must all submit ourselves to either sooner or later...'*

The British regiments became constant targets, the perpetrators native Indians, wolves, or furious colonists. Jeremy was to record some of the happenings and skirmishes his regiment encountered. His book *'Concord Fight'* published by Harvard University Press/Oxford University Press is a remarkable record of the day-to-day battles including major confrontations in Boston, Concord, and Lexington.

Jeremy was promoted to Captain on the 17th February 1781 before returning home with the defeated British in 1783. In 1788 aged thirty-five, he married eighteen-year-old Rebecca Battle and later resigned his commission and returned to civilian life. Anne was two years old when Jeremy used Rebecca's inheritance to buy Skelfler estate in Market Weighton a small town and civil parish in the East Riding of Yorkshire. The estate consisted of a modest house named Skelfler along with the surrounding fields and two leased-out properties Low Grange Farm, Grange Farm, and farmyards. The family moved into Skelfler Farm in 1793. Later Jeremy sold his commission he began farming.

In 1808, Jeremy, with his family left the Skelfler House (now known as Skelfrey Park Farm) due to his foolish spending and financial difficulties, which left him unable to afford the cost of running and maintaining the property. Jeremy took his family to Halifax where he rented St Helen's House, North Bridge owned by the Lister estate. The Skelfler property was let out to a tenant and much of its farming equipment sold. Jeremy died at the family estate Shibden Hall in 1836.

Rebecca Battle (1770- 1817)

Rebecca Battle, Anne's mother born in 1770 came from North Cave in the East Riding of Yorkshire. She was Baptised on the 22nd of Sep 1770. Baptism Place: Welton With Melton, York, England. Her father was William Battle, Mother, Rebecca (Fearn) Battle. Rebecca took to drink in her later years, which caused her family a great deal of upset and pain. She died in 1817 and buried in Market Weighton, East Riding of Yorkshire.

Jeremy and Rebecca had six children:

1. John (b 1789) died at the age of 7 weeks
2. Anne (1791 – 1841)
3. Samuel (1793- 1813)
4. John (1795-1810)
5. Marian (1798-1882)
6. Jeremy (b 1801) who died at the age of 5 months

While Jeremy, Anne's father was stationed in Galway, Ireland in 1789, Rebecca gave birth to her first child, John who died at the age of 7 weeks. When she fell pregnant a second time Rebecca returned to Halifax as her pregnancy advanced. Their second child was born in St Helen's House, New Bank. Rebecca produced a daughter on 3rd April 1791, she was named Anne, after her twenty-six-year-old aunt... *"she who took me on her lap the moment I was born, gave me the first food I ever tasted, lifted me within the pale of Christianity"*.

Anne Lister had joined through birth, Halifax's small-scale gentry, though at the time of her birth her branch of the family had little in the way of wealth, unlike the orthodox Lister dynasty, tenants of the ancestral home Shibden Hall.

Out of their six children, only she, her younger sister Marian and her brother Samuel survived into adulthood.

There was no abundance in Anne Lister's household, money was tight and luxuries few. Jeremy earned relatively little and had always spent his money frivolously. Age had not necessarily made him wise, especially in business, and he had incurred a great deal of debt. Years of giving orders and accustomed to rough army life, his refinement had diminished, he lacked the refinement expected of a gentleman. He was too familiar with the wrong kind of people, particularly those of a lower rank and social class. He was well known both for his lack of social graces and for drinking with the lower classes. His inability to prosper must have affected the respect that Anne might have held for her father, being an astutely intelligent child, she would have been aware of his failings.

Anne and her mother did not get on well: at least, Anne did not seem to have much respect for her mother. Rebecca found Anne's conduct unacceptable and unmanageable, Anne seemed to deliberately go out of her way to be obstructive and to be defiant and unbending to her mother's wishes until Rebecca was almost at her wit's end to know how to control Anne's behaviour. According to Anne's diary and correspondence, alcoholism progressively destroyed the health and social abilities of her mother who featured rarely in the diary entries.

When Marian, Anne's sister was born, seven-year-old Anne also benefitted from her mother's excess milk... *"my mother had nursed me when my sister was born,* Anne recalled... *"She had too much milk. I liked it exceedingly"*

Anne's sister, Marian Lister was born 13th October 1798, she was the second daughter of Captain Jeremy and his wife Rebecca. Baptism: 16th Oct 1798 in Market Weighton. Marian seemed to get on better with their father than Anne did, she did not appear to find his rough manners offensive.

Anne and her sister Marian never really bonded, they loved each other as siblings do but they had little in common. Marian unlike her sister Anne did not have as much enthusiasm for knowledge, she did not share the same pursuits or ambitions to better herself. In Anne's eyes, Marian had a foolish soft spot in her heart for hard-pressed tenants and parted too freely with her money. It must have been difficult for Marian growing up and living in the shadow of a clever, more outgoing, and more forceful personality like her sibling Anne.

The last remaining Lister son, Samuel was born in 1793. If he had lived, he would have inherited Shibden from his uncle James. He and Anne where close, she wrote to him... *"you my dear Sam, are the last remaining hope and stay of an old, but lately drooping family. Seize it in its fall Renovate its languid energies; rear it with a tender hand and let it once more bloom upon the spray. Ah! let the well-ascended blood that trickles in your veins stimulate the generous enthusiasm of your soul, and prove it is not degenerated from the spirit of your ancestors"*
They rode their horses together and relished in each other's company. Anne being a boisterous, exuberant, and spirited personality was the perfect companion. As children, Anne loved to play the games more suited to boys, rough, energetic, masculine pursuits such as fencing with wooden swords and climbing. One of their calmer games was chess where Anne would pit herself against Sam, two years her junior, another competing tournament was translating passages from Latin, Anne would always be victorious.

Being a boy and the last remaining son, Samuel was next in line to inherit Shibden Hall their ancestral home. Uncle James paid his school fees to ensure he got a good education in readiness for his ultimate role. It was a result of Samuel's death that Anne Lister being the eldest daughter would eventually inherit the 400-acre Shibden Hall estate, in 1826, on the death of her uncle.

OWNERS OF SHIBDEN HALL

Shibden Hall, originally called Schepdene (meaning Valley of the sheep) was built around 1420 by William Otes/Oates, (b1399) a wealthy sheep farmer and cloth merchant who was part of a prominent family from Southowran. The arms of the family a black cross and crosslets can be seen on a windowpane at Shibden Hall.

The property passed through to his grandson William, then his half-sister before it was subsequently lived in by the wealthy Savile family after a court case that took place sometime between 1491 and 1504. The judgement meant that the property passed to Joan (nee oats) Savile who had entered the Savile family through marriage, later passing ownership to the Waterhouse family. Shibden Hall was inherited by Sir Edward Waterhouse who was forced to sell to stave off impending bankruptcy. It was bought by Caleb Waterhouse a cousin who was later bankrupt in 1614, who then sold it to a member of the Hemingway family cousins of the Listers.

This was John Hemingway, (1602-1615) son of Robert and Edith (née Lister) Hemingway whose aunt Mrs Jane Crowther (nee Hemingway), bought Shibden Hall from Caleb Waterhouse for the sum of £1,600 pounds in the year 1612 on John's behalf as he was underage. After both his aunt and father's death in 1615, John still being underage was made ward of the crown and his uncle Samuel Lister was appointed guardian to John and his four sisters, but when John later died in 1615 still underage, Shibden Hall passed to his sisters.

In 1614, Samuel Lister (1570-1632) a clothier was the tenant at Shibden Hall, son of Thomas Lister, he married Susan Drake in 1598 and they produced seven children. Samuel owned coal mines on the estate, and served as High Constable of Halifax, and governor of Heath Grammar School. The Hemingway children, John, Sibella, Edith, Phebe, and Martha, went to live with Samuel's family when he was appointed their guardian after their father's death.

The marriage of Samuel's sons to their cousins, brought Shibden into the Lister family ownership. Samuel Lister's eldest son, Thomas (1599-1677) married his cousin, Sybil Hemingway, followed in 1625 by another son, John, marrying Phoebe Hemingway. The girls who had inherited Shibden Hall had to relinquish their ownership to the Lister family. The Lister owners became one of the chief landowning families of Halifax, England in the late eighteenth and nineteenth centuries.

The estate then passed down through two further generations: both with the name Samuel, the first (1623-1694) who married Ester Oates, heiress of the Oates family. The second (1673-1702) married Dorothy Presley. The latter inherited Shibden in 1694, dying without an heir in 1702.

On Samuel's death, Shibden passed on to James Lister. An unsuccessful challenged regarding the ownership was made by Richard Sterne on the grounds that the hall belonged to the late Samuel's widow, Dorothy Presley who he had himself married on the 16th of November 1703, but James was successful in gaining ownership in 1709.

Dr James Lister (1673-1729) was an apothecary who made and sold medicines at his shop near Hall End, Halifax. He married Mary Issot in May 1699. The family later fell into financial difficulties trying to support twelve children -- John, Samuel, James, Thomas, William, Jeremiah, Martha, Mary, Phebe, Joseph and Japhet. Their first born, also called Samuel died soon after birth. The upkeep of Shibden must have been a drain on James's resources.

Reverend John Lister (1703-1759) eldest son of James Lister, was appointed first Headmaster of Bury Grammar School (1730-1740) he remained a bachelor, dying on Sunday September 2nd, 1759 in a hunting accident when he was out riding with Mr. William Walker, of Crow Nest. It appears that John was talking with his companion when he was seized with an apoplexy and dropped dead from his horse, the ownership of the Hall then passed to his brothers James (1705-1763) and then Samuel (1706-1768).

Jeremiah Lister (1713-1788) was a son of James Lister of Lower Brea, Leeds Road, a 27-acre part of the Shibden Hall estate. Jeremiah married Ann Hall in 1744.

In June 1735 Jeremiah, who eventually became Anne's grandfather, followed his brother, Thomas who had left in 1733 to travel to Virginia, to seek his fortune and after which he hoped to raise the sagging fortunes of Shibden Hall. After emigrating to the American colonies, their plans were to go into the tobacco trade. Thomas's disastrous three-quarters purchase of a sloop named 'Yorkshire Defiance,' and their plan to transport pork and pickle to the West Indies in exchange for rum and sugar was a failure. After living in Virginia for 12 months Jeremiah returned to Britain in December 1736.

In December 1736, brother William (1712–1743) also sailed to Virginia following in the footsteps of his brothers Thomas and Jeremiah. William set up home in Appomattox and in 1738 he married Susanna Lewis, sister of Thomas's wife Anne, they had two children. In his correspondence with Jeremiah who was then living back in Yorkshire, William had the idea that deerskins would be a valuable commodity in Halifax, however the skins they purchased were ruined because Thomas had not strewn them with tobacco. What might have been a profitable shipload left William with a huge loss. Disaster continued for the brothers for in a letter to Jeremiah, in Halifax, William wrote... *'You must know Thomas has purchased about 3,000 bushels of wheat...There is a report raised in Virginia that the sloop was seized in Cadiz upon the account of money on board..."*

After this setback William decided that North Carolina would prove a more profitable base and moved to New Berne on the Neuse River. Writing to his sister Phoebe in Halifax he lamented the fact that he had lost his only companion, his brother Thomas who died of distemper in August 1740, a situation so familiar to immigrants in an often-hostile land. Thomas's widow Anne had been left with four children.

William later drowned along with two negro slaves on the 21^{st of} October 1743 as he returned from collecting goods which had been sent from Shibden Hall. The letter that widowed Susanna wrote in 1743, with the news of her sudden bereavement, to the family in Halifax is on display at Shibden Hall.

James Lister (1748-1826) being the eldest son of Jeremiah Lister, inherited Shibden Hall from his father. James never married and lived at Shibden Hall with his last remaining sister Anne as housekeeper. James Lister's siblings: John (1745 -1769), Phoebe (1754 -1771), Mary (d1786) and Martha (ne Fawcett) (1763 -1809) had all died leaving Joseph (1750-1817) Anne (1765-1836) and Jeremy (1752-1836). Apparently, there were also four more siblings.

While some of the Lister ancestors had been merchants, the family had increasingly detached itself from concerns related to trading and textiles. Anne certainly refused to acknowledge the fact that she was a descendant of trades people. Anne Lister's class background is especially important in trying to understand her as an independent woman managing a landed estate in an urban-industrial setting. Much of Anne's income was derived from extractive industries, investments in canals and roads, and property acquisitions. The Lister wealth was not wholly restricted to Yorkshire, West Yorkshire Archive Service Calderdale, hold Lister deeds relating to properties acquired by the Lister family through marriage, in Buckinghamshire, Cambridge, Essex, Kent, Lancashire, Lincolnshire, London, Nottinghamshire, Suffolk, and Surrey, dating from 1473-1880.

On his death, James left the Hall to his niece Anne, who was the most capable and qualified to undertake the responsibility and who was unlikely to marry (a man), rather than to his last surviving brother Jeremy, who was poor in business dealings, therefore could not be trusted as caretaker, also wisely because James feared that his brother Jeremy, would in turn, leave Shibden to Anne and Marian jointly, and if Marian were to marry, her half of the estate would pass to her husband and be absorbed into his estate therefore lost to the Listers.

Commenting later regarding her accession to the estate, Anne explained that she did... *"many things ladies, in general, could not do but did them quietly"* ... *"My education had been different from the common rule. I was suited to my circumstances. On my uncle's death should come in for my uncle's estate, at my own disposal. He had no high opinion of ladies - was not fond of leaving estates to females. Where I other than I am, would not leave his to me"* ...

(Source: Some entries taken from 'Malcolm Bull's Calderdale Companion')

CLASS, STATUS AND INHERITANCE

To fully understand Anne Lister, who she was and how she conducted her life both in her private and business dealings, we must consider the times in which she lived, the restrictions brought about by the social code of behaviour, the limitations and inequality of the sexes, the industrial revolution which brought huge changes for industry and which affected all other areas of life, the geographics of the area where she lived, and how she conducted her business.

The class system in England was traditionally divided hierarchically within a system that considered social status, political influence, and occupation. England was divided into several classes and those classes were further sub-divided accordingly. During the 1700's and early 1800's the class system had propelled the gentry into the highest social class alongside nobility and even royalty. The system was therefore controlled by the landed gentry and aristocracy, to which the Lister family belonged, wealthy landholders who gained their status through family lineages.

Class and gender where categories around which Anne's primary experiences of identity were organized, and it is difficult to say whether one took priority over the other. Her material resources enhanced her ability to make a variety of choices in all areas of her life. But her social status was not entirely dependent on experiences of wealth. Her income was at the lowest end of what might be considered "gentry."

Anne Lister being a member of the landed gentry, developed an attitude of superiority with people from the lower classes. Certainly, in the eyes of the upper classes, the emerging middle class were on a lower rung of the social ladder, even with the wealth that they might have accrued.

Anne Lister was enormously conscious of class differences between herself, who by the late 1830s was perhaps able to generate an income of £2,000 a year, and carpet manufacturers like her neighbours the Crossley's, they would perhaps have an income of £60,000 a year. The Crossley family of West Yorkshire began making carpets in 1621 and continued until 1989, they were the largest carpet manufacturer in the world throughout much of the nineteenth and twentieth centuries. Based in Halifax, Yorkshire they held a Royal Warrant to supply Queen Victoria. Crossley carpets graced the rooms of Buckingham Palace and many prestigious buildings around the world. Interestingly Francis Crossley (1817–1872) operated a policy of paying women equal wages to men for doing the same job. It is extraordinary that it took another 100 years before the Equal Pay act was finally passed through Parliament in 1970. In the record Anne Lister has left, she appeared to be secure in the knowledge that her social status was superior to the Crossley's.

Anne consistently demonstrated her disapproval when her sister was found to be engaged to a Mr. John Abbott a man who had made his money from the wool trade. She avoided him if possible and rarely spoke to him or acknowledge the engagement. When she found some eighteenth-century letters and cloth patterns in Shibden archives relating to her tradesmen Lister ancestors, she burnt them all, destroying evidence of unfavourable connections.

'Class' was not a word Anne Lister used to describe social and economic hierarchies. She understood these things in terms of 'rank' and 'respectability.' From about 1815 to 1830 she concentrated much of her energy on enhancing her status by associating with women on a higher rung of the social ladder than herself and through her ability to create the persona she wished others to admire, was not only accepted but enthusiastically welcomed into their midst.

Working-class, middle, and upper-class women experienced sexuality in vastly different ways. The experience of women who desired other women varied by class, there is factual evidence of working-class cross-dressers and female husbands. There is certainly evidence of erotic desire among Victorian middle and upper-class women's passionate friendships. Although female same sex relationships were known of by a few enlightened people, it was not until late in the 19th century that the term Lesbian and Sapphic came into use.

For the ruling classes, the thing to consider is the importance that ownership of land had in Victorian Britain; it was a time when inheritance was a national obsession. Land ownership was what made a family part of the aristocracy or gentry. The land procured an income that was predictable and continuous. That income freed the family from the necessity to earn their living by daily effort. It enabled them to enjoy a good education, pursue the arts and sciences, become involved in politics, or lead a life of idleness and refinement. The idea of work to make money was beneath the dignity of someone who had inherited "gentry" status.

This gave ownership of land a cachet that went beyond ownership of cash or tangible goods. A landed estate was the 'Patrimony' which conferred status in society, not just on one person for one generation, but on the family so long as it lasted.

On the death of the head of a family, the eldest son would inherit all family assets. Subdivision of an estate divided between all sons would make them gentlemen, but over several generations was enough to make smaller patrimonies that, individually, do not qualify their descendants for the same social status because they cannot generate enough income. The answer to this problem is primogeniture (the rights of succession of the firstborn) but among male heirs only, which keeps 'The Patrimony' itself intact and under the control of the head of the family in each generation.

The survival of the family is considered more important than the individuals, even though it might be at the cost of unfairness to other surviving children. If the family head dies without sons, then one might imagine that the estate would be inherited by the man's eldest daughter. However, the daughter almost surely will marry — Once women married, their property rights were governed by English common law, which required that the property women took into a marriage, or acquired subsequently, be legally absorbed by their husbands. This means that the original family patrimony ceases to exist and becomes part of the husband's estate.

Jill Liddington writes a revealing exposé on primogeniture in 'Beating the Inheritance Bounds: Anne Lister (1791-1840) and her Dynamic Identity'. Blackwell Publishing Ltd 1995.

The complexity of the laws governing the rights of women meant that it was widely accepted that the law deterred women's ownership of land and property. Through the early records of railway surveyors laying out new routes in the 19th century who made detailed maps and recorded the usage and ownership of every affected property, indicating statistical information revealing that women-owned, either singly or jointly, only about 12% of that land.

Before the 1882 Married Women's Property Act, wives were constrained by common law: they could own real property but lost independent control of its management and the use of any rents or profits unless they had a settlement or trust, which was excessively expensive to set up. Women who owned with men were regarded as having limited control over that land. Women who owned with an institution had the least control given that institutions had statutory powers and often protracted decision-making.

Benjamin Disraeli's novel Sybil, published in 1845, goes to the heart of one of the most controversial subjects of 19th-century history – Class *"Two nations between whom there is no intercourse and no sympathy; who are ignorant of each other's habits and feelings, as if they were dwellers in different zones or inhabitants of different planets; who are formed by different breeding, are fed by different food, are ordered by different manners, and are not governed by the same laws...THE RICH AND THE POOR".*

THE JOURNAL - A RECORD OF A LANDED LADY

Anne Lister was, without doubt, an intellectual, an academic with a thirst for self-improvement and knowledge of language, science, classics, and literature. She was fluent in Greek and Latin and absorbed classical writings with great energy. She obtained a workable use of Hebrew; she also spoke French well and in later years picked up a smattering of Italian, German, Russian and Dutch.

Besides classical studies, she had an ongoing interest in mathematics, biology, and natural history. Whilst most women of her time were prevented from studying such subject matter, Anne took the opportunity and advantage her position in society gave her and devoured convoluted subjects that only men were thought capable of understanding.

She was incredibly adventurous and courageous, she not only travelled to popular places around the world, but she also travelled to locations where Europeans had never set foot before. One of her real joys was to climb mountains (because the challenge was there). Without the benefit of modern equipment made the climbs so much more difficult even for the most experienced climber. Anne was the first woman to ascend Monte Perdu (*Lost mountain*) in 1830, it is the third highest mountain in the Pyrenees and in 1838 she was the first recorded person ever to reach the peak of Vignemale at 3,298 metres, the highest of the French Pyrenean summits. Women, though few who climbed mountains at this time risked their reputation as being 'well-bred young women'. It was said of them 'they risked their lives without the justification of a useful end view' If men climbed to prove their masculinity then women climbed to prove their equality.

Lister's interest in travel may have been instigated by the knowledge that no gentleman's education would be complete without the experience of travel and the benefits and advantages that could be gained through experiencing culture from outside of their normal day to day existence.

Travel for the wealthy young gentleman was considered an education necessity for the upper classes; made popular by the aristocratic society since the beginning of the 17th century. The Grand Tour was a traditional adventure around Europe, taking in the fine, majestic buildings, works of art and all the culture, richness, and splendour that Europe had to offer. Upper class young men from privileged background on reaching the age of 21 years old, accompanied by a chaperone, would gain knowledge of the world that would set him apart from the provincial man. By the mid-18th century, the Grand Tour had become a regular feature of aristocratic education until the riots and revolutionary unrest that swept Europe made such adventure risky.

Whilst living at Shibden, Anne tried to keep herself to a rigorous schedule of study, keeping her accounts, managing the estate, day to day running of the business. She was not afraid of manual work on the estate, often working alongside her employees, planting hedges, working in the stables with her horses. Anne donned the clothes of a man whilst undertaking manual duties such as a man's greatcoat and boots, she supervised the farm, estate, and industrial concerns, and what is so crucial to history, writing her journal. Her aunt continued in the role of supervising the household staff and organised the domestic duties.

During the 18th and 19th centuries growing literacy rates and more literate culture, changes in the education system, and an awareness of the importance of national events resulted in the more privileged in society, such as Anne Lister, devoting some of their leisure time to writing their journals, recording the events happening around them, though it seems few recorded such detailed accounts, especially not the intimate, sexual revelations which Anne Lister did. Diary writing was a hobby that was part of a daily routine which declined as time progressed. Many who now record events happening in their lives prefer to document them using social media.

So much is known about Anne Lister's life due to the survival of those diaries, which extend to 27 volumes, 6600 pages or almost 4 million words, nearly every volume of the diary with an index of, among other things, books read, people visited, letters sent and received, ailments, sexual encounters, orgasms, and bowel movements.

The encrypted passages require deciphering. The key is easily available and the work for the transcriber might be described as daunting. Lister generally employed a clear legible hand for her cipher, printing out each symbol distinctly. Some ingenuity is required, however, in deciding where words and sentences begin and end, for there are no spaces between words, little punctuation and few capital letters in these passages. Each dedicated transcriber has adopted a different approach to presenting the encrypted hand entries.

The passages that are written in plain hand present just as many difficulties to the transcriber than those in encrypted, for, particularly in the diary and draft letters, Lister's writing is small and cramped, and she uses many idiosyncratic abbreviations and spellings, although conventional punctuation usually appears in these passages.

Throughout this book I have included some of the entries from Anne's Journals, which have been translated by researchers' and historians. These are set between quotation marks. They give Anne her voice and allow her to speak for herself in her own words.

Anne was not only a keen diarist, but she was also a prolific correspondent, frequently writing twenty or so business and personal letters a week, some over seventy pages long. She occasionally used the 'Cross writing' method, a popular cost saving technique to fill a page with writing at a 90-degree angle, over the top of horizontal written words, to fit in as much writing as possible on each page. She kept letters received (often also copying them out in full in her diary) and drafts of letters she had written and regularly reviewed. During Anne Lister's lifetime the cost of paper was high and would have been the reason why Anne used small letters and abbreviations to allow more words per page, and of course speed of writing. There are 1000 letters held in the Calderdale Office of the West Yorkshire Archive Service, and together they are a wealth of information.

Lister lived in a relatively huge, clean, though somewhat draughty ancient manor house. Her diet was also different from that of most of the town's population. The gentry and aristocracy, because of the game laws, had access to a wide variety of foods. Lister's diary records the receipt of gifts of various game birds such as pheasants and partridges.

Anne gave gifts of food to her friends. When she was traveling in Marseilles, Anne Lister thoughtfully sent a box of figs to Vere and Lady Stuart at Richmond Park. She sent them braces of moor game by coach from Shibden to London. She also sent gifts of moor game, shot on the estate, to the Norcliffe's near Malton and to the Duffin's in York. There were no restrictions for the wealthy, however, the game laws restricted those without rank and wealth the number of animals per person. It was claimed that the restrictions were to limit the species killed and numbers harvested, it also limited the use of weapons and fishing tackle used with which to capture them. The Night Poaching Act of 1828 ensured that penalties were severe. Persons caught taking or destroying game by night were for a first offence, imprisoned for 3 months with hard labour and a fine. A second offence was 6 months imprisonment, hard labour and a fine and for a third Offence, the offender would be liable to transportation to Australia, specifically New South Wales and Van Diemen's Land (modern-day Tasmania).

Lister's account books from the years 1798- 1830 record the frequent purchase of foods which the poor would undoubtedly describe as luxury goods, and therefore unaffordable for the masses, such as sugar, tea, coffee, cocoa, raisins, figs, oranges, lemons, butter, cheese, mutton, beef, veal, fish, salmon, and lamb. In 1825 the butcher's bill alone came to £35.11/7, while an indoor servant such as Elizabeth Cordingley, received £10.10/0 for a year's wages.

The Lister's food was prepared and served by servants, they undertook all other household chores, including emptying chamber pots, making the beds, laying the fire, cleaning the house and windows, running errands etc. Anne's lady's maid helped her dress and coiffured her hair. In 1825 she tried to get her uncle to pay for an inside water-closet, but he refused. She did have a toilet and sewer system put into the Hall by the late 1830s, this is a particularly early example of such sanitation, which did not come to most middle and working-class houses in Britain until much later in the century, or even in some instances, well into the 20th century.

Anne Lister grew up as a relatively privileged member of the gentry. While she occasionally visited the women of manufacturing families like the Crossley's, most of her visits were to other old, landed families like the Waterhouse's, Rawson's, and Walkers. She also visited the Priestley's, who perhaps were considered 'middle-class' in 1770; by the early nineteenth century, they were more akin to the gentry.

It was a John Lister a descendant of Anne's, the last inhabitant of the Lister family seat, Shibden Hall, Halifax, who discovered the diaries in the late 19th century hidden in the panelling of an upstairs bedroom. He began to publish extensive extracts from the diaries in the Halifax Guardian in the late 1880s and early 1890s. These extracts focused primarily on Anne Lister as an electoral manipulator and canal shareowner.

When John's friend Arthur Burrell assisted him to try and decipher the encrypted sections between 1887 and1892 they grew alarmed at what they discovered. According to Burrell, the code contained evidence that Anne Lister's "friendships were criminal" In fact, that was not the case as sexual acts between women was not illegal in Britain, though the subject had been a contentious issue for centuries. However, there was no respectable language at the time for lesbianism and the revelations would have been shocking and entirely unacceptable and certainly unpublishable.

Realising the sensational nature of the contents, Burrell was so disturbed by the revelations they discovered that he suggested the diaries should be burned. John Lister was reluctant, believing it wrong to destroy a part of his family's history, the responsibility of what to do with them was best avoided. John was reputed to be gay himself so he may have felt that any revelations regarding the contents concealed in the dairies, may inadvertently draw attention to his own sexuality. Thankfully, he did not take Burrell's advice but instead, returned the diaries to their hiding place where they stayed for almost another sixty years.

Following the Criminal Law Amendment Act in 1855 which made all male homosexual acts of 'gross indecency' illegal in the United Kingdom, the attitude toward gay men in Britain was to worsen, particularly after the trial and conviction of Oscar Wilde in 1895. This had an impact on lesbians because of gaining a homosexual identity, being gay prompted a greater self-consciousness and a taboo subject, the diaries remained hidden.

Once rediscovered no major work was done until the 1950s when Vivian Ingham and Dr Phyllis Ramsden learned the code and set out to read the entire diaries. Their research took them into the early 1980s, but because of fears around the sexual nature of much of the coded passages and possible prosecution by violating the Obscene Publications Act 1959, both Ingham and Ramsden expurgated their research and only published a few accounts of Lister as a traveller and scholar in the local history journal. In November 1968, Vivian Ingham published 'Anne Lister's Ascent of Vignemale'.

Anything anyone wanted to publish about Anne Lister was at that time subject to the approval of the Libraries and Museums Sub-Committee of the town of Halifax, as the 'best way to retain their right of ensuring that unsuitable material should not be publicised'. It was in the 1980s almost a century after they were first discovered that the code would be once again broken by historian Helena Whitbread and the true nature of the contents exposed to the public at large.

I give grateful thanks and appreciation to those historians and researchers who have worked tirelessly and conscientiously to decode the diaries and letters, so that we too may discover the way

Anne lived her life, which has been invaluable to me in the writing of this book.

ANNE LISTER'S HALIFAX

Halifax one of the nation's greatest industrial towns is steeped in history, much of the architecture is of national importance. Halifax reflects its prosperous past in the many grand buildings built by the wealthy Georgian and Victorian industrialists. The hills and moors which surround Halifax provide a backdrop which is vast, dramatic, and brooding but always beautiful. It has spectacular views; the best can be seen from Beacon Hill.

During the 18th century Halifax was a small but busy market town, served by a network of ancient packhorse causeways. The surrounding land had long been divided up into enclosures by a series of dry-stone walls. The growing number of inns and alehouses must have given the town something of an urban atmosphere. There were some areas of immense poverty, so much was needed by the way of charity. To try to alleviate the resultant issues, Alms-houses, orphanages, workhouses, charity schools also made their mark on this landscape.

In this extensive Pennine community, which reflected most of the major themes of English social, political, economic, and industrial history between 1750 and 1850. Halifax one of the largest parishes in England, ranged some 100 miles or some 75,740 acres across the foothills of some of the most scenic land situated on the backbone of England. The earliest settlers built scattered stone houses along the hillsides, using the characteristic dark grey stone, known as millstone grit, a course, grey, sandstone, found in a wide area in the north of England, beautiful in summer, stark in the depths of winter.

The farms and cottages built for the working class, many of which are still standing today are distinctive, partly because there is such a close link between the appearance of the buildings and the surrounding rugged landscape. Most of the properties were built with workrooms on the upper floor, where 'weaver's windows' were constructed to allow as much daylight in as possible enabling the tenants to work at their looms in their own homes.

Between 1700-1850 Halifax changed from being an area where people were primarily employed in their hillside farms spinning and weaving pieces of cloth to be sold in the specially built Piece Hall, a grand, quadrangle building with 315 rooms. Opened on 1st January 1779, the magnificent and unique cloth hall where trading took place of 'pieces' of cloth, hand woven by local people, gradually changed to an area that increasingly focused on valley-bottom mass manufacturing of worsted thread. Worsted thread though wool, differs from woollen thread by the length of the wool fibres, (long staple vs short staple). Under magnification, worsted yarns look smooth with long fibres, and woollen yarns are much hairier, with short fibres. Worsted wools are woven, woollen wools are knitted, crocheted, or woven into softer, fabric. Worsted wools are better at keeping out the wind and rain.

At the beginning of the eighteenth century the Halifax area had begun to specialize in the production of worsted cloth. The increasing focus on worsteds influenced the whole structure of the industry. For instance, technological changes limited to this type of cloth meant that local women and children composed most of the work force in the new spinning mills. It also meant a more hierarchical system of organization, with power increasingly concentrated in the hands of larger merchant-capitalists, rather than with the smaller cloth manufacturers, as in the woollen industry still prevalent in Huddersfield some 4miles away where a plentiful supply of wool and fast-running streams of soft water necessary for cloth production was prevalent. Of the main processes involved in the manufacture of worsted cloth, spinning was the first to be mechanised.

Steam engines did not predominate in Halifax until the 1870s. As trade increased in the eighteenth century, it became imperative for Halifax to have greater access to outside markets. The merchants of

Halifax did a large export trade, but their cloth had to be transported by packhorse over Swales Moor to the canal docks in Leeds. It was decided to build a canal which could serve Halifax more directly. In the mid-eighteenth century the Calder and Hebble Navigation company was formed to capitalize the venture. The Listers were early shareholders.

The old road that went in front of Shibden Hall, was close enough for the occupants when looking out of their windows to see the coaches travelling to Wakefield and surrounding areas. It was a turnpike road from which the Lister family also derived a regular income. In 1830 it was replaced by another new toll road which was partly constructed by means of shearing off many tons of earth off the top of Bank Top hill, a move which Anne Lister hailed as a... *"feat of engineering."*... The Godley road-cut went behind instead of in front of the Shibden Hall estate, and allowed for a grander, if more secluded entrance to the grounds. Improved roads made mail delivery and travel by coach more economic and more comfortable. In 1830 some thirteen daily mail coaches left the White Swan Inn in Halifax, bound for various destinations. Coaches also left from the yards of other Inns. Anne Lister's diary records her constant use of this means of transport.

The mail coaches pulled by horses were originally designed for a driver, seated outside, and up to four passengers inside. The guard, the only Post Office employee on the coach, travelled on the outside at the rear next to the mailbox. Later a further passenger was allowed outside, sitting at the front next to the driver, and eventually a second row of seating was added behind him to allow two further passengers to sit outside.

Passengers were obliged to dismount from the carriage when going up steep hills to spare the horses (as Charles Dickens describes at the beginning of 'A Tale of Two Cities'). By the time Queen Victoria came to the throne in 1837, the roads had improved enough to allow speeds of up to 10 mph (16 km/h). Fresh horses were supplied every 10 to 15 miles (16–24 km). Stops to collect mail were short and sometimes there would be no stops at all, with the guard throwing the mail off the coach and snatching the new deliveries from the postmaster.

The guard was heavily armed with a Blunderbuss, often referred to as a 'Thunder Pipe' or 'Thunder Gun' a short barrelled, short distance firearm which gave a spread of shot to cause the maximum damage, and two pistols. The guard smartly dressed in the Post Office livery of maroon and gold was also supplied with a timepiece, to ensure the schedule was met, and a Post horn, a valveless, cylindrical, brass trumpet type instrument with a cupped mouthpiece. This was crucial in alerting the post house to the imminent arrival of the coach. It warned tollgate keepers to open the gate (mail coaches were exempt from stopping and paying tolls: a fine was payable if the coach was forced to stop). Since the coaches had right of way on the roads the horn was also used to advise other road users of their approach.

However, the development of the railways in the 1830s had a huge impact on the stagecoach. Stage and mail coaches could not compete with the speed of the new railways. Soon the post was travelling by rail and by the mid-19th century, most coaches travelling to and from London had been withdrawn from service.

Between 1779-1837 some thirty-two banks were established, though only a few of these continued in operation. The 1830s particularly saw a burgeoning of local banking institutions, including branches of the Commercial Bank of England (1834-1835), the Northern and Central Bank of England (1834-1837), the Yorkshire District Bank (1834-1837), the Halifax and Huddersfield Union Banking Co. (1836-1910), and the Halifax Commercial Banking Co. (1836-to date).

The most important banks for this discussion were those of John, William, and Christopher Rawson & Co., (1811-1836), and the Halifax Joint Stock Banking Co., (1829-1910). Anne Lister's sister Marian wrote to her in 1829 to tell her of the founding of this bank, saying... *"They have allowed no one to take shares who would not keep their account with the Bank, and I believe ladies have not been privileged, probably you might be excepted..."* Marian would know these facts as her bow Mr. John Abbott was a founder member of this Bank, however Anne did her banking with the Rawson's Bank.

Certainly, the Halifax experienced by Anne Lister and that known to 'the working classes' seem to be almost two separate universes. The comparatively enormous quantity of time available to her for such activities as reading, writing, social visiting is particularly striking.

Anne Lister's Halifax was provincial but active. For a town of its size, it appears to have had a flourishing cultural and intellectual life. According to the estate account books, in the early decades of the nineteenth century, the Listers of Shibden Hall attended plays and oratorios, subscribed to a public library and financially supported grammar schools and charities. Anne Lister obtained both printed books and blank journal books from Thomas Edwards [1762-1834] The booksellers of Halifax, whose father founded the business and was considered... *"one of the best and most elegant binders in England."*...

While Halifax was growing into an industrial town, its growth was never as rapid nor as extensive as other nearby towns such as Bradford, primarily because of transportation and growth limitations imposed by topography. It was changing, however. Anne Lister commented in 1831...

"In passing along, I could not help observing on the comparatively fine, clear air of Halifax. Never in my life did I see a more Smokey place than Bradford. The great, long chimneys are doubled I think in number within these two or three years. The same may be said of Leeds. I begin to consider Halifax one of the cleanest and most comely of manufacturing towns"... By 1837, however, she found that even Halifax was... *"brightening into the polish of a large smoke-canopied commercial town."*...

ANNE'S EARLY YEARS

Anne Lister describes her early childhood as ... "A great pickle" Commenting on a childhood memory... *"Scaped my maid & got away among the workpeople. [...] When my mother thought I was safe I was running out in an evening. Saw curious scenes, bad women, etc. I was a curious genius and had been so from my cradle"* ...

Anne was a 'tomboy', the descriptive title given to any young female who due to their brash, boisterous, or self-assured code of conduct, with rough boyish physical characteristics and behaviour, is likened to a male rather than a sweet feminine child. Anne's interactions with young females were not questioned in her early years as it was thought normal for young persons to have harmless 'crushes' and romantic friendships. However, later in her early teens Anne's interactions with her peers at school became even more flirtatious and sexual and whenever the opportunities arose, she would not hesitate to seize them.

Initially, Anne was educated at home, first by the Revd Samuel White, later vicar of Halifax. Anne proved to be a keen and adept student. Anne's father Jeremy being in the military was away from home so much, Anne's mother dismissed Anne as... *"unmanageable"* ... so in 1798 at the age of seven she was packed off to boarding school in Ripon run by a Mrs. Hagues and a Mrs. Chettle in Agnes Gate, where she proved a relentlessly rebellious pupil, she was fiercely intelligent and full of boundless energy. Her teachers at the Ripon school regarded her as a... *"singular child, and singularly dressed, but genteel looking, very quick & independent & above telling an untruth"* ...

In her teacher's attempts to curb her over-exuberance Anne recalls that she was whipped every day, though it is doubtful that any excessive force was applied judging by the lack of detail in Anne's accounts of her punishment. Eventually, in 1800 Anne was asked to leave because the teachers feared she was 'corrupting' the other girls. Apart from being able to whistle very well, she claimed to have learned nothing at school. She admitted to... *"always talking to the girls instead of attending to my book"* ...

At home Anne refused to learn how to cook or keep house and managed to disappear when domestic choirs were being dished out. Anne was unable however to dodge learning how to sew, as it was entirely her responsibility to repair her own clothes. Anne often visited Shibden Hall, her time there was filled with interesting assignments to fully occupy an intelligent, inquisitive personality like Anne's. Uncle James and Aunt Anne got on very well with their wayward niece, her behaviour with them was far less troublesome and never problematic. Anne respected James, a quiet bookish man, and her childless godmother treated her niece as the daughter she never had. They became very close and it certainly appears that she had far more love and respect for her aunt and uncle than she had for her parents.

She stayed for long periods with her uncle and aunt at Shibden Hall during 1802 and 1803, the later visit lasted nearly a year, and to continue her education she was taught by the Misses Sarah and Grace Mellin of Halifax.

Whilst staying with her Shibden relatives she participated in work around the estate, enthusiastic to learn the lessons of land management and animal husbandry, which would put her in good stead in future years and would eventually convince her uncle that she would be perfectly capable of maintaining the family home and heritage.

A formal letter of February 1803 to her aunt at Shibden Hall reveals not only that she read precociously for her age, but that she had acquired a taste for purchasing books, an activity that later led her to establish a fine library at Shibden Hall. She mentions in this letter reading Georgical Essays, by A. Hunter (1803), a study of agricultural methods which is... *"very improving and at the same time entertaining I was always fond of Farming"* ... an unusual interest for a twelve-year-old girl, though not for one who had set her mind to the serious contemplation of estate ownership and management or had a desire to impress upon others that she had the necessary knowledge and qualifications to look favourably upon her.

When Anne was just eleven years old, she wrote to her parents about harvesting oats at Shibden Hall and considered the political and socio-historical meaning of her favourite subject of Farming.

ANNE'S TEENAGE YEARS

Anne's classical education began in 1804, when she returned home to Market Weighton, where she had lessons with the Vicar of All Saints, the Rev. George Skelding who taught her Latin, a classical language which Anne found fascinating particularly as it was a subject normally on the curriculum for boys.

He supplied her with the vigorous programme of study for example:

Monday - From eight till nine Writing and Accompter (accounts). From nine till half after ten Practice Till twelve. Draw Till one. read from three till six Geometry, Astronomy, Geography & Heraldry.

Tuesday - From six in the morning till eight and from nine till ten Geometry, Astronomy, Geography & Heraldry. From ten till half after eleven Practice. From half after eleven till one writing & accompter (accounts).

Each day of the week is laid out in this way. In addition, the Rev. Skelding recommended that Lister have... *'Two Latin Grammar Lessons every day except Tuesday & Saturday one in the morning & one in the afternoon"* ... Lister observed the studious practices established under the Rev. Skelding for the rest of her life and they were to have a profound effect on her reading and the development of her social and sexual self.

In 1805 at 14 years, she was sent to the Manor House School in York, where she mixed with young women from wealthy, professional and minor aristocratic backgrounds, several of whom became her close friends, and in one case at least, her lover.

Anne was schooled in reading, writing, and arithmetic, geometry, astronomy, geography, history, and heraldry. Because of her eagerness to learn, a broad range of classical, technical, and artistic subjects were on the curriculum. The Drawing lessons were given by the artist Joseph Halfpenny, who had published detailed architectural drawings of York Cathedral, only two minutes' walk from King's Manor. Anne showed a greater talent for music. She practised the flute and pianoforte every day. There Anne continued her Latin lessons at her own request, for eight hours a week. Although, as a girl, she could not attend a regular grammar school, she still wanted to learn the language of the sciences like her brothers did and for this she was known as the Solomon of her school.

From an early age, Lister had ambitions to rise in society above what she perceived as the sunken fortunes of her parents. Education itself unlike wealth, could not affect what was also essential to this ascent, but the educational benefits lent an air of superiority and would allow her proficiency to converse with scholars and with cultured and sophisticated members of high society. Marriage was the more usual route to these objectives for women, but simultaneously with her social ambitions, Lister began to develop her sexual identity, which precluded the option of Marriage.

Her life changed dramatically when 15-year-old Eliza Raine – the half-Indian daughter of a British doctor – was sent to join her in the attic room above the chapel with Miss Burn and Miss Manners. Raine had the least comfortable position under the slope of the roof. Six other rooms accommodated between three and eight pupils.

Teachers tried to limit her disruptive influence. However, Anne was asked to leave Manor School after two years following an incident which resulted in her dismissal due to what was considered an unhealthy association with a fellow pupil. She was told that she could return after Eliza had left the school. When Anne finally left after the second period at the Manor School in 1806 at the age of fifteen years, Lister had by no means finished with her education, on the contrary, she did not consider her serious study to have begun until later in her teens, Lister recognised the limitations of the education provided by a private girls' boarding-school, though she conceded that for boys it was different... *"Eton is good, and Westminster is good ... A boy may be made a scholar at either"* ...

After leaving the York school, when she began to spend protracted periods at Shibden Hall, Anne arranged to continue her study under the Rev. Samuel Knight, Vicar of Holy Trinity Church, Halifax. learning algebra, rhetoric, and classical languages – all subjects befitting a budding gentleman, but not considered necessary or fitting for a young woman.

After years of contemplating her feelings regarding her own sexual urges, Anne must have felt a great deal of consolation after reading the quote by Jean-Jacques Rousseau, the Genevan philosopher, one of the most influential thinkers of the 18th century. His political philosophy influenced the progress of the Enlightenment throughout Europe... *"I know my heart and have studied mankind; I am not made like anyone I have been acquainted with, perhaps like no one in existence; if not better, I at least claim originality, and whether Nature did wisely in breaking the mould with which she formed me, can only be determined after having read this work."*
– Jean-Jacques Rousseau, *Confessions* (1782)

In diary entries for 1806, 1807 and 1808 when Anne took up permanent residency at Shibden Hall with her uncle James and his sister Anne, Lister reveals that she had begun to study the classics more seriously and found solace in their teachings.

Anne learned Greek with the New Testament, but as early as 1807, she was studying Demosthenes and a year later Homer, Xenophon, and Sophocles; she also read Horace's Latin odes. The Classics interested her not only because they were part of young men's curricula; Anne soon realized that classical literature exalted in eroticism and desire in all its forms, without Christian moralising. The translations of the time censored what was considered obscene, so Anne had no other option but to read Greek and Latin poetry in the original.

Anne's reading revealed that women of Greco-Roman times not only behaved as lasciviously as men, but they also wrote about the fantasized sex they had. Whilst reading passages from the many books and pamphlets she acquired, she drew up a list of explanations of words such as the clitoris, eunuch, hermaphrodite, paedophile, and tribade. The Latin word for Lesbian is fricatrix (she who rubs) Other descriptive names are, Amazon, (used as either a compliment or insult) Anandryne, (a Greek word meaning without a man), Sapphist, (an admirer of Sappho), Tommy, (defined as women in the lesbian community who chooses to wear masculine clothes but may not necessarily be the dominant partner).

In Pierre Bayle's Dictionnaire Historique et critique (1695–1697, published in English in 1738), Anne came across an entry on Sappho (b C 630BC) Perhaps the most important lesbian poet of all time. Sappho taught young women on the island of Lesbos. But she also kept lovers through the years, which were referred to in her verse as 'hetaerae'. Whether because of the scandal and secrecy, or relationships, or simply because she was unlucky in love, the names of her female paramours cannot be found in Sappho's surviving verse. What has endured is the vivid memory of her love affairs. Her steamy writings secure her place in the literary pantheon. Bayle wrote the women of the Isle of Lesbos were very subject to this passion and Sappho had been made infamous by the island's young maids. Anne found Bayle's extensive articles interesting for they mirrored her own feelings and objectives, and systematically followed his references to Horace, Juvenal and Martial.

Martial (b38/41AD) a Roman poet from Hispana (modern Spain) wrote two infamous epigrams on women who desire women, for instance on a certain Bassa, who acted chaste and unapproachable in public but secretly fucked women; no other verb is better fitting to the original, in which Bassa penetrates other women with her prodigious Venus, (her prodigious clitoris). Another of Martial's epigrams deals with Philaenis of Samos, daughter of Ocymenes, who was a tribas, the name derived from the Greek word τριβάς, many modern scholars consider Philaenis a fictional character.

Tribadism refers to the sexual position of scissoring, a lesbian sexual practice in which a woman rubs her vulva against her partner's body for sexual stimulation. Philaenis began her literary odyssey with her book which she titled 'On Indecent Kisses'. Chapters include 'The Use of Aphrodisiacs'; 'Abortion Methods'; and 'Sexual Positions.' Her erotic manual was clearly popular gaining a mention by other writers of the period. It is recorded that Philaenis buggers' boys as vigorously as a man, she was remembered for her reputation of licentiousness, a masculine woman also known for having sex with women using a strap-on-dildo, [*"those strange and monstrous tools of lechery without semen"*] as described by Lucian of Samosata.

Anne studied Juvenal extensively, he used obscene language to satirize Roman society as populated by effeminate men, drunkards, and adulterous women were the aristocratic vices of his age. However, the Romans had no law on adultery when it was committed between women. One of the commentators Anne read on Juvenal, the Reverend D. H. Urquhart, excused the poet as a great republican spirit whose frank verses simply attacked the immorality of his time. Most contemporary translations of Juvenal were highly censored. Perspicacious Anne found a seventeenth-century Latin commentator, Lubinus, who revealed another layer of Juvenal to her, a mine of information about homosexuality, both male and female. When Juvenal refers to lesbian behaviour, it is in oblique and negative terms: for instance, when Tullia and her foster sister Maura pass the ancient shrine of Chastity, it's here they piss on the goddess' form, squirting like siphons, and ride each other like horses, warm and excited, with only the moon as witness. Then home they fly.

In commenting on such passages, Lubinus not only defined fellatio, pederasty, and tribadism, he also explained that Juvenal borrowed his image from an epigram of Martial, who much more explicitly referred to 'tribadism'. Martial's epigrams, which Anne knew, are even more negative than Juvenal about lesbianism. Philaenis exercises with dumbbells, guzzle wine, steak, and girl's 'juicy quims,' in the words of one late Victorian translator; but the poet attacks her for transgressing her sex and wishing she would... *"learn to suck a penis,"*... a vicious insult in Roman culture.

For Anne, it was a revelation to realize that she was not alone in her desire for women because although Martial's depictions of lesbianism were intended to be negative, they at least gave evidence that lesbianism existed. Female homosexuality began its metamorphosis in the second half of the 19th century as the term began to refer less to a practice than to an identity. She seems to have found reading Juvenal in Latin sexually stimulating. When Anne read these poems, she did not react with shock, and disgust, but rather with excitement and learnedly speculated as to whether Bassa used a dildo or not.

Lister noted that Christianity's strict hostility to sexuality was atypical among religions and therefore she adapted her own version of morality. Anne was religious with a strong Anglican faith. She struggled with the question about her affairs with married woman, believing that the act was fornication, and her association with Mariana Lawton was adultery. She believed that the most important personal obligation, as the single adulterer, was to herself as it detracted from her feelings regarding love, sex, and marriage. However, though her conscience told her it was wrong, she habitually committed the sin with women who took her fancy, whilst her feelings regarding women who married for money and rank was legalized prostitution.

The thing which caused Anne the real sense of sinning against God arose from her masturbatory practices. Anne struggled with her conscience when reading erotica, which resulted in her sexual fantasising and urges that she was only able to satisfy by what she described as '*self-pollution*,' about which she had an overwhelming sense of sinfulness. She regularly prayed to God for the willpower to resist such sexual indulgences...' (Whitbread, Helena (2016) *Secret Diaries Past & Present*,)

While Lister was accumulating the masculine accoutrements, such as pistols, and sword, deep masculine voice, fast gate, and stride, during her teenage years, she continued to receive attention from male suitors. Miss Marsh's letter of 24 September 1814 conveys the interest of Captain Philip Taylor... "*in short my dear Girl, it is plain he would give his Ears and Eyes for yo*"'...

However, although facts regarding sexual diversity were not readily available in the early 19th century, Anne had already come to terms with her psychologically and emotionally with her sexuality. She had spent time exploring her physical anatomy so that she was more able to understand herself, her discoveries revealed that she was certainly female, having 'normal', functioning, female genitalia. Through this informative exploration she must have gained the knowledge of how to please a woman sexually, vital in her future lovemaking technique.

A tragedy struck her immediate family when in the summer of 1810 when Anne was nineteen years old, her younger brother John died aged fourteen. Anne's father, Captain Jeremy Lister, presented her with the gift of a horse, which served to distract from some of her feeling of loss for her sibling and the tedium of her prosaic provincial life. Anne found the business of tending to the horses a comforting and welcome distraction…

"My father has got me a very spirited horse which is ready for me at any time in quarter of an hour. It is exactly what I wished for, though I confess it is at present quite as much as I can manage. The moment one mounts it begins prancing and capering, and as I am not a very steady [indec] scientific rider I daresay like Homer's heroes I shall lick the dust." …

A month later, on the 30th of September, she writes to Isabella, saying that riding around the countryside with her brother Sam had become a great source of pleasure to her … *"We take very pleasant and sometimes very long rides; indeed, we have every inducement as the landscape is everywhere interesting and, in many places, delightfully varied with the beautiful and the sublime."* …

ELIZA RAINE

Eliza Raine (1791-1860) became Anne's first lover.

The 14-year-old Anne Lister was sent In April 1805 to the Manor School, (now King's Manor, part of the University of York) an elite girls' boarding school for some 41 pupils, her education at the school was paid for by her aunt Anne, where she stayed after a short break until the early summer of 1806.

The most significant outcome of her time there was the development of her romantic friendship with fellow-pupil, Eliza Raine, a girl of Anglo-Indian parentage, the daughter of the late William Raine, who had been a surgeon with the East India Company, and a native Indian woman.

Raine's marriage was not registered here in the UK, they had been married locally in India. The Rain's had two daughters both children were born in Vepery the Eurasian area of Madras, Eliza was born on July 13th, 1791. Both girls were christened and considered illegitimate but British.

For Anne and the other pupils at Manor school a medieval building which still exists today, Eliza may have been the first person they had ever seen from another part of the world. Anne was besotted with Eliza's beauty; thirty years and countless lovers later, she still described her as *"the most beautiful girl I ever saw"*.

Eliza and her sister Jane had been placed under the guardianship of William Duffin, late Head Surgeon in the Service of the East India Company who had retired in 1792 but had worked closely with William Rain whilst in India and was made executor of his Will.

In 1800 William Raine on discovering that he was suffering from a terminal illness boarded a ship to return to England to settle his affairs. Sadly, he died on the return journey and was buried at sea.

William Duffin was informed of this sad event, so William being named as the guardian of the Raine children in the event of their father's death, set out to travel to India to bring the girls back under his care, which was a six-month journey to complete.

Raine had made provisions for both daughters in his Will, 20,000 Star Pagodas issued by the East India Company to be used for a trust fund to be in each daughter's name, which amounted to £4000 to each, to be paid at the age of 21 or on marriage. His three trustees were William Duffin, Lady Mary Crawford (Raine's niece) and his bankers Thomas Coutts and Coutts of London. Raine left his Indian wife the house, banana plantation, and a yearly pension of 10 pagodas for the remainder of her life. Though there is scant information regarding the circumstances of her death, it is known that she died in July 1802 the same year her daughters arrived in England.

Eliza and her sister Jane arrived in London just after the Christmas of 1802 aged 13 and 11 years. The extremes of the climate must have been a huge shock for the sisters. Both Eliza and her sister Jane were first sent to a small Tottenham boarding school for foreign girls, but two years later, in 1804 they moved to York to Duffin's home. As his wife was an invalid, he engaged a governess a Miss Marsh, to care for them. Later they were sent to Manor School, Eliza became a boarder and Jane who was the eldest, a day student.

Anne and Eliza shared an attic bedroom and began a friendship that developed in intensity, reaching the point where they wanted to spend the rest of their lives together. Anne was a 'Tomboy' she had always felt masculine she had always acted like a boy, spoke like a boy, and behaved like a boy, seeing girls as completely different to herself. On reaching puberty she had taken a stronger interest in girls more like a man and without doubt, the reason why she had been put into the attic dormitory, safely away from fellow pupils. It is thought that Eliza's dark skin was the reason why she too was accommodated in the attic.

Alienated from the other girls Anne and Eliza became very close, so much so and out of sight of prying eyes, they slept together in the same bed and shared each other's secrets, plans, and dreams; as their feelings for each other grew stronger, Eliza and Anne swore to stay united forever. Each craved what the other had. Anne had no money Eliza had no real family. They planned to live together as soon as Eliza came into her inheritance at the age of twenty-one in six years' time. The girls exchanged rings to seal their promise. They were reluctant to be parted even in the school holidays, so the two of them staying with Anne's parents in a rented house in Halifax.

Two years later their love affair was discovered, when they were caught by their teacher sending love letters to each other. Anne's aunt was summoned to the school and told that her niece had to leave, but that the school would accept her back when Eliza had finished her schooling.

Their sexual relationship continued until around 1812. Anne's departure from the school had far-reaching consequences both for Anne and for posterity because it was the trigger that prompted both Anne and Eliza to spend more time with their journals and writing long affectionate letters to each other.

Lister did not permit her family access to her diary. It is thought that it was in fact Eliza who contrived the encrypted code so that their most private correspondences would be known only to themselves. When recording the details of the day Anne would often make notes of happenings at the time they took place, then write them up in her diary when she was able to spend more time on her writing.

By using a cipher, they ensured their correspondences, intimate parts of them at least were, without the key, unreadable, even under scrutiny. In her plaintext hand, Anne employed many abbreviations, some conventional to eighteenth-century writing practice, some idiosyncratic. These may have been intended to speed up the writing process, but they also served to disguise its content from casual observers.

Her plaintext handwriting is so cramped that it is frequently illegible. However, while many diarists have used secret writing and cipher to provide extra security for their private journals, Lister complicated her encrypted hand's function by distributing the key to her lovers, who subsequently used it in their letters and diaries. She also occasionally read out extracts from her diary to her lovers. After Anne left Manor school Anne and Eliza remained close friends and lovers; Eliza it seems had become besotted with Anne Lister. Both families had welcomed their friendship, each made many welcome visits to stay at each other's homes and could sleep together in each other's bed. Romantic friendships (a term coined in the 20th century) were close relationships between friends, that often involving a degree of physical closeness beyond that which is common in the contemporary, Western societies. It may include holding hands, cuddling, hugging, kissing, and sharing a bed, but without sexual intercourse or other physical sexual expression. Close relationships of this type were commonplace, and often mentioned within novels written in the eighteenth and nineteenth centuries.

Female romantic friendships were acceptable and generally encouraged in British society. For propriety, middle-class society made great efforts to separate male and female social worlds, it seemed natural that women would find their soul mates among other women. Raine and Lister exchanged letters very regularly, sometimes once or twice a day until their relationship ceased completely in 1814.

In 1808, free from the routine of school and discipline Anne was kept busy and adapted her life without Eliza's constant company, and with no more school, she was enjoying her newfound freedom. She was seventeen, masculine in mind and manner, and no one to object or criticize her actions.

With an introduction from Eliza, she made friends with the Alexander family, Dr Robert Alexander, and Harriot (Disney) Alexander, of Hope Hall, York. One evening on the 4th of January unchaperoned she played cards with Dr Disney Alexander one of the Alexander sons, and his friend Sam Dyson. Anne's inappropriate behaviour peaked when she pretended to faint and had to be revived by Disney, who was a doctor. Anne, of course, found it rollicking good fun, but when her father got to hear of it, he was furious, damage to Anne's reputation would have consequences regarding her marriage prospects in the future not to mention the reputation of her family.

He immediately cancelled all her social engagements, and this time imposed a strict curfew. Even this event did not deter Anne, she ignored all he had said and spent the whole of the following day at the Alexander's. When she arrived home, her aunt and uncle from Shibden were waiting for her and must have used some sobering words to remind her that their financial support was dependant on how she conducted herself in the future. At that time in her life Anne was far more concerned about her prospects than her reputation.

Anne began to give flute lessons to the unmarried Miss Maria Alexander (1776–1822) Lister was seventeen when they became friends, Maria was fifteen years older was distraught that she would be unable to marry or have children without a dowry. Maria's sister Anne (1779-1822) had married (4th November 1805) Walter Edward Hodgson, a London solicitor, the remaining siblings still living at home were all unmarried men. Dr Disney Alexander (1769–1844), Lieutenant Robert Alexander (1771-1795) Dr Gervase Alexander (1773-1856), Lewis Alexander (1774-1857) a solicitor who practiced in Halifax, Captain Nicholas Alexander (1785–1858), Captain John Alexander (1785–1859).

It is apparent that Alexander's enjoyed social gatherings and although Anne's parents found card games and musical evenings acceptable, "routs" were not, because of their riotous and unruly reputation. Rout parties were popular in the Regency period, a large evening party or assembly. It is otherwise described as a tumultuous or disorderly crowd of persons. The concept of these events was according to etiquette writers of the day, to invite as many ladies and gentlemen as you can, place them in a room with a Piano Forte or Harp with a few packs of cards and a good supper with plenty of wine, all then will make merry... Anne was staying out later and later much to her family's displeasure.

Although the two families did not make social calls on each other, Anne persuaded her Shibden Hall relatives to invite Maria Alexander to dinner. Although the Alexander family reciprocated and invited the Listers, their invitation was declined which was a great social rebuff and caused them much embarrassment. This resulted in Maria's aunt calling on the Lister's, but Rebecca refused to see her, and Jeremy was rude and then forbid Anne to visit them ever again.

Anne was again defiant, took little notice of her father's wishes and continued to go there with Eliza. This allowed Anne to flirt with Maria even in Eliza's presence. According to Anne's diary, Eliza even encouraged Anne to sit Maria on her knee and kiss her. Anne continued to visit the Alexander house against her parents' wishes. She records in her diary that on the 28th of December they finally agreed that she could stay over for the New Year festivities, which gave her the opportunity of forming a more intimate relationship with Maria, when she took advantage by sharing the same bed.

The Lister's were still reluctant to allow further contact between their daughter and the Alexander's but as the Alexander house was but a short distance from a relative's home at Northgate House, Anne offered to paint the birdhouse there as an excuse for her unaccompanied walks into town, enabling her to call upon the Alexander's without her family's knowledge. One evening when walking home in the dark she met Tom Dyson a local man in the woods. Precisely what happened Anne did not specify in her diary except to say that she suffered an acute sense of shame and embarrassment. What ever happened between them must surely have been mutual, as two days later when her father got to hear of the incident and immediately made a curfew of 4pm, he took no further or robust action against Dyson. However next day Anne always ready to defy, did not return until 5.30 pm.

It was during this period that Anne's mother Rebecca proposed her adopted Irish son, Mr. Stubbs, as a match for Eliza, as her considerable dowry would be welcome in their impoverished family. However, Eliza, having secretly married Anne, did not want to meet him. Mr. Stubbs went to York to propose marriage to Eliza, so Anne wrote a short letter to her to reveal his intention. Anne revealed, *"My mother wrote to E.R. to ask her over intending to make the introduction"* ... to be forewarned is to be forearmed, and as Eliza was aware of the point of his visit, she was able to use some delicacies in handling her refusal. Eliza's letter sent on January 2nd, 1807 was a long explanation to Mrs. Lister asking for her

46

forgiveness, at the end of which she signs herself... *"I remain forever your affectionate & grateful Daughter"* ...

The outbreak of influenza that spread through York and surrounding areas in 1809 brought an epidemic fever that killed many people. Anne's brother John was one of those who died. Anne's father called her back home to Halifax when John got sick, but despite round the clock nursing by Anne and her younger brother Samuel, John's condition deteriorated. On the 24th of January 1810, John died peacefully at five minutes after 3 am, John would have been 15 years old on 3rd February.

It was a dreadful shock for the family, poor John the eldest boy would have inherited Shibden after his uncle's death. John's passing would make Anne the second in line after her brother Samuel to inherit their ancestral home. After this sobering event, Anne ceased her rebellious behaviour and concentrated on improving her somewhat tarnished reputation.

Eliza left Manor school at Christmas of that year so Anne who had requested that she might return to continue her studies asked Mr. Duffin if she could stay with his family in York. She intended to return to Manor School as a day pupil, boarding due to the past indiscretion was not an option. Anne was given Eliza's old room and Eliza went to stay with Lady Crawford. Although Eliza's sister Jane had found Lady Crawford difficult to live with, being of a softer more rational personality, Eliza felt sure that she would fare much better than her sister.

Eliza's sister Jane was also a ward of the Duffin's and in 1811 had been a day student at 'Mr Lumley's Boarding School for Ladies' (1712-1835) also known as the Manor school. After leaving school she went to live with her cousin, Lady Crawford, who was later the custodian of Eliza's finances during her committal and executor of her Will on her death. Unfortunately, Jane found her impossible to live with, so after a year she returned to Duffin's house.

Feeling that she did not fit into the Duffin family she often went to stay with her uncle James Raine and his family in Seamer near Scarborough. After one visit she took the coach to make the return journey and during the stop whilst changing horses in Malton, Jane made the acquaintance of Henry Boulton, a handsome cadet on leave from Calcutta. They chatted about India and she enjoyed his company; he then proposed marriage. Jane was twenty going on twenty-one and due to inherit £4000 the equivalent in today's money of £355,000.

She was an unhappy girl and the thought of all the financial and social independents gave her a great deal of worry. Thinking of India, the place where she had been happiest, must have played a part in her decision to accept his proposal.

Henry Boulton, older than Jane, born on the 8th of April 1787 in Malton, had joined the Madras Infantry as a cadet in 1807. As a fourth son, he had no fortune; and like similar families, most of his family's money would be spent on a dowry for the eldest daughter and a good education for the eldest boy. He had no chance of any promotion unless he paid for it, so he desperately needed an heiress to marry.

Jane catastrophically as it turned out accepted his proposal and despite server warnings from Mr. Duffin they married on the 21st May 1808 at Trinity Church, right opposite the Duffin's house in Micklegate leaving immediately for Calcutta. Eliza was distraught, believing that she would never see her sister again.

Anne attempted to comfort Eliza and invited her to her parent's house in Halifax for the summer. In Eliza's account of the occasion, she includes the word 'Felix' when writing about their adventures. 'Felix' is Latin for 'happiness' and successful. These entries coincide with Anne's notebook journal of August 1808.

Lister began to pursue an affair with a fellow student Isabella 'Tib' Norcliffe in 1810, a young woman from a wealthy county family. Tib was herself a masculine woman and appears to have been as exclusively devoted to women as Anne was, and who at one point hoped to become Anne's permanent partner. They remained friends and occasional lovers throughout the years. Although Anne was very fond of Isabella, her masculine proclivity was not a turn-on for Anne. However, Anne found her company particularly useful in times of sexual famine when other more favourable love interests were few. Anne's rejection of Isabella as a life-partner was a bitter blow, she remained single all her life.

Through her relationship with Eliza, Anne was introduced into the York social scene, and as her circle of friends widened, Eliza soon began to realize that she was losing Anne to Isabella Norcliffe. Raine's diary for July 1809 to November 1810 has survived. It anxiously rehearses the terms of her relationship with Lister, as these entries for August 1810, when Raine visited Halifax, demonstrate:

Sunday 5th... *"Dined at Ellen Royd I dined at Mrs. J. Lister's & heard an account of the amiable I N [Isabella Norcliffe]. Dear Lister & I had a reconciliation ... Lister & I had a dy'ference which happily was made up before the conclusion of the day but left me e (exceedingly) ill... my husband (Ann) came to me & finally a happy reunion was accomplished"* ...

Anne and Eliza made many visits to each other's homes. Staying with the Duffins at Red House, York, allowed Anne the opportunity to flirt with young Miss Duffin, niece of William and his first wife. Anne records a long letter of May 1811 from Eliza who was staying with the Lister family and hears all her news of the joy and love she receives from Anne's parents. Eliza did not waver from her devotion to Anne in the financially difficult times when Anne's parents were unable to keep up with pocket money, Eliza began to send her money, writing the amounts in code so as not to enlighten Mr. Duffin of her generosity.

When Norcliffe introduced her to Mariana Belcombe, a York doctor's daughter in 1812, Lister fell passionately in love. Anne still saw a great deal of Isabella and later in their friendship, Isabella took to snuff taking which apparently was the epitome of elegance for ladies some 200 years ago, it was a habit that Anne found most disagreeable. Another irritant for Anne was that Isabella was partial to partaking of the odd glass of wine or two, or more. Anne disapproved of Isabella's excessive drinking. Isabella was also known for her bad temper which became worse as the years passed.

Miss Marsh was also introduced to Anne by Eliza Raine, Marsh being Eliza's governess, and a mistress to her guardian Mr Duffin. It appears that Miss Marsh was never one of Anne's lovers but perhaps if Anne had pursued the opportunities presented to her, she would have achieved success with Miss Marsh. Whilst staying at the Duffin's home Anne wrote, ... *"very much in the amoroso.... She kissed me & put her tongue to my lips. I almost involuntarily called out God bless me. Kept wiping my lips. Said I had never had such a kiss before, and it was the oddest sensation in the world. We all laughed most heartily. In opening the front door, she gave me another such kiss, saying, can you not put your tongue between your lips? Shewing me how. I said no, it was such an odd sensation it set my teeth on edge"* ...

In June 1812, perhaps because Anne was showing interest in other women, Eliza took interest in another suitor, an old friend, Captain John Alexander who served in the Royal Navy. He was decorated for gallantry and wounds received off Toulouse France 1814, the final battle in the Napoleonic Wars and youngest brother of Maria. At first, she put him off by insisting that she had a... *"pre-engagement of her heart"* ... He repeatedly insisted on knowing who it was, and she eventually confessed that it was Anne Lister whom he knew very well being a family friend. Eliza had some concerns that on the coming 13th of July she would be 21 years old and would receive her inheritance. He swore that his feeling for her had no connection and mockingly made comments about his *"dreaded rival"*. Indecision made Eliza ask Anne's opinion and advice who told her to stay single and make this clear to Captain Alexander in a final meeting.

Captain Alexander had no intention of giving up, he had strong feelings for her and pursued Eliza at every opportunity. He told Eliza that she was delusional if she believed that she and Anne would eventually live together, which upset Eliza into writing to Anne to ask if this was true, but Anne was in York and did not reply. Anne did, however, inform Mr. Duffin of selected facts about the Capt. Alexander situation. She also informed Capt. Alexander that all his letters to Eliza and her replies had been copied and sent to her guardian and that nothing had been kept private. Capt. Alexander went to see Duffin immediately, but he was told that there would be no marriage. In despair, he wrote a final letter to Eliza...

"Almost horror-struck at the gloomy prospect for my future life, and acutely afflicted for the shame I have had in occasioning that anxiety and horror.... To Mr. Duffin and Miss Lister, I have asserted that I have had encouragement to persevere in my addresses until a late period, if this be incorrect you will pity my self-deception. ... I told my father and brother and Mrs. Veitch what claims I thought I had upon you. When I see them again, I shall say simply that tho' my hopes are disappointed, my gratitude for past kindnesses and respect for your general conduct will always be yours".

Eliza made an entry in her diary for 2nd August 1812, with a reminder of past joys and in anticipation of future delight...

"This day, month, hour I first saw you judge that in such reflection how many past scenes of my life rise to swell the pleasures of memory! Yet I do not look back to departed joys as if I had them not equally or in any degree now. In contrasting the past & the present, my judgment declares, the latter, to be more replete with solid happiness - & blessings seem greater than I have ever known them before - What says my Welly [Raine's pet-name for Lister, alluding to the Marquis of Wellington conqueror of India) *For affection & our long friendship tell me that our fates are ever inseparable; & that in the detail of the one we include if not all of the other's - Eight years then I have been blessed with, & invariably happy in our friend[ship] - Time seems only to swell the tide of our affections & our joys"...*

The effect of all this on her friends and acquaintances was to make Eliza a pariah. Capt. Alexander was considered an honourable man and a good catch; her conduct was thought cavalier and cruel... she was considered too rich, too isolated, too childish, too much the wilful temptress. She was shunned by York society, ostracised by all her friends. Anne meanwhile was spending the summer with the Norcliffe's. Eliza, on the other hand, was now very lonely.

Anne's feelings for Eliza cooled considerably in 1812. Soon after, or in the midst, of the Captain Alexander events and her acquaintance with Mariana Belcombe. Anne was in love with Belcombe, the two young women would be intensely involved for many years. The effect on Eliza was devastating. In a letter to Anne the following year, 1813, when Anne was 22, Eliza wrote:

"Of the instability of your character of which you so complain that you are complained of, I have ceased to believe, tho' you know that I once yielded my credence to the charge, & if your own conscience that infallible tribunal acquits you, you may not only not care for the injustice of mankind but be happy...The lovely Mariana will be happy to be so closely enjoying your friendship & conversation - she seems most amiable & none can wonder at your predilection for her. On Wednesday I dined at the Belcombe's".

Meanwhile, Eliza appears to have conceived of real affection for another young officer named Montagu. Eliza confessed to Anne that she was... *"in love"*... with him. The passage from this letter is a notable one:

"It is very odd; I am always wanting to write to you & yet when I get my pen, I don't know what to say - Once! How different was it! Now I feel afraid of appearing a fool by being natural; but if not to you I speak the undisguised feeling of my heart, to whom then shall I do. My heart says that if I ever many, Montagu must be my husband; for I know that he doats on you, that you approve him & I have heard you say, 'You would be fortunate indeed Eliza if you married Mr. Montagu - Welly (Eliza's pet name for Anne) *teach me if you think my regard foundered upon an empty foundation, teach me to root up this prepossession; if you would have me never marry tell me so - & I obey - I can say no more - than that Mr. M. is going soon to Sea & I perhaps may never see him again".*

Was this written to make Anne jealous and rekindle their own love affair?

Rebecca Anne's mother who was very fond of Eliza did not give up her attempt to matchmake on Eliza's behalf; Edward Priestley of Cliff Hill, who would eventually inherit all of Miss Walker's senior's fortune was attracted to Eliza. But though Eliza was flattered to receive such attention, she politely refused as she still believed that she and Anne would eventually make a match.

Among the circle of friends, there was an incident with a Captain Bourne that occurred when Anne had accompanied him to his room to see his pistols. Anne claimed that sexual impropriety had not occurred. Anne certainly did not feel that this had been a cause for such a fuss, she felt like a man, and had acted like a man and she had a strong interest in firearms. It was known that Anne had been accepted and treated as a young man by other young men although some did think her attractive enough and worthy of their amorous interest.

One Sunday morning Anne walked to church with the men instead of the ladies. Such an obvious statement was provocative. The next day Disney Alexander made a pass at her. Two days later she met Captain Bourne again and, at his invitation, returned to his room to see his "flageolet", (a woodwind instrument and a member of the fipple flute family) and drank wine with him. He proposed a closer relationship, but she demurred, instead offering to introduce him to her parents. They, however, were less than pleased with the impropriety of the suggestion; besides being alone with a man ran the risk of him accusing her of privately agreeing to marry him, and therefore making a case of 'breach of promise' where he could then claim substantial damages. Anne's parents re-imposed the curfew on the Alexander household.

It seems that several parents of Anne's close friends had become concerned for their daughter's reputations by their association with Anne Lister. A Mrs Bramley from an affluent family enquired about a rumour concerning Anne and a Captain Bourne. On hearing more details Miss Bramley was sent to a finishing school in London, as was Miss Maria Alexander a month later to remove them from a bad influence.

When Mrs. Greenup, sister of Miss Marsh, made an acid comment about Anne, Eliza duly defended her reputation but thought it her duty to repeat Mrs. Greenup's advice to Anne, to play less chess because it made her seem so masculine and importantly, she was sure it would injure a woman's brain.

Eliza was at this time living with Lady Crawford, her concerns were raised because the frequent letters she usually received from Anne Lister ceased. She continued to write perplexed that her letters had been ignored. The last letter Anne received from Eliza was blotched with tears; Eliza was desperate for news of her sister Jane, and knowing that Anne was in contact with Miss Marsh, she was sure that Anne would have heard reports of her whereabouts and surely would have news:

... *"now I am fearful there is some alarming cause for such unusual negligence from you therefore dear Lister if you have any consideration for my feelings answer me by return of post tell me why I am thus forgotten at a time so interesting. I know I gave you a day or two beyond Tuesday thinking you might have more to communicate respecting my unfortunate Sister but at last Saturday has arrived & I am still ignorant of Mr. Duffin's determinations or whether you received my first long letter"* ...

Her letters continue to beseech Anne for clarification about the cause of the noncommunication. She also reports that she has had a serious altercation with Lady Crawford.

Eliza eventually discovered that Anne had been writing regularly and that Lady Crawford had hidden all the letters, including urgent news about her sister. Invitations and social involvements had all been turned down and rejected without a word to Eliza.

When Eliza discovered what had happened to the absent letters she wrote:

My dear dear Lister
"What happiness do I experience from the long looking for epistle from one of my best & dearest of friends Oh Lister little can you conceive what a burden my heart is rid of. But amidst all my joy I cannot help being very seriously alarmed at ye fate of those letters I have written to you & that from yourself to me which it seems we have neither of us seen & are ignorant of until this mutual & I trust

happy disclosure. My dear L. how painful I have thought of you many days, have endured a tormenting solicitude. Illness I feared was the cause of your silence but thank God your health is unimpaired & that the mistakes & errors originated solely in those who have had the management of the parcels & letters". In this letter she also talks about her sister: *"No doubt you have letters to me from Jane & much have to tell me too but dear Lister if those letters are very distressing burn them & let me not have the pain of reading them".*

Anxious about her sister and increasingly nervous about her cousin Lady Crawford, Eliza demanded that Anne should be allowed to visit her in Doncaster, but Lady Crawford refused at first, unwilling to let anyone disturb her routine, especially Anne Lister, after suspecting that an unnatural association had formed between the two girls. Eliza eventually wrote:

You may now expect to hear from Lady C. with her long-intended invite; come to us dear L., I have set my heart upon having you & you well know how ill I can bear disappointment, I will not disguise that I am not always very comfortable with my relative but this I think will die away when I have become more familiar with her conduct; Remember dear Lister mine is become a peculiar situation I feel orphan like & unprotected in the society of Lady C, she is a Child & sometimes a tyrant in action but my trust is in that last & forever remaining consolation my Religion & my God may he protect me"...

Anne's next letter to her was smuggled inside a parcel from their friend Mrs. Swann. Three days later Eliza learned that her present accommodation with her cousin had been covered by a £100 allowance to Lady Crawford paid annually by Mr. Duffin out of Eliza's trust fund. This put their relationship on an entirely different footing. The amount was generous and thus paying her way to such an extent she felt entitled to invite her friend for a visit. This time there was no refusal; Anne arrived in Doncaster on 30th April.

The situation in India was not going well for Jane and her newlywed husband. After they arrived in Calcutta their relationship deteriorated to such an extent that Jane felt she had no option be to return to England. Young Mr Boulton took over her inheritance as was the law at that time. This made him at liberty to buy a higher rank in his regiment and as soon as that was accomplished their marriage completely failed. Jane packed her belongings and took a ship that would eventually return her to these shores.

English law held that when a woman was married, she became, in a sense, her husband's property. Married women had few legal rights and were by law not recognized as being separate legal beings. Therefore, she had no claim to her property including her wealth, as her husband had full control and could do whatever suited him regarding his wife's assets: A woman, on marrying, relinquished her personal property—moveable property such as money, stocks, furniture, and livestock--- to her husband's ownership; by law, he was permitted to dispose of it at will at any time in the marriage and could even Will it away at death. Only the extremely wealthy were able to afford the cost of creating a trust for a wife or her children's use. A married woman was unable to draft a Will or dispose of any property without her husband's consent.

It came to light that her poor dark-skinned sister Jane had suffered a traumatic journey home; for six months she had been alone, unchaperoned on a ship with mostly male passengers. When she arrived in France penniless, she had been arrested and sent to prison until she could prove her British nationality. There she had been raped or bought necessities with her only asset. Exhausted, distraught, and now pregnant, with no more than the clothes she stood up in, Jane, at last, made it to London.

When she arrived in York William Duffin refused her money; she was deemed no longer part of the Duffin family, she was now technically a Boulton. To add more woes in 1810 it was a criminal act for a wife to have another man's child, which a plea of rape was no defence, so she, therefore, could not ask the Boulton family for help as they could have her sent to prison.

Eliza was in a terrible position, Duffin was still holding her money in trust until she was 21, she was therefore unable to help her sister financially, and had to hold her tongue as she was still reliant on the Duffin's benevolence herself, besides, it was the custom at that time to ignore the plight of one so unfortunate as her sister. Eliza was living with her cousin Lady Crawford, so she could not offer her sister accommodation there. The situation had it been known, would have been a huge scandal, one that had to be hidden from society even though it was none of poor Jane's fault and she had been a victim of all which had happened to her.

Jane was now classed as a 'fallen' woman without the necessity to keep her illegitimate child. Penniless, the only option was to go to the parish and throw herself onto their mercy and work for her living. Duffin eventually found her a place to stay in Fulford, but this was only a short stay during her pregnancy. After which to avoid scandal and shame her guardian had her put away in an asylum.

The first known asylum in the UK was Bethlem Royal Hospital in London, also known as 'Bedlam', a name meaning chaos, confusion, disorder, and lunacy. One of its most famous patients being Daniel, who was reputed to have been 7'6" tall, and an employee of Oliver Cromwell. During the 18th & 19th centuries, women were admitted to private asylums on slender evidence, notably those who contravened expectations concerning their modesty, conduct, duties, or behaviour or those who would not bend to their husbands' will. Admissions were very much down to personal judgment and seem to have been heavily weighted against women. Indeed, there were often many more women compared with men confined in these institutions.

Reasons to admit a patient was Depression associated with various situations which were quite common. In many instances 'at the time of acquiring an inheritance', 'domestic trouble', 'immoral life' (often associated with carrying or delivering an illegitimate child), 'menstrual problems', 'the menopause', 'uterine problems', 'female disease' and 'nymphomania'.

Women at the time were expected to be demure, polite, and agreeable to the men in their lives. Should a woman dare to speak out of turn or argue with her father or husband, she could be considered hysterical and in need of treatment. Women could be admitted if they had 'overaction of the mind', This might be because they wanted to educate themselves, or for some, it may have been as simple as wanting to read. Indeed, 'novel reading' is listed as a reason for admission to the Trans-Allegheny Lunatic Asylum, West Virginia. Other reasons were religious or political excitement, sun stroke, masturbation, desertion by husband.

Once admitted, there was no procedure for the patient to appeal against detention. They could, however, be discharged on the application of a relative or friend, if they confirmed that they would take proper care of the patient and prevent them from injuring themselves or others.

Continuing friction between Eliza and Lady Crawford made for a very tempestuous situation in the Crawford household. Eliza was in misery from Lady Crawford's bad temper; she considered Eliza a very degraded moral indeed because of her association with Anne Lister, whom she described as '*the devil incarnates*', and that the vengeance of heaven would fall upon her. Lady Crawford accused Anne and Eliza of having acted together in some deep plot against her to injure her.

Another letter in which Eliza tells Anne of yet further friction she was enduring living with her cousin, it illustrates the misery Eliza's life had become.

"I exert myself to amuse her & according to her request in company use every deceit & speciousness, but 'tis well there is to be an end to all this soon, for I feel my sprits sometimes so broken I don't know whether life or death more desirable. I anxiously wish for Miss Mellin's letter in about a week I shall look for it if she cannot accommodate me what is to be become of me; Ask Mr. Duffin if he will approve my leaving off my pelisse in June you forgot in yr last. To Mr & Mrs. Duffin every best & affectionate love & do not omit my gratitude for his last kind message".

It was decided that the best thing would be for Eliza to leave her cousin. To avoid any scandal regarding their rows and Eliza's departure Lady Crawford requested that they should appear as cordial as ever; visit together, walk together, etc. Anne assisted her to escape the misery of Lady Crawford's home and moving into Miss Mellin's accommodation. Grace Mellin (1766-1831), with her sister Hannah had established a boarding school in 1788. Grace Melling had tutored Anne Lister at Shibden Hall in 1803. Even after all that had happened, Eliza stated that she would never desert her cousin, though she would never live with her again.

On June 3 she went first to Red House the home of the Duffin's where Anne was staying and where Miss Marsh joined them five days later. On July 30th she took the coach to Halifax to join Miss Mellin. Eliza was overjoyed at moving closer to the Lister family where she anticipated living there with Anne very soon. However, Anne had already decided never to return to Halifax, she regretted her pledge of undying love because of her association with Isabella Norcliffe who was six years older. The Norcliffe family had extensive connections within local society and Mrs. Norcliffe was a local judge by descent. Anne was also in love with another girl from her old school, Mariana Belcombe whom she had met at a house party at Langton Hall.

In 1812 As the time approached for Eliza to receive her inheritance the agreed time when Anne and Eliza had planned to live together, Anne felt she was too young at 21 years to be joined in marriage to another, to forsake all others and settle down. A week later Eliza's summer visit ended, Anne said goodbye after paying for Eliza's luggage to be sent back to York. It was early November when Eliza left Halifax much disillusioned that her darling Welly was insistent that they should wait longer before they would be together properly. Eliza's mournful letter expresses her emotional state.

'It is a sweet moonlight night; this and the murmuring of the water which we have both delighted to hear brings to my mind a thousand pleasing scenes, which I hope will one day be realized. How my heart throbs for thee! Here I turn my eyes to my bed. This I hope after a few years which confidence in your affection will shorten, you will share with me and thus complete my worldly wishes. Never did I feel as on Friday night; you were continually before my eyes; I could scarcely believe you were not with me. And yet when I stretched out my arms you were not there in the warmth of my affection. I almost cursed our separation and declared to myself that I would rather die than live long without you. A thousand plans for our soon meeting, being together,

presented themselves, all of which, though then likely, afterthought convinced me were absurd. But my adored since much exquisite happiness cannot yet be mine, I will endeavour to bear it patiently, though how I can wait for ten years I know not. But I have every confidence in my lovely W. and this will support me. I will always tell thee every thought and every remnant of desire and will not my W. do the same. Yes she will and then I will be happy, and let us wait buoyed up on the wings of hope and expectation".

When Raine came into her inheritance in August 1812, she at once communicated in crypt hand to Lister her intention to withdraw... *"two hundred & fifty of the principal' with which she intends to furnish her house, to make her guardian, Mr. Duffin, 'a handsome present' and 'have in reserve for your Bath jaunt ... thirty or forty pound and this I shall give you"* ...

In another letter to Lister, she wrote...
"remember welly that you send for more when you want it if I come to York my purse shall be yours & myself the source of all wants & necessities, I shall send you a pair of stays & some nice cambric pocket handers".

Anne knew that Eliza had made out her Will to her *'husband'* to inherit everything she had after her death. Eliza involved Anne in all her life just as a loyal wife should.

After Eliza gained her inheritance, she left Miss Mellin's residence to set up a home of her own in anticipation of the time that she and Anne might live together. Her letters are full of detail to keep Anne up to date with the progress she was making in creating a fine home. *"Everybody flatters me by admiring my house. ... First let me tell you in brief that my house is nearly on the finish, & to my no trifling joy the front parlour is ready for the paint. Next loved welly my Servant's arrival I announce, a nice-looking girl of 20, she havg a greater appearance of juvenility than her age declares. – She seems as if she wd suit me, I hope it anxiously, for well you know the trouble I have had in searching for these needful aids to our domestic comforts'* –

In 1812 Lister was not only writing to Eliza she was also corresponding with Miss Marsh. After the death of Mr. Duffin's first wife, who had been much loved by Raine, things became even more difficult for Eliza. When Raine came into her inheritance her position in the Duffin household seems to have declined rapidly from that point.

Mary Jane Marsh an unmarried woman of outwardly genteel appearance that hid an astute scheming mind was a clergyman's daughter that instituted herself into the household of the Duffin's as a companion to the ailing Mrs. Duffin. She quickly assumed the role of mistress to Mr. Duffin intending to become the second Mrs. Duffin when his first wife expired. At this time of their lives, Mr. Duffin was 62 and Miss Marsh was 38 years old. It would be seventeen more years before she was taken as his wife. Mrs. Duffin died in 1823, but for decency sake they were not married until the 20th of September 1826 at Holy Trinity Church, Micklegate York. Mr. William Duffin died in 1839 aged 92.

Eliza and Samuel Lister had been close, she had taken over the schooling of Anne's brother Sam and sister Marian, so she loved and knew them both well. Eliza often spoke of the increasing likeness Sam was becoming to his elder sister Anne. She also spoke of Sam's attention to her wants. Sam encouraged by his father Jeremy, had enlisted into the army much to his mother's alarm fearing for his safety, but with much anticipation he left to join his regiment. Samuel kept a personal journal covering his travelling to Liverpool and going to join the battalion in Ireland.

The York Herald, County & General Advertiser on the 10th of July 1813 reported the accident:
On the 19th of June at Fermoy, Samuel Lister Esq of the 84th regiment, aged 20, and only son of Jeremy Lister, Esq of Halifax. The melancholy accident which cut off, in the prime of life, this truly excellent young man, must ever stamp his loss with humble grace upon the hearts of his disconsolate family and friends. He went out with some of his brother officers, to bathe in the Blackwater. Hardly had he plunged in, before the current forced him from his depth. His friends saw him sink, beyond the power of assistance. And Oh! He sunk to rise no more.

Though every exertion was immediately made, the body was not found until it had been two hours underwater. All means to restore life proved ineffectual – his sainted spirit had escaped forever. He had left all those that knew him to lament and say He was the best of sons, of brothers, and friends and lasting tribute is all the worthy tribute they can pay.

In July 1813 Anne Lister (senior) wrote to Eliza informing her of his death.

"the most lamentable event, which has plunged our family into the extremity of affliction ...he had gone to bathe about 2 o'clock on Saturday...along with three or four of his brother officers, got beyond his depth almost instantaneously and sunk... when Anne came yesterday, her mother received her alone, and broke the dreadful tidings to her by degrees, but when the word was told, her sorrow and anguish of mind was extreme"

Eliza was distraught by the news which deteriorated further by not being invited to the funeral, nor was she invited to Halifax to support the family. She had loved Sam as much as any of them, she felt wronged and slighted. At last, she realized that she and Anne would never live together, or would Anne pay her much attention in the future. Amid Eliza's misery, Jane Boulton unexpectedly turned up at the door of Red House, home of the Duffin's. Her pathetic appearance must have been a shock. Drunk, raggedly dressed, and desperate, she asked that Mr. Duffin would give her back her property he still held, accusing him and the trustees of stealing her rightful possessions. She was once again rejected and banished into the night.

This incident made it abundantly clear to Eliza that she too had been treated badly by those closest to her, which greatly affected her metal stability. Eliza began to think that even Mr. Duffin only tolerated her because of her money, or was he influenced by Miss Marsh, whose sister, Mrs. Greenup, had so often upset her during her time in Halifax. Eliza had completely trusted Anne, but it had become clear that she had betrayed her too.

Now living at Red House, the situation continued to be uncomfortable for Eliza, she noticed that family invitations did not include her. When Anne wrote it was to Miss Marsh and never made any mention of Eliza. This naturally upset Eliza who wrote to Anne, drawing attention to the money she had spent continually for some years in recognition of their mutual promise. Anne informed Mr. Duffin who sent Eliza away to stay with lady Hoyland, a kind, elderly aristocrat of limited means who lived within a day's ride of York.

Anne, on the other hand, joined the newly established York Friendly Society and had started to take particular care of her appearance. Now she was moving in more affluent circles it was necessary to look the part and certainly look respectable. There were important aspects to consider when hoping to be excepted and to impress the high end of social connections. Would Eliza's dark appearance be detrimental to her own respectability? The exotic nature of her Indian background had faded completely in Anne's eyes and then there was the issue of her "fallen" sister and an illegitimate child to consider. Letters between them grew fewer until there were none for many months. Mariana after hearing of Anne's cavalier attitude towards her devoted friend wrote to Anne ...

"My beloved Anne, Eliza has said everything, I dare only to add a Request that you will immediately reply minutely to all her Requests – Why have you so long neglected writing to her. Don't be guilty of the like again. She feels tho' she says nothing. You possess a Heart & a Disposition incapable of voluntarily giving Pain, & ye from Inattention, you do cause it to those most fondly attached to you".

That summer Anne arranged a meeting between Eliza and Isabella hoping that if they got on well together then perhaps, they would transfer their affectionate feelings towards Lister, to each other instead, and that would free her from her close involvement with these two possessive women. Eliza after the failed meeting with Isabella wrote to Anne in their secret code,

"How can I refuse my darling husbands' solitude to bear the events of Isabella's visit? Nothing glaringly strange took place, my love, but....it may illustrate most clearly the resemblance that dear

creature has arrived at to you. On entering I was accosted rather roughly; we sat down and after looks that really now, L, made me blush the tray was brought in. She ate heartily and drank freely, insisting on me drinking your health with all the airs of masculine fervour, forgot everything she had to say and spoke more in her eyes than I liked; put her hand into her habit; sat with all the freedom of a man, and thought, I daresay, that she could not be too near to me. These are singular traits, L...and the consciousness of a certain something, being but human nature, occurred to me so strongly as to influence me to the elevation of my dignity... or consequences would have inclined myself to rudeness.........

At the end of the letter, Eliza revealed that she had asked after Mariana and it seems she had begun to realize that there was more in Anne's friendship with Mariana than she had previously believed. *"I asked after Mariana Belcombe, on which she gave me the strongest look and said, "What makes you ask me after her?" "I replied "Merely from the idea of their great intimacy.... In future, I shell learn discretion in communicating to my friend, finding that she tells you everything".*

Anne, wrote back to deny any physical relationship with either Mariana or Isabella and demanded an apology from Eliza which she immediately got, her relationship with them both continued unabated.

Because of Eliza's isolation and the realization that Capt. Alexander's was right in his assumption that Anne would never live with her, she decided that she utterly understood what her sister had been through; a failed marriage and social stigmatisation. She decided to live near Jane in Fulford, a part of York. Jane was now 23 years old and consumptive.

Eliza wrote to Anne about her decision, but Anne advised her to keep her distance from Jane, who now had to work for her living, and their association would most certainly tarnish Eliza's own reputation. Anne must have informed Mr. Duffin because he wrote to Eliza demanding that she "sink £200" of her capital to clear her debts. Although after her inheritance she was a wealthy woman, the money was distributed to her in an annual allowance. She had spent so much in the seven months since her twenty-first birthday that she only had £80 left for the remaining half-year and large debts had to be put on hold.

In 1813 Eliza and Miss Marsh were staying with Mr. and Mrs. Duffin in Red House, York. Eliza began expressing her dislike of Anne Lister who had been keeping her distance to avoid being tainted by association with the Duffin's and there was her friendship with Isabella & Mariana which now occupied all her attention.
Marsh wrote to Anne:

" No one sees her, what a miserable wretch she must be... She desires nothing from you to whom she has & does [behave] with the [blackest] Ingratitude - My Lady Crawford has taken no notice of her nor invited her all summer I think has [vexed?] her & made the black Blood to boil however I have got forever quit of the Rubbish even to speak to".

The following extract gives some further clues as to what was happening to Eliza Raine. Her expressions of sadness, jealousy, or any behaviour not in keeping with that expected from a respectable young lady, were attributed to her race with discriminative language to underline the prejudice against this unfortunate girl.
Marsh writes:

"Miss Raine is still about I shall not be surprised to find she quits York for ever which I think would be a wise act - for she will not long have many friends there or perhaps anywhere - for kindness seems to make her bate People or why that inveterate Dislike to the Belcombe's which she was constantly shewing whilst here - I gave her some good Lectures upon it. What can all this be but Derangement or the Waste of a Heart, or if she has one, it is a black one. She has never been herself since She lost your Intimacy & Friendship - I have often heard of Pearls thrown. it is fully [justified?]. You are a good Christian to be interested about her now. I admire it in you - tho' I do not feel the least inclined to follow your Example - I have done with her & all the black Progeny for ever - being now quite of my former opinion that where black Blood is there can be nothing amiable - I congratulate you that you

are so soon to have that dear Girl Mariana - in her Society you will feel completely happy, wanting nothing".

While Lister wished to keep secret their sexual and financial intimacy, the crypt hand produced for Raine an illusion of power and control in the relationship. Raine's impulse to secrecy was slight and seems to have been brought on less by concern for social respectability than by fear of jeopardizing her inheritance. After her twenty-first birthday, in possession of her fortune, Raine was far from cautious in her conduct to her guardian and there was an imminent danger that she might reveal details of their true association.

With her financial and emotional dependence on Raine successfully hidden, Lister could with impunity take an opposing side in the uproar that attended Raine's fall from grace. She chose to support Raine's principal accuser, Miss Marsh. Marsh makes it clear in her letters to Lister that she believes that Raine has been the recipient of Lister's beneficence rather than vice versa and refers to Raine as ungrateful and having taken an unreasonable and 'virulent antipathy'.

Throughout all that was said and done to her, Eliza appears always to have written with respect, love, and gratitude for those around her, sending her warm regards, concerned for their health and wellbeing and never it seems wrote harshly or with malice for those who on occasion wronged her. In 1814 Anne Lister declared that she would not live with Eliza though Eliza kept in touch with the Lister family and thought of them as her own.

On the 23rd of August 1814: Jane unexpectedly turned up at Eliza's lodgings in Blake Street. She was drunk and Eliza's first thoughts were to turn her away, her maid said that she should consider it wrong to turn her sister from her door, so Eliza agreed to allow her to enter. It was obvious to Eliza that the way her sister was dressed, and the incoherency of her speech was that she was not only inebriated but mentally deranged. So concerned was Eliza that her heart went out to this poor retched, pathetic soul and told her that if she would place herself under her protection, she would find her a place of warmth and safety for the rest of her life.

Jane readily consented and stayed with Eliza for a week whilst she sought confirmation on her sister's condition. Eliza thought it best to withdraw Jane from the life that was killing her to find her a place of safety and tranquillity. She first wrote to Mr. Duffin to find out the address of Mr & Mrs. James to recommend someone to consult on a case of insanity before she was placed in an asylum. She begged them to enquire for her the most eminent physician in London. Mr. James recommended a friend of his, a physician to the Middlesex hospital a Dr Munro.

Mr. Duffin acknowledged that she was justified on the steps she had taken. However, he felt that although poor Jane had brought on her situation herself, he insisted that before she was confined to the rest of her life in an institution, she should be permitted to have her liberty for six months as a trial, if she violated her promise to be steady, he would certainly comply with Munro's certificate authorising her detention.

Jane had in the past appointed a trustee a Mr. Dickinson from Coutts Bank, to care for her interests both financial and her person. He took Jane, placing her in lodgings near to him, promising to take care of her in the future. Sadly, this arrangement did not help Jane or to regain her right mind, and the disappearance of Eliza allowed people to judge both Jane and Eliza of unsound mind. Of course, Miss Marsh had plenty to say on the subject to Anne Lister...

"She has acted in this affair completely by herself. Therefore, let the issue be what it will, she has none to blame or thank but herself. I think with you that Eliza is a little in the same way as Jane.... I have been very anxious about the Asylum business ... I think all has gone off very well for Dr Best as second physician & 300 a year salary" ...

Miss Marsh certainly appears to have been a rather venomous creature who thrived on tickle tackle and was without compassion for the two sisters. Her eagerness to impress Anne Lister is displayed in all her letters and can only indicate a jealous, resentful nature.

The following summer, in 1814, Eliza began to have serious mental health problems. The earliest indication of the severity of her condition came in a letter from Miss Marsh to Anne in August 1814. She says Eliza was just recovering... *"from a dangerous illness."*... She gives a long summary of Miss Raines behaviour in the previous three weeks and says she never intends to speak to her again, as Miss Raine has been extremely rude to her. Marsh's description of the onset of Raine's illness during an evening when she was staying with the Belcombe's gave the full force of Eliza's derangement ...

"The last night she stayed there - such a Night, I suppose was never passed ... - She is dreadfully abusive when a Paroxism [Paroxysms]comes on & her Imprecations are most dreadful as Dr & Mrs. B[elcombe] found" ...

What happened unsurprisingly resulted in Eliza's mental breakdown; so, William Duffin declared Eliza insane, and handed her over to his colleague, Dr Belcombe who removed her to his asylum in York. Anne made her feelings clear siding with the Duffin's standpoint and criticising poor Eliza's conduct. Following this betrayal, Eliza broke off all contact with Anne Lister. However, after Mariana learned of this, she believed that a great injustice had occurred, realizing how much Anne might have played in Eliza's breakdown. She begged Anne to go and spend some time with her. Anne however, preferred to keep her distance.

Eliza was sent to the Quakers' Asylum known as The Retreat. A private asylum for people with mental & psychological problems. Both Dr William Belcombe (1813) and his son Dr Henry Stephen Belcombe (1817) were physicians there. The Retreat occupies a central place in the history of psychiatry. Opened in 1796 by William Tuke, a retired tea merchant, the original Retreat was intended to be a place where members of The Society of Friends (Quakers) who were experiencing mental distress could go to recover in an environment that would be both familiar and sympathetic to their needs.

Raine's letters written after she was committal lack the intimate assumptions of former times, and are pathetic in their attempts at the formality,

"My dear Miss Lister, Your last letter to me has afforded me more pleasure than I have experienced & I thank you for kind assurances of affection & friendship – You have always been my friend - I have sometimes doubted it - but now I hope never more to do so - Whatever pique resentment & ill-will I may have hitherto shewn to you, I request you will be so generous as to bury in oblivion - I acknowledge it not only to you - but to those to whom I have during the last two months sought only to injure you - I trust there has been an apology for me - will y think it - will you forgive all I may have said of you in the months of my derangement" –

In a letter to Lister of 7th December 1814, Miss Marsh's opening lines are as dramatic as any Gothic novel...

"the poor unfortunate Eliza. She continues much the same, sometimes giving hopes by a long interval of Reason that She is coming about when again She falls into her Wildness & is as bad as ever ... She strained her faculties with writing so very much [long] strange wild incoherent Letters to Mrs. B [Belcombe, Marianna's mother] -2 or 3 times a day - now She has taken to Sketching & has done many little things - of the melancholy kind - all wretchedly bad except one which She calls Mariana's Tomb" ... When the rift between Raine and Lister occurred, Raine wrote to Lister that... *"I shall be obliged to you to collect Capt. Alexander's letters to you, to me, & mine that you may have, to him"* suggesting that Lister was already beginning to construct the archive of letters and written material that was to play an important part in the production and management of herself.

The letters of Eliza Raine and Miss Marsh were kept at Shibden Hall in tied bundles. Lister did not return Raine' s letters as requested, for they are still in the Shibden Hall Muniments. It is clear from the 1822 document, 'Contents of my letter-Drawer', that Lister probably burned several of Miss Marsh's letters.

The last letter in the collection of Eliza Raine's letters to Anne reads in part as follows:

"will you forgive all I may have said of you in the moments of my derangement - to my dear friends Dr & Mrs. Belcombe I am

indebted for the care and kindness they have shown me since I have been at Clifton -... From Dr Belcombe you must learn how far I am or am not restored to my reason. He & Mr. Mather are in constant attendance at this Retreat - where every gentle, thoughtful method is adopted for the recovery of unfortunate patients of Lunacy. Write to me soon - assure me that you believe I will try to deserve your regard".

Eliza Raine remained confined to Dr Belcombe's private clinic near Clifton Green for some years. In May 1815 there was some discussion of making her a Ward in Chancery [minor under the guardianship of the Court of Chancery; today referred to as 'ward of court'. This was an idea put forward by Anne Lister. It must have always been in Anne's mind that Eliza may speak of their true relationship, and she possibly thought who would believe the ramblings of a lunatic that was under the restrictions of the court? Eliza's moments of lucidity were so frequent that Mr. Duffin was afraid they might not be able to convince the examiner of her derangement. However, in 1819 Mr. Duffin told Anne that Eliza was incurable. In 1820 Anne and Mr. Duffin quarrelled about Eliza's Will and its beneficials and the legalities. Eliza's trust fund had left her a wealthy woman and Lister remembering the contents of the Will when Eliza declared that the main beneficiary would be her 'husband'! whom she believed at the time of writing would be Anne Lister, therefore Anne had much to gain if she had been successful in convincing others of her legal rights.

At one-point Lady Crawford temporarily removed Eliza from the asylum after it came to light that there had been some scandal associated with this establishment. Lady Crawford had been appalled that Eliza had been held under Dr Belcombe's care. She, therefore, insisted on lodging Eliza privately in a rented house in Gillygate in the centre of York.

Eliza could recover in peace with the help of a widow and her three daughters. Of course, Mrs Duffin (nee Marsh) had a lot to say on the matter claiming it was a case of... *"one maniac looking after another"* ...The home where Eliza was placed had... *"no insanes"*. ...At this time Eliza was still in possession of most of her original £4000, less what she had spent on furniture bought in Halifax, rent in Hot Wells and York, and travelling expenses, which amounted to approximately £500. After Jane's death, she had inherited three thousand more plus interest.

Jane's estranged husband, Lieutenant Henry Boulton was killed in action in Calcutta in 1819; therefore, Jane inherited £3000 which was left over from her own money that she had been forced to relinquish to her husband on marriage. Only about £1000 of her original sum had been used. Sadly, all were returned too late as poor Jane's health had deteriorated so drastically, she now constantly spat blood, later dying of consumption in November aged 30 but apparently looking 60. As her only living relative, Eliza inherited all her fortune.

Lady Crawford said she was happy to care for Eliza who quickly recovered. Eliza's health improved, she was physically fit and calmer so efforts were made to find her former servant, Grace Whinray to help care for her after noting that Eliza had left Grace £10 in her Will. When it later materialized that none of Eliza's money would devolve to lady Crawford, curiously Lady Crawford proclaimed that Eliza had had a sudden relapse and was returned to Clifton Green asylum.

In 1835 Mr. Duffin asked Jonathan Grey solicitor of York to have a last look at Eliza's papers, to see if anything could be done about the Will. A year later after much badgering by Mrs. Duffin (nee Marsh), Mr. Grey stated that he could find no evidence to validate the Will. This did not go down well with Mrs. Duffin now aged 45, that Eliza should be... *"happy, healthy and most likely to outlive us all"* ... and importantly *"her vast fortune could not be available to those who could use it best"*. After Mr. Duffin's death in 1838, his widow continued to visit Eliza. Were these visits an act of compassion, guilt, or obligation, we will quite possibly never know for sure. We are only able to speculate - perhaps the visits where a show of reconciliation to gain Jane's trust in the hope that a new Will might be drawn up in Duffin's favour?

Eliza was later admitted to the Clifton House retreat or Quakers' Asylum at Clifton in December 1814 which was publicised as being for the 'Reception and cure of persons afflicted with nervous complaints and insanity'. In 1853 she became a resident of Terrace House in Osbaldwick (numbers 59 and 57 Osbaldwick Village). This was the local asylum for ladies founded in 1821. The asylum for men was housed in Hollytree House (no. 47 Osbaldwick Village).

According to the book 'Osbaldwick, the History of a Village' published by Osbaldwick History Group in 1980, "The female patients lived in what is now Stanley House, Osbaldwick Village (No 57) with Mrs (Elizabeth) Toes and later Dr Ure living next door." Eliza Raine died there on 31st January 1860 aged sixty-nine years after suffering a stomach and bowel haemorrhage, having spent all her adult life in an Institution. At that time, her fortune had increased to £8000, (approx. £980,000 today) having no relatives her money was claimed by the crown.

Her body was buried in St Thomas churchyard Osbaldwick across the road from her last home. Her simple gravestone was filmed for television as part of a documentary and visited by the presenter Sue Perkins.

In 1832 Anne recorded in retrospect a discussion of this relationship with the woman with whom she was eventually to settle, Ann Walker...

"Talked of my attachment to Eliza Raine that began at thirteen or fourteen each unknowing at first. That there was a break between us. My fault. I too giddy tho' not caring for anyone else and the poor girl from that time began to be not quite herself"...

Anne did take an interest in Eliza's welfare for many years and made many visits to see Eliza whenever she was in York. This would prove to be a painful exercise for both parties. During one visit Anne made in 1831 Eliza was lying incoherent on the floor, mumbling, recognizing no one, and unable to clean up after herself.

ISABELLA (TIB) NORCLIFFE

Lister was nineteen and Isabella Norcliffe twenty-five when Raine introduced them. Norcliffe's born in 1785, the eldest child of a wealthy landowner, Lieutenant-Colonel Thomas Norcliffe Dalton, and his wife Ann of Langton Hall an estate of around 2,500 acres near Malton in the Vale of York. They had three more surviving daughters, Charlotte, Mary (married Charles Best MD) and Emily (died in Brussels 1817) and two sons, Norcliffe and Thomas.

Tib was an accomplished horsewoman and a keen member of the hunting fraternity... *"I have taken entirely to coursing, and can think or dream of nothing but horses' hares and greyhounds"* ... *"I have had no falls as yet and consequently am very courageous"*. Anne and Isabella became great friends and lovers. Lister enjoyed the social benefits of such a liaison.

Their affair began in 1810 and ran desultorily for many years but began to peter out in the late 1820s after Lister reconsidered Norcliffe's suitability as a possible partner. She wrote of their nights spent together, from their first sexual experience to the later, lack lustre connections when Lister's regard for Isabella was waning. In 1821, for example, a year after Lister's pronouncing the match impossible, she 'slept' with [Norcliffe] at the Black Swan in Halifax and received... *"A kiss (sex) of Tib, both last night & this morning ... but she cannot give me much pleasure & I think we are equally calm in our feelings on these occasions"* ...

The Norcliffe's, however, felt that Anne was a good influence on Isabella and encouraged their friendship. Mrs Ann Norcliffe, Isabella's mother, became fond of Anne and a friendship grew, which remained until Ann Norcliffe's death in 1835. They acted with generosity and invited Anne to family gatherings and excursions around the countryside like the trip to Bath when Anne wrote... *"it was the first time I had left Yorkshire"* ... It was with them that Anne learned the rules and manners of privileged society, cultivating her

73

conversational skills and internalizing the differences between an upper-class accent and her native Yorkshire dialect which she would emulate with great success. Before they returned to Yorkshire, Anne and Isabella were permitted to spend a week alone travelling as far as Stonehenge and enjoying the sites of interest along the way, which gave Anne a taste for travel that she would continue for the rest of her life.

MARIANA BELCOMBE

Mariana Percy Belcombe, (1790-1868) was the daughter of Dr William Belcombe, he was in partnership with a Dr Charles Best, doctors in charge of the York asylum, the 'Retreat' to which Eliza Raine was eventually committed. Anne was introduced to Lister by Isabella Norcliffe in 1812. In that year Mariana Belcombe was 22 years old and Anne was 21 when the pair fell head over heels in love.

Mariana's mother, Marianne (1760-1842) had become uneasy at the deep friendship that had developed between her daughter and Anne Lister. They both strenuously denied any physical relationship, which appeared to satisfy Mrs Belcombe's concerns. Even though Mrs Belcombe had raised her suspicions, the rebellious lovers took liabilities. Anne whilst visiting their home encouraged by Belcombe, bedded Mariana even when all the family were in the house... *"A little before 11, she herself [M] suggested our having a kiss. I thought it dangerous & would have declined the risk but she persisted & by way of excuse to bolt the door sent me downstairs for some paper, that she was going to the close-stool"*

A close stool *was* used from the Middle Ages, an early type of portable toilet, made in the shape of a cabinet, a box or a chair at sitting height, normally with a lid or cover and fitted with a receptacle that could be removed in order to empty. Used until the introduction of the indoor flush toilet ... *"The expedient answer & she tried to laugh me out of my nervousness. I took off my pelisse & drawers, got into bed and had a very good kiss, she showing all due inclination & in less than seven minutes the door was un-bolted again & we were all right again"* ...

Lister committed herself to Belcombe and they went through a type of marriage ceremony conducted themselves of course in private. But four years into their idyllic relationship, Belcombe married on the 9th of March 1816, Charles Lawton, a 56-year-old widower for economic stability. Charles Bourne Lawton (1771-1860) was a wealthy businessman and landowner owning Lawton Hall in Cheshire with an income of £6000 who dearly longed for an heir. His first wife Ann (Featherstone) died in childbirth in 1814; the child also died.

The Belcombe's were delighted at the match, viewing it as the most favourable prospect they could have ever imagined, especially as they had three more unmarried daughters to support. Mariana Lawton's male relatives were able to raise a £10,000 dowry for her marriage to Charles, she was guaranteed £300 a year out of the income of the Lawton estate both annually and in the event of Charles's death.

However, if Mariana had chosen to remain faithful to Anne Lister instead, her relatives would not have provided anything, and she would not have gained the same status in society at that time because although Anne was to become a woman of property and status, that would be achieved only after the death of her uncle. No doubt Lister would have tried to create some degree of financial security for her though she, in turn, was reliant on the allowance that was given to her by her aunt and uncle.

The married couple was to reside in Lawton Hall, the family home of the Lawton's for 13 centuries, a grand country house estate to the east of the village of Church Lawton, Cheshire England. Mariana's new residence was a magnificently refurbished mansion. They had servants to wait on them, fine furnishings, up-to-date facilities, stables and coaches and every luxury that an affluent family could wish for. Little wonder perhaps that Mariana chose absolute luxury over passion.

The building has since been used as a hotel, requisitioned for use as a Civil Defence Reserve Camp, then a school, and in 1999 was converted into separate residential units. It is recorded in the

National Heritage List for England as a designated Grade II Listed building.

In front of the Hall stands a permanent memorial to 'Bullie' the Bullfinch, the cherished pet of Mariana Percy Lawton, the former lady of Lawton Hall. Bullie housed in a cage outside the kitchen window was trained to sing the National Anthem on request. The gravestone was originally engraved in 1853 with a dedicated poem written by Mrs. Lawton to Bullie.

Dear Bullie thy voice which so often did charm

Is silenced forever by Death's mighty arm.

God gave thee thy beauty; man gave thee thy song

Such perfection combined to few Bullies belong

Thy notes were so loyal, so sweet and as gay

As any free bird that sang on its spray

And all who ere heard thee thy loss will regret

Thy ready obedience I ne'er can forget

Then farewell my bird. I give thee this grave

In return for the pleasure thou often me gave

The sun will shine o'er thee, thou art free from the storm

These flowers will be freshened by the tears of the morn

M P Lawton March 31st, 1853

Local councillors, English Heritage, local historians, and residents held a ceremony to reinstate the restored gravestone following the completion of the redevelopment of the Estate.

Anne was devastated by the news of Mariana's coming marriage although she had originally accepted that there was much to gain from this union. Charles was twenty years older than Mariana, so they had both believed his life expectancy would be short and they would benefit from his wealth enabling them to live comfortably together at Shibden after his death, more so if Mariana could produce a son and heir who would inherit all of Charles Lawton's wealth, preventing any of Charles's estate falling in the hands of his nephew who was the next in line to inherit everything. However, Mariana was confident that even if the nephew inherited Charles's estate, being on good terms with him she was sure that he would take care of her. After a terrible accident, when the nephew was killed, she realized that the estate would pass to some other relative, who would not be so caring, and she would be left destitute. In the event their idea that Charles would succumb to an early death was very wide of the mark as he remained in relatively good health until his 89th year!

Anne attended the wedding as did Mariana's sister Anne, both even joined the couple on their honeymoon, with Anne venting continuously about the... *"legal prostitution"*, as she saw the union... *"She believed herself, or seemed to believe herself, over head and ears in love,"* she ranted... *"Yet she sold her person to another. "Surely no-one ever doted on another as I did then on her."* ...

The two women were determined to keep seeing each other. Anne travelled weekly to see Mariana – who lived 40 miles away from Shibden Hall, much to the dismay of her aunt and uncle who were concerned at the expense Anne incurred with these jaunts. Belcombe still wore the ring that Lister had given her at their marriage ceremony, and Lister wore the ring Charles had given Mariana. In September 1825, Belcombe and Lister had a recommitment ceremony. They exchanged wedding rings and gold lockets that contained each other's pubic hair. These rituals did nothing to eliminate the guilt Anne endured, knowing that she was committing adultery with another man's wife. In the stolen moments that they managed to be together, she lamented that... *"I felt that she was another man's wife. I shuddered at the thought & at the conviction that no soffistry (sophistry) could gloss over the criminality of our connection"* ...

Although Lister often declared her passionate attachment to Belcombe, a consequence of their progressive separation, meant that Anne needed to find other liaisons to satisfy her strong desire for physical connections. Even at the height of their affair her diary reports many other flirtations, liaisons, and affairs. In August 1816, Anne Lister stayed at Buxton, the famous Derbyshire spa. She was on her way to visit Mariana at Lawton Hall, Cheshire. She was accompanied by Mariana's sister, Anne Belcombe.

During the day, the two women bathed in the curative waters, a very fashionable pastime in the pursuit of good health and wellbeing; walked on the promenades, met with acquaintances to enjoy tea and a *tête-à-tête* in the pretty cafes. At night they shared a bed, a routine practice for genteel women on a tight budget. One night, on the 15th of August, according to her diary, Lister confessed to Belcombe of having a... *"partiality to the ladies"*, although the next day she hurriedly... *"contradicted all"*. Anne had to proceed with caution when disclosing anything to do with her sexuality, a careless word in the wrong ear could spell disaster for her reputation and status.

Later that year Anne Belcombe stayed with Lister at her home, Shibden and the matter was broached again. While once more they passed their days in the peaceful visits, walks, and gossip typical of women of polite society, their nights together in bed were altogether more eventful. Lister reiterated to Belcombe her... *"penchant for the ladies"*, and... *"expatiated on the nature of my feelings towards her and hers towards me"*. Belcombe was a thirty-one-year-old unmarried woman, six years older than Anne Lister and it was likely she had little experience of matters of a sexual nature, and unlikely to have had experience of lesbian connections. Though undoubtedly, she was infatuated with Anne Lister she was apprehensive about where the situation might be going...

"I mentioned the wickedness said to be practised by girls at schools, but explained how this was quite different, such as making use of instruments. Named the girl in Dublin who was obliged to have a surgeon to extract a stick from her (Jane Duffin's story to Eliza Raine). Secret and solitary vice in all, which I had never any concern. That in fact they would have given me no pleasure and

that I abhorred them all, in naming my peculiar detestation of solitary vice."

Anne Belcombe's hesitation began to frustrate and wear Lister down, so she decided to talk to Anne candidly to illustrate the ramifications she experienced due to Belcombe's conduct...

Sunday 9th November... *"Talked to Anne almost all the morning telling [her] she should be either on or off, that she was acting very unfairly and ought either to make up her mind to let me have a kiss (sex) at once or change her manners altogether. I said she excited my feelings in a way that was very unjustifiable unless she meant to gratify them & that, really, that sort of thing made me far from well, as I was then very sick, languid and uncomfortable – not able to relish anything".*

This frank discussion must have made an impression on Belcombe because she surrendered her inhibitions readily enough to Lister's overtures of seduction, the act of surrender rapidly led Anne to attempt *'great lengths'* of physical intimacy with Belcombe... *"such as feeling her all over pushing my finger up her etc".* Anne added... *"Enlightened her on many subjects, telling her the good of being moist, etc. etc. and that there can be no pleasure without it."*

But when Lister asked her several times to... *"let me get nearer to her and have a proper kiss (genital connection)",* Belcombe declined the offer 'languidly' though... *"as if she would by no means have disliked it but as if she thought it right to refuse".* Questioned by Belcombe about the propriety of such behaviour, Lister said... *"urged in my own defence the strength of natural feeling & instinct".*

Monday 11th November the situation then advanced, Belcombe making the total act of surrender... *"Had a very good kiss (full sex) last night. Anne gave me with pleasure, not thinking it necessary to refuse me any longer"* ...

However, Anne Belcombe's conscience was bothering her... *"she asked if I thought the thing was wrong – if it was forbidden in the Bible... I urged in my own defence the strength of natural feeling & instinct, for so I might call it, as I have had the same turn from infancy."*

Lister's diary account shows her cleverly conniving that neither sister should know of her sexual relationship with the other, writing in the index to November 1816... *"Sat. 23rd: Anne does not suspect M'* and *"Mon 25th: wrote to M- deny the affair with Anne"*.

Her attitude towards Anne was predatory and cavalier... *"Had a very good kiss last night. Anne has always an abundance of moisture and never fails to give me full gratification"* ... She admitted to using her for casual sex, as this diary entry 8th November demonstrates...

"I do not admire but rather frel disgust for her she is not nice & her breath is disagreeable however her manners made me feel desire", But in her dairy, she depicts Anne as being in love with her...

In one letter Anne Belcombe concluded... *"from your ever sincere affectionate, Anne Belcombe."* The seal she applied to her letter, depicted Cupid in a boat guided by a star. *"Si je te perds, je suis perdu,* [Maybe you lose everything, but if I lose you, I'm lost!]. However, Anne Lister confides in her dairy... *"I shall not think about her but get out of the scrape as well as I can, sorry & remorseful to have been in it at all. Heaven forgive me & may M(Mariana) never know it"* ...

All five Belcombe sisters, Mariana, Harriet, Anne (Nantz), Louisa (Lou), and Eliza (Eli), were the objects of Lister's amorous interest and apparent success. A diary entry for 8th November 1816 recounts how she told Anne Belcombe that she had sexual feelings towards' her sister Eliza ... saying that... *"I admired her as a pretty girl". She later considered "sleeping with Eliza Belcombe".* Anne refers frequently to receiving encouragement from Louisa.

Harriet Milne (nee Belcombe) was married to Lieutenant-Colonel Milne and had a romantic liaison with Anne Lister. Mrs Milne was known for her scandalous behaviour earning a reputation with York's high society by conducting numerous love affairs with other men whilst married to Milne. Anne said of her... *"she is a heartless unprincipled woman, and I will not even flirt with her much longer"* ... *"promised to keep the little turquoise ring she gave me and give her another. Lovemaking but too old a bird to entangle myself"* ... (Source: Whitbread's "No Priest But Love" pp 146-153)

COMING TO TERMS WITH SEXUALITY AND IDENTITY

Throughout her life Anne's "oddity" intrigued her; she trawled books on anatomy to comprehend where her feelings came from, to no avail. But as she came to terms with her sexuality, there was no self-loathing. Her feelings were entirely natural she concluded, she could not change what she was, and excepted fully how God had made her. Heterosexual women, while usually confused about their feelings for Anne, were typically captivated by her. Anne was promiscuous and arguably predatory, with always an eye on her next conquest, moving efficiently from one lover to the next.

Anne held masculine views when it came to seduction and surrender, a sexual double-standard which told Anne's masculinized subjectivity that she was free to form as many sexual liaisons as she wished, but if feminized women did so they were no longer worthy of respect. She preferred a woman to be chaste and have reserve at the beginning of the affair, too eager too soon to allow Anne's sexual advances quickly lost Anne's respect.

Lister considered her sexual attraction towards women, 'natural' she certainly did not question as 'unnatural', other feminine women's attraction to her, that may be explained by her feeling of a masculinized identity. She saw her role as masculine, a partnership would have separate spheres of activity for each partner. It is obvious that her idea of masculinity was that the male partner takes the lead in love making and is never penetrated.

Following in the traditional heterosexual ideology for long term relationships, Anne believed that both parties should reveal financial information of their assets. The revelation would then allow Anne to assess that partner, whether they could be an asset to a comfortable future together.

There is little doubt that Anne was a charismatic character; it is obvious that other women found Anne sexually attractive considering the number of females who she indulged in a spontaneous flirtation with. Her manner was such as to beguile them, she excited their feelings, she fascinated even heterosexual ladies, and must have successfully seduced several who submitted to her amorous overtures.

"The girls liked me & had always liked me. I had never been refused by anyone". Anne Lister, 13th November 1816...

To most people it must have been apparent that Anne was somewhat masculine in her mannerisms and flirtatious conduct with other women, though their lack of knowledge and acceptance of homosexuality, would not necessarily associate Anne Lister's attachment to various women with her sexual practice. It was widely thought that a woman had no sexual desires and that loving and affectionate relationships between women were entirely innocent. Unquestionably a male egotistical perception.

The upper classes, representing less than one percent of the population, dominated social life in society, and this was almost entirely controlled by women. Mistakes could cut you off, even if temporarily, from wider human contact. It was this social system that enabled Anne Lister for many years to carry on complex behaviour patterns of nonmonogamy within the women's community without suffering an open scandal.

Anne Lister's relationships with various women over the years since puberty, form a central theme of her life. Without a doubt, Anne Lister for most of her life was a philander her libido, influenced by biological, psychological, and social factors. When attempting to understand Anne Lister's psyche, we must accept that she had a healthy sex drive and longed to settle down in a lasting, loving relationship. The separation from the woman she most loved, Mariana Lawton, reduced her to search for other more available company. Because of this she has been perhaps unjustly labelled predatory.

In her attempts to achieve her goals, Lister tested the boundaries of sexual decorum; the ease in which she was able to take liberties and engaged in same sex petting had surely roots the fact that middle and upper-class women were somewhat repressed from sexual interaction with men and warned to constrain their desires. Certainly, in the circles within which Anne Lister moved, sexualized play between consenting women was acceptable and perhaps more prevalent than we might imagine. Sexuality and desire are a force of nature, which if supressed, could bubble up under the pressure of puritan control and repression, finding other outlets for channelling urges with willing and participating alliances.

From a young age, Lister had emotionally and psychologically come to terms with her sexual orientation. She expressed her feelings about men and women in her diary entry for Monday, 29th January 1821...

"Burnt Mr. Montagu's farewell verses that no trace of any man's admiration may remain". [This is probably the same Mr. Montagu of whom Raine wrote to Lister in July 1812, *"If I am to marry Montagu must be my Husband'*] Lister wrote, *"It is not meat for me. I love and only love the fairer sex and thus, beloved by them in turn, my heart revolts from any other love than theirs..."*

Anne Lister's sexual practice did not exclude her from respectable society if the explicitly sexual practice remained unspoken and hidden. She was a clever chameleon, never open about her sexual practice except for potential lovers, her true sexual identity was concealed, and she was naturally accepted as a female by other members of society. She could thus remain comfortably within the boundaries of respectable society. Anne was a careful observer of lesbian 'signs' amongst other women. One of her techniques of seduction was to mention in conversation, books which touched upon lesbianism or male homosexuality and then to observe her companion and judge their reaction.

Masculinity in the time of Anne Lister was based in sport and codes of honour derived from military prowess, finding expression in hunting, riding, drinking, and wenching. This is not only a critical, upper-class concept of gentry masculinity but is still inordinately linked to a certain physical, material form; Anne Lister does incorporate a gentry discourse on masculinity into her subjectivity, but because of dominant discourse (including laws) about her physical form is unable, for example, to enter the military, University, vote, or drink in public. However, this does not inhibit her from the "wenching" aspect of masculinity.

The ideology of Separate Spheres rested on a definition of the 'natural' characteristics of women and men. Women were considered physically weaker yet morally superior to men, which meant that they were best suited to the domestic sphere. Women in affluent society were considered delicate creatures, frail and emotional, to be treated with gentleness and respect. They were expected to be pure, virginal, untouched by the realities of life. It was accepted that men want sex women want relationships.

Anne Lister was a complicated character. She was considered to have a somewhat masculine appearance and stride, and certainly stood out in Halifax thanks to her decision to dress only in black. The relative ignorance regarding lesbianism would not necessarily associate her mode of dress with her sexual preference and simply be recognised as eccentric or odd. Anne's unusual choice of clothing became an integral part of her image. In the 21st century, we are seldom shocked by mode of dress, almost anything that was once thought scandalous is perfectly acceptable today. In Anne's time, there was much less tolerance for diversity and divergence from social norms, making her determination to wear the outfits that pleased her, brave. We might describe Anne's code of dress as gender-neutral a balance between male and female and therefore marked her out as different, even impressive.

Males held most if not all the power in the 18th and 19th centuries in British society, so we might imagine that if women dressed as men, it was a way for them to get a little of this masculine power. Masculine clothing was a practical choice for independent, active people. Lister found the mannish style suited the independent active life she led on Shibden Hall estate and the image she wished to project. At an early age, she adopted a style of dress that was considered eccentric or odd for a lady, her Halifax neighbours certainly thought so. A diary entry for November 1806, when she was fifteen, describes her attending ... "*Mr. Stafford's concert in a Habit Skirt...*" that is, the split riding skirt, the garment in which the Ladies of Llangollen were frequently depicted. It was the closest a woman could get to trousers at that time and was more usually worn on the farm or at a hunt meet. Lister writes that she... "*was much stared at and well quizzed as an original*", for this outfit. Her response to this attention was that "*care [was] despised on my part*".

Some of the items which Anne wore would have, by the strict social conventions of the time, such as corsetry, (the term corset was first used for this garment in English in1830), Stays (a fully boned laced bodice worn under clothes), pelisse (a woman's ankle-length cloak with armholes or sleeves) and ankle-length skirts be perfectly fitting for a woman and considered normal. But the diaries reveal several items of masculine type clothing that she wore to form a picture of her individuality, an important manifestation of identity.

There's mention of several things including a spencer (*a short waisted or bust-length jacket)* a greatcoat (a protective outer long woollen or worsted coat worn by the more affluent members of society), wool waistcoats, gaiters, or spats (gaiters made of leather or cloth with expensive buttons for the wealthy to wear in cold weather, worn over the shoe and lower leg. Spats made of either leather, white cloth, grey or brown felt material, which fitted around the ankle over the top of footwear) and male drawers worn over female corsetry that marked her out as different, even intrepid. The gentleman's pocket watch which hung from a chain about her person and concealed in her waistcoat pocket was continually being retrieved for time checks then is snapped shut.

At the age of 18, bought a pair of gentlemen's braces for 2/6 - but the braces she wore under her dressing-gown, petticoat, or pelisse.

She wore skirts because trousers were considered a blatant outward sign of masculinity. Additionally, existing laws such as anti-vagrancy statutes were pressed into service to ensure that women would dress in accordance with the gender norms of the time.

For much of history the wearing of trousers has been restricted to men. In Britain it was never officially considered as a crime for women to dress as men, but women living as men, who married other women were accuse of stealing the woman's goods. In many regions of the world, the wearing of trousers by women was forbidden, enforced not only by social custom but also by law. In France, a law made in 1800 forbid the wearing of trousers for women. It was necessary to have the permission of local police if a woman wanted to 'dress like a man' and wear trousers. Various US cities, in the 19th and 20th centuries, passed legislation barring women from wearing trousers. Representative among these was an 1863 law passed by San Francisco's Board of Supervisors criminalizing appearing in public in 'a dress not belonging to his or her sex',

This same law was used to prosecute women for cross-dressing because their dressing outside of gender norms constituted a 'disguise'. In 1851, early women's rights advocate Elizabeth Smith Miller introduced Amelia Bloomer to a garment initially known as the 'Turkish dress', which featured a knee-length skirt over Turkish-style pantaloons... Bloomer came to advocate and promote the dress, including instructions for making it. 'The Lily' newspaper dedicated to the 'Emancipation of Woman from Intemperance, Injustice, Prejudice, and Bigotry, inspired a craze for the dress, which came to be known as 'Bloomers'. It was not until the 1920s and 1930s that wearing trousers became fashionable and acceptable for ladies in the UK.

However, some female laborers in the late 19th century, notably the 'Pit Brow Woman' also known as 'Pit Brow Lasses' in Lancashire and areas of the north, 'Tip Girls' in South Wales, and 'Pit Bank Women' in Staffordshire, (woman surface workers) began wearing trousers beneath a short skirt as a practical component of their uniform. This attracted the attention of the public, and various photographers produced records of the women's unconventional manner of dress through the mid- to late 19th century.

Anne wore her hair in a conventional style with a middle parting and drawn into a bun or coil at the back, adding false curls. These she wore pinned on each side of her head. To keep the curls looking smart and tidy she regularly took them to Crossley's on Horton street to have them done up. Ladies could purchase a variety of hair pieces that gained popularity throughout the 18th and 19th century— from clusters of false curls to pin at their temples to friezes to wear at their foreheads. Anne's choice of hats was also to her singular taste, usually small and round and not the fashion of the day for either woman or men but entries in her diary's also reveal that she did wear a variety of headgear including a bandana and a lady's riding short, top hat. Ladies in general wore bonnets, far more feminine, but Anne had always refused to wear such womanly attire claiming they inhibited her vision.

Commentators have described Anne's fast walk and upright gait as 'if hounds nipped at her heels', the purposeful stride and her kinetic energy defines her. Most people in her time for relatively short distances walked to reach their destination and certainly, Anne's energy enabled her to cover long distances in a noticeably short time. Due to her stride, she was able to cover the six-mile walk from Ripponden a village on the River Ryburn near Halifax in West Yorkshire, to Halifax in just two hours, even though the terrain was rougher than it is today. Due to the amount of exercise her body was slim and wiry. She wrote of herself…

"8st 4 ½ lbs and 5ft 4 ½ ins. tall. It is a very difficult thing to make a bad figure look like a good one" …

However, like many women before and after, she attempted to increase her curves on occasion by adding padding to her chest. She deviated from social norms, but her androgynous look was both provocative but also attractive. Anne said of herself…

"My manners are certainly peculiar, not all masculine but rather softly gentleman-like. I know how to please girls".

In 1817, she describes herself sitting, *"before breakfast, in my drawers put on with gentleman's braces I bought for 2/6 on 27th March & my old black waistcoat & dressing-gown"* ... She appropriated masculine mannerisms, sleeping with a sword, and loaded pistol by her side. By 1820, when she was twenty-nine, she reports being reprimanded by Mariana Belcombe for *"having too much of the civility of a well-bred gentleman"*. Mrs. Simpson mentioned her deep-toned voice. She recounts all this with self-satisfaction, though she noted that her demeanour disturbed Belcombe: After Anne had flattered and complimented Harriet, Mariana's sister whilst in Mariana's company, the obvious jealousy caused Mariana to state... *"Speaking of my manners, she owned they were not masculine, but such was my form, voice & style of conversation ... that if this sort of thing was not carried off by my talents & cleverness, I should be disgusting"*.

Lister makes it clear in her diary that her self-presentation arose in conscious imitation of a man, rather than from a desire to be a man. She undoubtedly had come to accept that her gender is more mental than physical that alone indicates a perceptive, deductive insight and meditative thinking. When she twirled her watch about to impress Mrs. Priestly, she did so in a..." rather *gentlemanly sort of style"* ... rather than as a gentleman; when Miss Browne requested that she take the leather strap off the handle of her umbrella, she did so because it... *"made it look like a gentleman's..."* The greatcoat she ordered from a gentleman's outfitters in London was for... "a *lady's measure'* and *'sufficiently wide in the sleeves to be easy over my pelisse'"* ...

The evidence presented indicates that Lister conceived of her sexuality, not simply in terms of sexual relations, but as a sexual sensibility, acknowledging it as an integral part of herself. Her strong sense of homosexuality as an identity and practice with a historical past was gained from her classical studies. Other enlightening reading from lesbian eroticism was also available at that time in pornographic texts such as the pseudonymous, Abbé du Prat's *'The Venus in the Cloister: or, the Nun in Her Smock',* published in 1683, focusing on masturbation, flagellation, voyeurism, and female same-sex relations. Oxford don William King's vicious satire *'The Toast'*, written in 1732 fictionalizes the

Duchess of Newburgh (Lady Frances Brudenell) as a witch and lesbian named 'Myra. King writes... *"This little Woman gave Myra more Pleasure than all the rest of her Lovers and Mistresses. She was therefore dignified with the Title of Chief of the Tribades or Lesbians..."*

It is obvious that there were concerns in the spiritual and judicial quarters regarding homosexuality. Laws against lesbianism had been suggested both in England and America but not enforced. In 1636, John Cotton (1585 – 1652) who was a clergyman in both England and the American colonies, proposed a law for Massachusetts Bay, to make sex between two women (or two men) a capital offense, but the law was not sanctioned. In 1655, the Connecticut Colony passed a law against sodomy between men and included women, but it was not upheld. In 1779 Thomas Jefferson proposed a law for, "W*hosoever shall be guilty of rape, polygamy, or sodomy by man or woman shall be punished, if a man, by castration, if a woman, by cutting through the cartilage of her nose making a hole of one-half inch diameter"*, but this too failed to become law.

The only prosecution for female homosexual activities in United States history, took place in Plymouth Colony, in 1649, Sarah White Norman and Mary Vincent Hammon were prosecuted for ... *"lewd behaviour with each other upon a bed"*... their trial documents are the only known record of sex between female English colonists in North America during the 17th century. Hammon however, was only reprimanded, possibly because she was younger than sixteen, but in 1650 Norman was convicted and required to acknowledge publicly her 'unchaste behaviour'... This is the only prosecution for female homosexual activities in United States history. (Source: - Days of Love: Celebrating LGBT History - One Story at a Time by Elisa Rolle. Publisher: CreateSpace Independent Publishing Platform; 1 edition, July 1, 2014).

The affair between Lister and Lawton continued though sporadically due to infrequent opportunity for togetherness with Lister feeling like an occasional companion who will always came second. Later in their association, Mariana became embarrassed to be seen in public with Anne, because of Anne's obvious underlying masculine characteristics, which was remarked upon by others, and which could have reflected badly on herself as to what their alliance involved. They are a butch/femme couple. A woman friend told Anne that Mariana is ... *"plus femme que moi"* (woman than me) ... *"I have the figure & nature of a man. Have not beauty but agreeable features tho' not those of a woman. I joked, pretended to be shocked..."*

Anne comforted herself with the idea that togetherness would eventually resolve Mariana's concerns. ... *"For if we once got together the world might say what it pleased. She should never mind. . . She shrank from having the thing surmised now, but declared that if we were once fairly together, she should not care about it. I might tell our connection to all the world if I pleased"* ...

Perhaps Mariana's claim that she was agreeable to such openness was because she knew that the fulfilment of this plan would never materialize.

It was not until the mid-19th century that the word Lesbian and Sapphic came into general use as terms for female relationships. Such practices were due to be criminalised in the Criminal Law Amendment Act 1885 legislation until Queen Victoria declared them impossible, whereupon the clause was omitted, an amusing naivety that serves to underline a common, and commonly welcomed ignorance, at a time when lurid, fictionalised lesbianism was often figured as an especially repulsive/seductive French vice. In 1921 Parliament attempted to extend the Criminal Amendment Act of 1885, to add a clause making lesbianism into a criminal offence. However, this was ultimately dropped out of concern that legislation would only draw attention to the 'offence' and encourage women to explore their sexuality.

DIARIES OF 1817

It was in 1817 that Anne's mother, Rebecca Lister, and her brother-in-law Uncle Joseph Lister of Northgate House died. Uncle Joseph had been Anne's earliest benefactor, he left Anne 'twenty pounds for Mourning'. Aunt Mary, Joseph's wife was left the home they shared, Northgate House in Halifax but when she died in 1822 the property reverted to Uncle James to embellish the Shibden estate. Uncle James then increased Anne's allowance to £50 a year afforded by the rent gained from the property, which aided Anne's travelling expenses visiting friends and lovers.

At the time of the earliest journal entries, Mariana has already married, and her husband who intercepted their correspondence, which included speculations on Anne and Mariana forming a household together after the husband's death. Understandably when their plotting was discovered, Charles was incensed and refused to allow their association to continue.

At this point, Anne began to use her cipher in the infrequent correspondences for key passages, as well as in her journals. Relations between the two women were becoming strained from the separation. The opulent lifestyle that Mariana now had living with Charles, helped to compensate the loss of her lover's company, she appreciated her affluent position above the less lavish prospects with Anne, who relied on hand-outs from her relatives and was in no position to support anyone other than herself.

Anne laments...

"I now begin to think seriously that she and I will never get together. Strange to say I feel as if I was weening myself from wishing it. I begin to fancy I shall not like another man's leavings and that by the time Charles is out of the way I may have suited myself as well all things considered. I have no fault to find with

Mariana as to her conduct, but her letters have ceased to be those best calculated to keep alive my affections and the present impossibility of our seeing each other may have made a wide difference in both before we meet again. I love her yet still I never felt till now that I could love without her. God knows how the thing will end. I feel a sad want of someone, and I am sure I will be anxious to fix as soon as I have a fortune and establishment of my own" ...

Anne's thoughts turned once more to an earlier lover, Tib (Isabella Norcliffe), who was part of the York social circles of her youth. Tib and her family, however, were traveling in Italy. And so, Anne befriended a Miss Browne, daughter of a Mr. Copley Browne, a self-made businessman of Westfield Cottage, Halifax, a woman from a socially inferior family—an association which caused jealousies among some other Halifax families to whose company Anne was indifferent. But this new friendship was interrupted by Miss Browne's removal to Harrogate for half a year. Was this to separate the two woman and keep Miss Brown from harm's way and the influence of Anne Lister?

In May, the Lister's whilst quietly seated together downstairs at a few minutes to 10 pm were disturbed by loud rapping and hysterical female voices at their door. The callers were Mrs. Walker of Crow nest and her two daughters, Elizabeth, and Ann all in a terrible state of fright and shock. They had just been in a dreadful accident after their carriage had overturned into a field after taking a bend at the top of the lane. The reins had broken, the coachman had lost control, the horses had been running full speed and were now lying in a field possibly dead. The coachman had sprung a bone in his left ankle and was badly bruised. The ladies came off much better, and though shook up and in shock, they were otherwise in good condition. After a soothing glass of wine and very much recovered they were given cloaks and lanterns, the ladies set off to walk home, their coach broken and undrivable but the horses which had fallen had quite recovered, the ones which had bolted were caught and taken home by the Lister's servants.

During a visit to York Anne took the opportunity to see Mariana and her family and try to repair some social ties by pretending to be less affectionate to Mariana to give the impression that their association went no deeper than friendship. This reaching out led to a very brief return visit from Mariana at the end of the month. Anne joyfully discovers that Mariana is still a virgin because of her husband's obvious incompetence; Anne describes in detail how she uses her middle finger to break the membrane and so takes Mariana's virginity, which gives Anne a feeling of euphoria.

Tuesday 2nd September: *"Spent the whole morning vamping up a pair of old black chamois shoes. As soon as I was dressed went to drink tea with the Miss Walkers of Cliff Hill – went in black silk, the first time to an evening visit I have entered upon my plan of always wearing black"* ...

Saturday 18th October: *"From a little before tea till near 11 at night looking over poor Eliza Raine's letters. My heart bled at the remembrance of the past, poor girl! She did indeed love me truly"*.

Wednesday 22nd October: *"Looking over the correspondence between Mariana and me in the beginning of 1815: whatever might be her regard for me it is very plain it bore but a very subservient portion to her regard for the good things of this world. I was in love or surely, I could not have been so blinded and acted with such doting folly. Oh, that I then could have given her up without a struggle"* ...

On Saturday 27th December: Anne received tragic news that 18 years old Emily Norcliffe who was with her family travelling the continent had sadly died of consumption whilst in Brussels. Charlotte her sister was sick too; her symptoms were the same as those suffered by her brother in-law Charles Best who had died during their stay in Italy. However, the Scottish physician attending Charlotte had prescribed medication that had done her good, but the family were sick with worry after the tragedy of already losing two of their party and the trauma they had been through.

DIARIES OF 1818

The first part of the year was noticeably quiet, in April Miss Browne returned to Halifax and Anne becomes quite attentive to her, despite considering her family vulgar. This resulted in much speculation as the friendship was between the two women alone and not between their families. Anne finds many excuses to encounter her casually, in the library, on the street, she feels despondent if she does not run into Miss Brown but there are no formal visits.

Halifax society began to gossip, making comments regarding Anne's unlikely relationship with this young lady. When writing accounts of their meetings in her dairy Anne has given Miss Browne the nickname Kallista (derives from Callisto, from the Greek, meaning 'most beautiful', who was a nymph, the daughter of King Lycao). Anne also records encounters with more lower-class persons who mock her for her masculine appearance and habits.

Thursday 28th August... *"Did nothing but dream of Miss Brown and though I awoke at six yet had not resolution to get up but lay dozing and thinking of the fair charmer. She is certainly very pretty, she seemed evidently not displeased with my attention and I felt all possible inclination to be as foolish as I ever was in former days, in fact I shall be much better out of her way than in it"* ...

When Anne writes of Mariana, she is cooler, she has doubts that they will ever be together. Each passing month without meeting only confirms their drifting apart and propels her thoughts to whether she can shape Miss Browne into a suitable companion. In general, Miss Browne though it seems is flattered by Anne's attentiveness, she was also flustered by it. Anne appears to believe Miss Browne understands the nature of her affections, but this is not at all clear to an outside observer. Anne it seems is unable to compel any sort of intimacy with Miss Brown and her desire for female closeness was overwhelming.

The Norcliffe's, including Anne's friend Tib, returned from their travels to the continent, with a recovered Charlotte. *"Mrs Norcliffe seemed glad to see me & I very sincerely rejoice to find them in spirits so much better than I fancied they would be"* ...

Anne planned to spend September and the following few weeks with the Norcliffe's in York. The family were having a house party and Anne was both excited and apprehensive about the meeting with Isabella after almost three years separation and after such tragic events during the families' ill-fated travels abroad... Anne and tib were soon reunited in the bedroom ... *"After all, Tib's passion last night, or rather in the evening, she was dry at night. But oiled her with rose oil and then had a good kiss"* ...

In late November Anne spends time with the Belcombe's (Mariana's family). There is an interesting conversation with Lou (Mariana's sister) on the topic of female companions and Anne gets the impression that Lou seems to be hinting of her own feelings for Anne. In December, Anne returns to Halifax where she again takes a strong interest in Miss Browne still hoping that they might at last become more intricately connected.

In 1818 she wrote...*"The people generally remark, as I pass along, how much I am like a man. I think they did it more than usual this evening. At the top of Gunnery Lane, as I went, three men said, as usual,"That's a man' & one axed 'Does your cock stand' I know not how it is, but I feel low this evening."* ...

Although Anne appears to accept and on occasion even gratified with comments on her apparent masculinity from friends and individuals from polite society, the more brutal, scornful utterances from the lower classes, cause her great pain.

DIARIES OF 1819

Anne is disappointed when she discovers that Miss Browne is evidently in love with a man that she has known for several years and is unhappy that her parents are set against him. It was becoming clear to Anne that Miss Browne had never seen Anne's interest as romantic. After much internal conflict recorded in February and March, Anne's acceptance of this impossible situation is quite evident as her interest fades significantly.

In 1819 having saved up an adequate sum, Anne was determined to travel in France, perhaps with Tib or with her aunt Anne, as a distraction from her frustration at the separation from Mariana the woman whom she desperately loved. Letters arrive from Mariana, but these do little to elevate the fear that any hope of sharing their lives is unlikely as she... *"will be worn out in service to another"*.

In May, Anne and her aunt Anne spent a month in Paris. Turning her attention almost entirely to the subject of natural history she discovered the... *"Jardin des Plantes* (Garden of the Plants) *biological gardens and found that there were thirteen professors attached to this noble establishment, each gives an annual course of lectures gratis, and equally open to foreigners as to the French themselves!"* ...

In June, after they return home, Tib comes to visit and though Tib was eagerly affectionate, various discussions made it clear to Anne that there was no future for them as a couple in part because Tib was saddled with responsibility for an unmarried sister.

With the growing disinterest in Miss Browne and the futility of making plans with Mariana, Anne's romantic prospects were looking bleak. Anne is also irritated by Tib as she has something of an annoying habit of teasing, repeating anecdotes, the snuff taking, the drinking and the inexcusable blabber telling their friends about Anne's coded journals. Anne prefers to keep such revelations from general speculation, therefore Tib's loose lip chatter, causes Anne a great deal of irritation.

In August, despite her dwindling interest, but forever the optimist, Anne finally brings Miss Browne to Shibden Hall for a formal visit. During which Tib who is staying with Anne at Shibden takes the opportunity when the three of them are alone in the garden, to kiss Anne in front of Miss Browne, so that would give Anne an excuse to kiss Miss Browne in turn, which she does rather *"moistly"*. Miss Browne appeared embarrassed with such familiarity, which made Anne feel awkward and which confirmed the fact that Miss Brown did not think of Anne as a potential lover. Throughout September, Anne comments regularly on how she will be relieved when Tib leaves and she can return to her routines, but also will be sad... *"left alone with none to love or speak to"*.

In late October, Mariana proposes a meeting while she is in transit with her mother and sister in Manchester, the opportunity arising because her husband would not be with them. This resurrects some of Anne's dwindling feelings for Mariana after their long separation and reminding her that she should not read too much into the invitation, for as always, she would be left devastated on their parting. However, she decides to go to Manchester anyway, which happened in mid-November. They spend the night together and discuss their sex life and how it relates to Mariana's marriage...

Anne feels that any commitment she had made was annulled by Mariana's marriage. As if to spite her, Anne brings up Tib's continuing interest, noting... *"Tib would really willingly marry me in disguise at the altar"*... At the end of the year, Anne is being bothered by a persistent (male) suitor--a stranger who has been writing her letters that she ignores. There is also an incident where someone put an advertisement in the paper in her name looking for a husband, evidently as a practical joke or more likely as harassment.

DIARIES OF 1820

At the beginning of the year, Anne is once more being annoyed by strangers accosting her on the road and by impertinent letters sent anonymously. After yet another comment about an advertisement taken out in her name seeking a 'sweetheart', she consults a lawyer about the letters, but he advises her to take no notice and do nothing.

In February she goes off to spend time in York with the Balcombe's and Mariana. In March they are joined by Isabella (Tib) Norcliffe and it is clear having all three women in one place is a rather uncomfortable situation as both Mariana and Tib are jealous of the other's close friendship with Anne.

Mariana returned to Halifax with Anne. At one point she found one of Anne's diaries with entries from around the time of her marriage to Charles and becomes upset to discover how badly it had affected Anne. They discuss some of the issues around Anne's too-attentive public behaviour to other women. There is an entry that concludes…

"Went upstairs at 11. Sat up lovemaking, she is conjuring me to be faithful, to consider myself as married, & always to act to other women as if I was M--'s husband."

Mariana seems to be overly concerned about Anne's faithfulness or lack of it. There are several emotional scenes where Mariana demands some sort of pledge, a promise to curtail all other liaisons with other willing partners. Anne evades the subject and tries to skip around giving a straight answer, convincing herself that she is free to form other romantic connections as Mariana chose marriage above her love for Anne. When Mariana writes to her in August, she continues to believe that Anne should not indulge herself with other loves and continues to refer to her promise. Anne cautions her to be more discreet and is concerned that their intimacy could be discovered and in retaliation asks Mariana to send her letters back.

This squabble lasted for almost a year, they kept their distance until the pair were reunited when Mariana accepted an invitation to visit Shibden, and after taking to her bed with toothache, Anne visited her bedroom and demanded a "*kiss*"...

Thursday 9th July 1820. After Anne returned to Halifax her account in her Journal recorded that both Anne and Mariana had both experienced some form of venial symptoms. Anne was sure their symptoms was a direct result of their intimate association. Anne strongly suspected that Charles, Mariana's husband who was known to have a reputation for extramarital affairs with young women, even members of his own extended family, had infected Mariana and in turn, she had passed it on to her.

On Saturday, Aug 4th Anne went to York to discuss Mariana's infection with her brother Steph, and he informed Anne that he was treating his sister for this condition. Anne to be discreet told Steph... *"Said I knew someone in the same condition. A young married woman, poor, who had tried much advice without relief and therefore asked Steph for the same prescription he gave M-. which he promised. I begin to look at home for the heat & itching I felt last night have been considerable today & I am persuaded of being touched with the same complaint"* ...

Whilst staying in York Anne writes, Tuesday 7th Aug.
"Nice clean bed & slept very comfortably. The people very attentive & civil, nor do I think their charges high. Dinner 3/6 dessert 1/-; bed, 2/-; & breakfast 1/9; my sitting room not charged. In fact, I have every reason to be satisfied & will go to the Bridgewater (Manchester hotel) in the future. The mail left Manchester so punctually at 9, that has obliged me to bring away a crust of roll & leave my breakfast untouched. Had an inside place but came the whole way on the box with the coachman... The man offered me the reins 2 or 3 miles on the side of Rochdale, gave me some good instructions & I drove 2 or 3 miles.... Got into Halifax at 20 minutes before 2".

Friday 10th Aug: *"Ordered Suter to make me up Steph's prescription for venereal & what I copied from Mr. Duffin long ago for an injection. A scruple of calomel gradually mixed in a marble mortar with an ounce of sweet oil. .... two or three drops to be injected two or three times a day after making water generally cure in two or three days. Asked Suter if he had ever made up Steph's prescription before. "Yes," said he, very frequently. I have felt the discharge a good deal today, & as if my linen, rubbing against my thighs, made them feel hot & irritated. There can be no doubt it can be venereal". From twelve until the time getting into bed, trying to use my two ivory syringes that were Eliza Raine's. Let the common one fall & broke off the top of the piston but afterwards got to manage very well with the uterine syringe"*

The following day Anne's servant George brought the rest of the prescription from Suter... *"liniment for the injection, fifteen pills, pulvis cubeb powers and lotions. The lotions contained, ten grains of hyd, oximur, that is a corrosive sublimate, with two drams of tincture of opium to be mixed in a quart of water administered with a sponge"* ... Anne was to suffer bouts of her venereal disease throughout her life.

In the 18th and 19th century, mercury, arsenic, and sulphur were commonly used to treat venereal disease, which often resulted in serious side effects and many people died of mercury poisoning. In the 20th Century, the advent of penicillin and other antibiotics led to an effective cure for bacterial STDs.

Though Anne had concerns over her health caused by her infection, she continued to have other affairs, though showing some restraint about full sexual contact until Mariana, jealous of her other lovers, begged her to... *"be faithful, to consider myself as married." "What would Mariana say to all this if she knew? I am indeed unable, it seems, to take care of myself with woman. I am always getting into some scrape with them"* ... But later she wrote... *"I shall now begin to think and act [as] if she were my wife"* ...

At the end of September, Anne goes to York to visit the Norcliffe's for a short break. Anne concerned at Tib's indulgent behaviour and takes her to task for the quantity of wine she drinks, which Tib strongly denies.

In October of 1820 whilst again staying with Isabella, Miss Mary Vallance another female houseguest attracts Anne's flirtatious attention. Tib takes exception to the attention Anne is paying to Miss Vallance and the three of them lay in bed. Anne recalls...

"I pressed her as well as I could for Tib not to know. In the course of the morning, she came into my room for my gloves to mend, sat on my knee & staid half an hour, both of us in a state of great excitement.... I see that may say & do what I like" ... *Later when they got the chance to be alone... Sucked her left breast very near quarter of an hour – She certainly did not dislike it"* ...

Anne made a point of explaining to Miss Vallance, who took the man's role in her relationship with Tib and made it clear that she would do likewise with her too. This revelation resulted in Miss Vallance inviting Anne again into her room later that night, Anne was more than happy to accept her invitation.

... *"I found her alone, and though Burnett (servant) came in, she whispered me to stay. Began rubbing her. I kissed and put my tongue in while I had the three fingers of my right hand pushed as far as they would go up there. Distinctly felt the stones of ovaria. She was ready and wide as if there was not virginity to struggle with. I spoke softly and asked if she liked me. She said yes and began to whimper and said her love was not worth having and would send me to Isabella"* ...

In November whilst in company Anne took the liberty of sitting close to Miss Valance... *"I sat by her, and unobserved by those around, got my hand up her petticoats and pushed my finger up her quere"* ...

Their apparent closeness had aroused Tib's suspicions, their body language was a strong clue to what was occurring, and that resulted in Tib's relationship with Anne becoming rather strained. Tib conceded that if she wished to keep Anne's attention, she had no other option but to share Anne's affections with yet another rival in Miss Vallance...

"Tib was very violent after she came into bed at night. We renewed the conversation & she was a good deal more violent than before.... I stood by the fire, talking very calmly, I daresay about an hour, while she was in bed, repeating what I had said before. She still swore by all that is sacred she never took more than five glasses a day: one at luncheon, one at supper, one at dinner & two at tea. I repeated that I could, if I chose, mention a time (alluring a time when she was last at Shibden) when for several days she not only took more than five but more than six or seven glasses. She called God and all the angles it was a lie & wished herself at the devil if it was not false. I still quietly persisted that I knew the thing to be fact. She declared it to be an infamous lie, that I could not mention the time & place where, because I could not.... I told her many home truths. When the conversation ceased, I began to curl & get into bed. She was soon snoring & we never spoke after me getting into bed".

In the morning Anne went to some length to tell Tib that her taking too much wine... *"was lamented by all her friends"* ... Anne explained how she did not know the injury she caused herself, with even the servants commenting on her drinking, and how much she had aged through overindulgence of drink. This made quite an impression on Tib who had to concede that she was making herself unattractive and therefore unlovable to Anne.

Anne's feelings were fickle, and perhaps Miss Vallance gave her too much leeway to do as she pleased to retain Anne's enthusiasm...

"Only a few minutes with Miss Vallance & felt no real desire to succeed with her. At last, she said, now you are doing all this and perhaps mean nothing at all. Of course, I fought off, bidding her only try me, but I felt a little remorse struck" .... *"then went to Anne, a little before twelve & stayed two hours. At first rather lover-like, reminding her of former days. But nor her or her room seemed very sweet to my nose. I could not help contrasting her with Miss Vallance & felt no real desire to succeed with her".*

Anne had been contemplating the pros and cons of a past conquest, Anne Belcombe, Mariana's sister, and notes in early December... *"I believe I could have her again in spite of all she says ... [she] owns she loves me & perhaps she has feelings as well as I. She let me kiss her breasts*" ... Anne records at least two other sexual encounters with Anne Belcombe in late December.

DIARIES OF 1821

While staying with the Balcombe's in York she is once again in the company of Miss Vallance. Anne gives her a copy of her secret cypher while at the same time saying she is... *"getting lukewarm about her."* ... Anne returns to Halifax in mid-January.

In February she writes a very loving letter to Mariana and refers to her as... *"my wife"* ...

Thursday 8th February 1821... *"Came upstairs at 11 a.m. Spent my time from then until 3, writing to M- very affectionately, more so than I remember to have done for long... Wrote the following crypt., "I can live upon hope, forget that we grow older, & love you as warmly as ever. Yes, Mary, you cannot doubt the love of one who has waited for you so long & patiently. You can give me all of happiness I care for &, prest to the heart which I believe my own, caressed & treasured there, I will indeed be constant & never, from that moment, feel a wish or thought for any other than my wife. You shall have every smile & every breath of tenderness. One shall our union & our interests be, & every wish that love inspires & every kiss & every dear feeling of delight shall only make me more securely & entirely yours... I do not like to be too long estranged from you sometimes, for, Mary, there is a nameless tie in that soft intercourse which blends us into one & makes me feel that you are mine. There is no feeling like it. There is no pledge which gives such sweet possession"* ...

In May she records a sexual fantasy about a local woman Caroline Greenwood, whom she admires, and there are regular notes through the summer about her attraction to various women, though none of these seem to go beyond admiration. Yet in June, in the context of writing to Mariana, she once again notes that she considers herself pledged to her...

"I love and only love the fairer sex and thus beloved by them in turn, my heart revolts from any other love than theirs." – 29th January 1821.

In July, Anne makes a visit to see Mariana at the home of her brother in Newcastle, two notable things are recorded. After making love to Mariana, they exchange ... *"an irrevocable promise forever"* ... and symbolize it with the same ring that Anne had previously given Mariana. Anne also notes that the suspicion that Mariana has passed on to her the venereal disease, mentioning the symptoms and treatment she is applying, this subject is reflected upon in many of Anne's future entries.

In September, Anne goes again to York and pays a great deal of time and attention to acquiring a carriage and horse. While there, she has a flirtatious encounter with Anne Belcombe though she notes to herself that she is... *"much altered"* ... in attitude to Anne since making her pledge to Mariana. But when Tib Norcliffe comes to visit her in York, it is clear they continue their sexual relationship, both from Anne's coded use of *'kiss'* (for orgasm) and from her concern after the passion that she might have passed the venereal infection on to Tib.

She is still in York in December when Mariana comes to visit her there (intending to return to Halifax with Anne at the end of the year). While still in York, there is again friction when Anne, Mariana, and Tib are in the same company. Anne is learning to drive her new carriage with only minor mishaps.

DIARIES OF 1822

Anne was depressed after Mariana left Halifax in January. During a visit from Tib, Anne tells her that she is no longer as interested in *'sleeping with'* other women because of her relationship with Mariana. Tib teases her about this and continues to believe that she would eventually settle down with her. Anne on the other hand was hanging on to the possibility that she would eventually be Mariana's life partner. Anne continues to be less than honest with Tib about her commitment to Mariana, of whom Tib continues to be jealous. This situation is mirrored by the scenario Anne found herself with Mariana. Both Lawton and Lister are less than honest about their intent, and both Norcliffe and Lister were waiting in anticipation for something unobtainable.

During that year of 1822, the Listers acquired three new horses. Naming them was a serious business for Anne. The names had to have meaningful associations and gave her the opportunity of celebrating something or someone who she held in high esteem. One of the horses... *"a very pretty, four-year-old, useful mare [is] to be called Vienne, from a little circumstance relative to Vienne in Dauphiny"* ... the birthplace of her lover, Mariana Lawton (nee Belcombe) who was born in Vienne in 1790 during the time her father, Dr Belcombe, spent working on the Continent.

Anne gave her next horse the name of Percy, again ..."*out of compliment to Mariana"* ... whose full name was Mariana Percy Lawton. Her stable was now complete and the attention she lavished on her horses did much to alleviate the pain and sadness caused by Mariana's marriage and the lonely days spent dreaming of their eventual union. On the 22nd January of that same year, it had become necessary to have the Listers' old mare put down.

Anne's relative, Aunt Mary (Joseph Lister's widow) died, her property Northgate House, passed to the ownership of the Lister estate and Anne and Tib quarrel over plans for the property whether they might share it living together. Anne alternates between making love to her and explaining that they would not work out as partners and happy when Tib eventually leaves. The summer passes mostly with social encounters. Anne has conflicts with her Halifax neighbours over her snobbishness.

Saturday, June 1st Anne writes... *"My uncle brought down the will that he has written... Everything is secured to me except for the navigation money, which will be at my aunt's disposal"* ...

The contents of the Will states... I give devise and bequeath all and every my real and personal estates whatsoever and wherever. To my Niece Anne Lister her Heirs, Executors, Administrators and Assigns absolutely forever. And I hereby appoint her, the said Anne Lister my Niece the sole executrix of this my Will, not doubting she will see the same carefully performed.

In June, Anne began planning a visit to Wales where she hoped to visit Lady Eleanor Butler and Miss Ponsonby, the famous "Ladies of Llangollen". Anne had a fascination regarding the two Irish gentlewomen who had run off to live with each other in Wales and whose relationship during the late 18th and early 19th century scandalized and fascinated their contemporaries. They provided a celebrated exemplar of feminine, yet respectable romance which Anne hoped to emulate one day with a love of her own. Anne's ambition was to visit them and witness their life together. They had moved to Wales with a servant, Mary Caryll, who lived and worked for them without pay for the rest of her life, and who was buried in the same plot and memorialized on the same grave marker.

Anne spoke with her lover, Mariana about the coming visit to meet the two ladies, as Mariana had made the same trip herself some years before. Anne was keen to know if it might be possible for her to meet them personally, and if so, what type of introduction she would need to make their acquaintance. She was assured that they receive... *"any literary person"*... who calls on them. Anne eager to meet them arranged the visit for herself and her aunt in July. Before they left for Wales, she had a brief tryst with Mariana in passing at Northwich.

Saturday 13 July [Diary in Crept hand:) Lister confided in her diary the concerns she had regarding the evasive attitude that Mariana had adopted during their planned reunion...

"When I asked M- how long it might be before we got together.... she seemed to fight off answering......She seems as fond of me as ever, yet all the night when I was convulsed with smothering my sobs, she took no notice, nor was affected at all apparently" ...

... "Two kisses last night, one almost immediately after the other, before we went to sleep and one just before getting up this morning, I felt better but was so shockingly low last night I cried bitterly but smothered it so that M– scarcely knew of it. At any rate, she took no notice, wisely enough. I told M– before we got up of my regard for and correspondence with Miss MacLean and M– told me of the gentlemanliness & agreeableness of Mr. Powis who, it seems, might interest M– more than duly had her heart no object but C– (Charles), with whom she has had no connection these four months"... It appears that a little tit for tat to instigate a little jealousy had entered their conversation...

"Not down to breakfast till 11 – settling 1 thing or other – M– went with me to the stables to see Percy & the gig & we then (leaving my aunt) went to inquire about servants – walked a little on the walls up & down the rows & did not come in till 1 – then, perhaps luckily for us, all in a bustle & M– off at 2 14"...

WALES & THE LADIES OF LLANGOLLEN

Anne and her aunt accompanied by their manservant George Playforth set off for their planned trip to Wales...

" We were off [from Chester] in 12.1/2 hour & got here (the King's Head, new hotel, Llangollen patronized by Lady Eleanor Butler & Miss Ponsonby) in 4.12 hours including the 12.12 hour we stopped at the church gate at Wrexham to the beautiful church which is kept with the greatest possible neatness – Beautiful drive from Chester to Wrexham. It was market day & the town seemed very busy".

The beautiful drive from Wrexham *was* described by Anne in all its splendid detail.

"The inn (kept by a Elizabeth Davies) is close to the bridge & washed by the River Dee, we are much taken with our hostess & with the place – have had an excellent roast leg of mutton, & trout & very fine port wine with every possible attention – I should like to spend a few days here – It is from here the Saltmarshes had the mutton sent – 5d per lb & the carriage might be about 1. 12 per lb making it in all 6.12 a lb. The waiter said we had come on the wrong side of the water – we should have crossed by a bridge on our left over the canal (the Ellesmere) & turned along the aqueduct – we sat down to dinner at 8.12, having previously strolled thro' the town to Lady E– B–'s & Miss Ponsonby's place – there is a public road close to the house, thro' the grounds, & along this we passed & repassed [deletions] standing to look at the house (cottage) which is really very pretty – a great many of the people touched their hats to us on passing & we are much struck with their universal civility" –

"After dinner (the people of the house took it at 10), wrote the following note to the Right Honourable Lady Eleanor Butler & Miss Ponsonby Plasnewydd. Mrs & Miss Lister take the liberty of presenting their compliments to Lady Eleanor Butler & Miss Ponsonby, & of asking permission to see their grounds at Plâs Newyd in the course of tomorrow morning – Miss L–, at the suggestion of Mr Banks, had intended herself the honour of calling on her ladyship & Miss Ponsonby, & hopes she may be allowed to express her very great regret at hearing of her ladyship's indisposition – King's Head Hotel – Saturday evening 13 July". In reply the message returned was that *should go to the grounds at 12 noon the following day, – "this will prevent our going to church, which begins at 11 & will not be over till after 1 – the service is principally in Welsh except the lesson & sermon every 2nd Sunday & tomorrow is the English day – Lady E.B. has been couched – she ventured out too soon & caught cold – her medical man (Mr Lloyd Jones of Ruthin) positively refuses her seeing anyone – her cousin, Lady Mary Ponsonby, passed thro' not long ago & did not see her – wrote the above of today & the last 16 lines of yesterday from 10.12 to 12.12 after dinner – It struck 12 before I came up to bed & I wrote 12.12 hour afterwards – Very fine day – merely a beam or 2 of sun, & no dust – consequence of late rain – they have had scarcely any rain here till last day or 2 – they were burnt up before – market day here – beef 6d per lb, veal 3d-3 1/2, mutton 4d to 5d* – [in code referring to her venereal condition*: a good deal of discharge both today & yesterday]* –

Sunday 14th July
"My aunt and I off at 8.12 to Castell Dinas Brân (a medieval castle occupying a prominent hilltop site above the town of Llangollen*) & got back again at 10 – 36 minutes in ascending to the summit – a boy, the under waiter at the inn, went with us as guide, and led us by the way[thro] the little garden of Evan Parry whose son, a boy of 12 or 13 accompanied us with 2 sticks pronged with iron – my aunt used hers, but I had no need of one – the way is perfectly good and considering the steepness of the ascent & the dryness of the ground not at all slipper[I never slipped once even with my bright iron-heeled boots on] – little steps cut which obviate whatever difficulties there might otherwise be – there was a light blue mist over the mountains which impeded our view – & after reading*

Bingley's description & that ascending Dinas Bran might be a substitute to those who had not ascended Snowdon. I was disappointed we could not see near to the end of the Vale of Llangollen – nor distinguish anything of Vale [sic] Crucis Abbey – the hills immediately around bounded our view very narrowly – the remains are very small – Mr .... (Lloyd?) of Chirk to whom the castle belongs is going to build a sort of gothic [cottage or] summer house at the top of the hill. The castle is to be walled round with an upper & lower wall, & the rest of the ascencottat pleasant all round – this will be a very great improvement – the waiter seemed to know something of the [underground] communications with the castle mentioned but disbelieved by Bingley – he (the waiter) said it was somewhere towards the north end of the castle now filled up with stones – In descending we gave the boy 1/ – for going with us and taking the sticks & went into his father's cottage – very neat – his wife and youngest daughter there very neat looking healthy people – a very nice old man – a slater by trade and slated "that grand house" the King's Head – He had been reading the "English physician" an old physic book – we asked him to read us a little of the 1st chapter of St John in Welsh – he did & I tried to read after with tolerable success – the pronunciation is very gutteral, but I think I could get the language in a few months so as to make myself pretty well understood – Had breakfast as soon as we got back – excellent bread & butter, hot home-made rolls, & good coffee – At 11. 34 my aunt & I, accompanied by Boots to introduce us, walked to Plâs Newydd – the gardener in waiting – we talked to him a good deal – he seemed a good sort of intelligent man much attached to his mistresses after having lived with them 30 years – he had walked about the country with them many miles when they were young – they were about 20 when they 1st came there & had now been there 43 years – they kept no horses but milked 6 cows – said I, "Can they use the milk of 6 cows?" "Oh! they never mind the milk – it is the cream" – he said Lady E.B. was a good deal better – He remembered Mr Banks – has been there 4 or 5 times – I told him I had longed to see the place for the last dozen years, & we have expressed our great admiration of the place – In St Gothens (for I know not how else to spell it & which we most particularly admired) was a little bookcase of 30 or 40 volumes, chiefly poetry, Spenser, Chaucer, Pope, Cowper, Homer, Shakespeare, & – I quite agreed with M– (vide her letter), the place "is a beautiful little bijou" shewing excellent taste – much to the credit of the ladies who have done it entirely themselves. The gardener said, "they were always reading" – the dairy is very pretty, close to the house, & particularly the pump Gothic iron-work from Shrewsbury (Colebrookdale perhaps ?) – the well 7 yards deep – It is an interesting place – my expectations were more than realized & it excited in me, from a variety of circumstances, a sort of particular interest tinged with melancholy – I could have mused for hours & dreampt [dreams] of happiness, conjured up many a vision of [illegible] hope – In our return we strolled thro' the church yard – I shall copy the epitaph to Lady E. B– 's & Miss P–'s favourite old servant, Mrs Mary Clark, who died in 1809, when we go back – Just peeped into the church stood in the porch – the service not concluded – for the benefit of the distressed Irish – got back to the inn at 1.14 and off to Corwen at 1.34 and get here [Corwen] in exactly 1. 40 hours at 3 35 – [dated at] Cernioge 8.12 p.m.) Very fine drive (10 miles vid. from Llangollen to Corwen, the Dee within a short distance on our right all the way – the banks shaded by rather large trees – perhaps chiefly alders – the valley narrow the hills on each side bold and beautiful and picturesque –this road like a bowling green –one of the best I ever travelled"

Monday 15th July

"Off at 7.12 to Capel Curig – detained talking to Mr. Weaver the landlord about our route, & bought of him Nicholson's Cambrian Traveller's guide, London 1813, 2d edition 1 vol. large 8vo price 18/) From the 1st turnpike (about 3 miles from Cernioge) the road loses all its naked dreariness & begins to be wooded & beautiful – we stopped according to Mr. W–'s directions about 6 miles or rather more from Cernioge & turned down a footpath on our left to see the beautiful fall of Penmachno – this took us altogether about 25 minutes & waiting 10 minutes for George to see it, we were delayed 35 minutes. Notwithstanding this we reached here, Capel Curig, at 10 .12 a distance of 15 miles – meant to have breakfasted at Bettws but passed on by mistake. [deletion] Stood up in the gig to see the fall of the Rhyddol & got out to look at the bridge built[over the river] on rocks [deletions] sublime scenery for the last 11 or 12 miles – Snowdon very majestic – completely

cloud-capt – Had breakfast at 11 – then walked into the garden whence a fine view of this king of mountains & a couple of small lakes just beyond the garden – [deletions] about 12 the day cleared so much we intended to ascend – all agreed with the guide & to be off in 12.12 hour (at 2) – the house, planned by Wyatt has a handsome exterior & some capital rooms – but the attendance & [breakfast are] the worst we have had so far".

Anne and her aunt enjoy a tour at the gardens at Plas Newydd but Lady Butler is indisposed and there is no personal meeting. Anne meditates on "dreams of happiness...many a vision of...hope" inspired by thinking about the Ladies and contemplating her future with Mariana. They enjoy the tourist sites at Bangor and are entertained by a prize-winning Welsh harpist. When they return to Llangollen, Lady Eleanor is still indisposed but they entertain Miss Ponsonby and are much taken with her.

Tuesday 16th July

Off to Snowden at 2 pm. went in the gig (the guide mounted behind us) as far as we had to go on the Beddgelert road i.e. 4 .14 miles, & sent George back with the horses – Began the ascent on foot at 3, & gained the highest point of the highest summit Wydfa [sic] (a distance of 5 miles) in 3 hours – we had hoped to see the sun set but this was prevented by intervening clouds – we saw however a magnificent prospect – seven lakes immediately among the Snowdonian mountains – the Menai Straights – the bays of Cardigan & Caemawr, Anglesea &c. &c. the ascent was much easier than I expected – no danger attending it, & the exertion required more on account of the length of the way than anything else – our last part of the ascent for a considerable distance (just above the Glas-Lyn lake) & passing by the copper works[49] which have killed the fish & turned green the waters of the lake) was along an artificial path 5 feet wide, cut in traverses, which brought us up to the ridge, as it were, on which stands [the pointed summit] Wydfa – the first view is certainly most striking and altogether we thought ourselves well repaid for our trouble. Neither the guide (Evan Jones) nor I expected my aunt to go to the top, & therefore took a boy with us to conduct her to Llanberis – as we went along in the gig we had perceived 2 men on horseback after us – they rode to the pass of Llanberis, sent their horses to the village & we soon found them at our heels going up the mountain – they continued to join us for the benefit of our guide to which I should have objected but one of them was the son of [our] innkeeper & the other's [a Mr. Reid, an attorney arm was taken by my aunt & he helped her up the mountain & was in fact the means of enabling her to get up to the top – arrived there, we looked about a few minutes, & then foolishly sat down in the little hut on the stone benches & were some minutes. All the party felt chilled and took a little bread & brandy excluding myself – Indeed the 2 gents drank almost all the two pint bottles of brandy[our guide had taken] at 3 or 4 different times of halt – the guide meant to have taken us to Llanberis by Dolbadarn Castle a route of 7 miles – but fancying that by going a shorter we might return to sleep at Capel Curig we ventured down a very steep & difficult pass just above Llanberis – had I had an idea what it was I should not have thought of doing it – However, by dint of patient labour & constant hold of the guide she got down – frightened as she was yet appearing less so than Mr Reid – yet tho' we saved three miles of distance we were 2. 20 hours in descending & did not reach the little inn at Llanberis till 9.40, too late to think of leaving it – the gents. returned to Capel Curig – we remained – had boiled milk & bread & butter for supper & went to bed – having nothing with us I only took off my pelisse & neck handkerchief & lay down in the rest of my clothes at 11 – to be called at 4 – For fear of damp sheets I wrapt my plaid round me – I know not that I was ever more heated – I had scarcely a dry thing about me – we had walked about 5.12 miles of ascent and about 4 of descent 10 times more fatiguing than anything which I had done before – my aunt's bowels very painful – doubtless for sitting in the cold hut & taking sheer brandy – I tasted nothing & felt no inconvenience – Very fine day – cool & pleasant & tolerably clear notwithstanding the clouds that shaded the setting sun" –

Wednesday 17th July

"about two hours dressing putting on clean things & siding my imperial &c] Went out to see the castle about 10 34. Had scarcely got there before it began to rain pretty heavily & continued the whole while that we... obliged to return: Gave the man two shillings for shewing the castle. I think one would have done. The

art of travelling requires an apprenticeship. Surely, I shall improve in time. I have given many a sixpence that might have been spare. Always take in your hand what you mean to give before you go. The castle is a most beautiful & surprisingly perfect remain all things considered – but we have seen it to great disadvantage in consequence of the rain could not see... interior of the keep tower – the boys of the town sometimes climb into it – but hardly anyone else *– it adjoins the great hall – Diganwy [sic] is just across the river about a mile from the ferry-house – the passage is 1 shilling each person – Conway seems a poor sort of town of 2 or 3 streets – we have been comfortable here – good, clean beds, tho' very small rooms – no window – curtains, no wash-stand – the pitcher & basin on the toilet table – good breakfast & great attention – the people seem clean, tho' the house looks dirtyish (second-rate) because, perhaps, it is old & not easily made to look clean – But, ongoing out I see it is evidently not the first-rate house – the White Lion, a little lower down the street appears a neat, new building &, as we passed, a gentleman's landau with his own post-boy & horses was at the door. We do not cut a figure in travelling equal to our expenses. My aunt is shabbily dressed & does not quite understand the thorough manners of a gentlewoman – for instance, taking the man's arm so readily to Snowdon &c &c. Indescribable. George too is a clown of a servant – too simple in the manners of the world. But we are not known. I will try to learn & improve in travelling matters &, by thought & observation, may turn all this to future advantage.*

During the visit to Wales Anne could not get Mariana out of her mind; a feeling of complete frustration and wretchedness caused by this hopeless situation of their relationship; their tryst before the planned trip has not proved to offer any assurance that they had a future together.

... "I feel very low. Somehow or other seeing M- has been no comfort to me when I asked her how long she thought it might be before we got together & she seemed to fight off answering. On pressing further, she said she felt some delicacy in this subject & did not like to talk openly of it even to ourselves for tho she did not love him yet kindness & obligation made her feel a wish to avoid

117

calculating the time or thinking of except in general terms – I promised not to press her on the subject again. All this has made a great impression on me & I know not how it is I cannot shake it off. She never did so before but talked [illegible] of so many – five or ten for instance – years as I did. She seemed fond of me as ever yet all the night when I was almost convulsed with smothering my sobs, she took no notice nor was affected at all apparently. I know not how it is but she as it were deceived me once & I feel that it is miserable to doubt. My aunt observed that she did not seem so fond of me as I was of her. I wish I did not think quite so much of all this but alas I cannot help – surely, I shall be better by & by. I feel miserably low. I remember too what she said of Mr Powis that if her heart was not engaged as it is to me, she might be in danger of very undesirable & uncomfortable feelings of interest towards him. I might have written her a few lines but feel as if I had not resolution. Where I fit for another world how gladly would I go there!" ...

Their tour of Wales continued until the 25th of July when they returned home after a night stay at the Royal Hotel Chester.

UPON THE RETURN FROM WALES

On their return to Halifax, Anne wrote to Mariana about her trip and meeting with Butler & Ponsonby, Mariana speculates on whether their relationship is purely platonic, Anne notes...

..."*I cannot help thinking that surely it was not [platonic].*"She finds it more likely that a relationship such as theirs was *cemented by something more tender still than friendship*" ...

While Anne was in Wales, Mariana and Isabella had visited Buxton at the same time, though not together. Each wrote to Anne jealously adding sarcastic comments of the other, to try and put each other in a bad light. Mariana wrote that Isabella ... "*looks fat & gross. She danced on Wednesday & looked almost vulgar. I could not keep my eyes off her or my mind from you.*" ... They had squabbled on Friday evening, just before Mariana began to write. Isabella, meanwhile, stated *that*...

"*Charles Lawton is certainly better looking than I expected, & is certainly very gentlemanly in his manners, but his figure is dreadful, Just before he took his leave, he said that he never saw anything so extraordinary as my likeness to you; M- exclaimed with silly face, that it was paying me a very great compliment; on any other occasion I should have said the same thing, but I was so astonished at hearing him mention your name, that I was (as we say in Yorkshire) perfectly dumbfounded*"...

In August, after Anne and her aunt's return from Wales, they found Jeremy and Marian at Shibden. The property Skelfler House where they had been living had been put on the market had not yet sold; in the generally poor economic climate, no one wanted to invest in a run-down estate. The livestock cows, sheep, horses, and pigs had all been auction off, along with all farm machinery and household goods.

Anne and her uncle discussed Jeremy and Marian's situation, and like Anne her uncle found that Jeremy's behaviour was objectionable, even embarrassing, both he and Anne decided that Jeremy and Marian would be better off living in France where they could afford a cheaper, and more comfortable life than they could in England. Anne knowing Paris well said she was willing to help them find a suitable place to live, so on the evening of the 29th August 1822, they set out for Kingston upon Hull to board a steamship arriving in London on the 31st and staying two days. Anne found her father embarrassingly vulgar... *"I am shocked to death at his vulgarity of speech & manner"*.

Much of her travel entries alternate between complaining of his behaviour, too loud, too vulgar, too jovial and his occasionally spitting... *"I am perpetually in dread of meeting anyone I know"*.

From Dover, they sailed to France, but they had barely set foot on French soil before Jeremy complained of digestion problems ... *"talks of being dead in two or 3 days"* ... Instead of continuing their journey on to Paris, they stayed to rest in Calais. Though Anne found her stay well enough, enjoying the walks on the beach and promenade, good food and wine her sister did not find any pleasure there, and complained much. Of her father Anne wrote... *"I do not think he likes France. He told me this morning he thought we should all go back together for he is sure Marian is tired already. What can he mean to do? He cannot belong at Shibden nor afford to live at Northgate"*.

After a week, they did travel to Paris where Anne searched for a home for them. Jeremy on the other hand showed little enthusiasm or interest then stated that he had never intended to stay longer than the money in his pocket lasted, and said he had seen enough of France on arrival in Calais... *"O that I could have guessed or divined this before we set off"* ... Anne wrote in her diary.

They returned to Halifax on the 28th of September. However, it is likely that Anne had not acted entirely unselfishly when she offered to accompany them to France. Anne loved Paris and felt at home there so the thoughts of what might be enjoyed once her family was settled was an opportunity too good to miss.

In November Anne again visits the Norcliffe's and simultaneously enjoys Tib's favours while discouraging Isabella's futile plans for their future together. Anne is still suffering from her venereal infection. One morning Isabella found Anne injecting into her vagina for her persistent discharge...

"I denied, but won't use the syringe again, however gently when she is in the room" ...

In the neighbouring village of Malton, where nobody knew her, Anne visited a doctor, offering him a part truthful explanation for her condition, caught it from a toilet seat at a married friend's home whose husband was a dissipated character, and after going to the water-closet just after, must have contracted it there. However, his diagnosis was as vague as that of Stephon Balcombe's, his prescription, mercury pills, was not helpful. Anne's dread of not effecting Tib did not stop her from having sex with her and denying herself of pleasure.

Thursday 25th Nov: Anne has taken receipt of the watercolour sketch done by Mrs. Taylor a miniature artist who charged Anne 2 guineas for the portrait. Mrs Taylor apparently had been at Ripon school at the same time as Anne was there, though Anne did not recognise her immediately. After showing the finished portrait to the Rawson's and Saltmarshes who thought it poor, Anne returned to Mrs. Taylor for her to improve some of the features, particularly the mouth area of the sketch which she did to Anne's satisfaction...

"The likeness was so strong I could not help laughing. My aunt came up and laughed too, agreeing that the likeness was capital. Ditto my uncle. We are all satisfied let others say what they may" ...

DIARIES OF 1823

In February, Anne struck up a friendship with a Miss Francis Pickford daughter of Sir Joseph Pickford Radcliffe, local magistrate, and a wealthy landowner. They met at a lecture series on science subjects. *Anne wrote of her... "I never met with such a woman before"*.

They met at a lecture series on science subjects though they were, in fact, distant relatives through marriage and had previously encountered one another ten years earlier in Bath in 1813 when Miss Pickford was staying with her elder sister Hannah (Mrs. William Wilcox) at Savile Hill in Halifax. Anne Lister thought Frances Pickford lacked the manners of her social class, being too accommodating when she went to meet visitors on the arriving stagecoach rather than sending a servant and found her sister, Mrs. Wilcox, 'Vulgar'.

Though they had similar interests, both being well educated and well read, Lister initially adopted a superior and slightly pitying tone in which there seems little irony... *"I daresay knowing me is a godsend to Miss Pickford. She can be more companionable than anyone here, but she is too masculine & if she runs after me too much, I shall tire"* ...

Anne had rebuffed all contact in the past due to Anne's aristocratic pride. Now, Anne established that Miss Pickford ... *"seems sensible & in my present dearth of people to speak with I should well enough like to know more of her. I talk a little to her just before & after the lecture & if she were young & pretty, should certainly scrape acquaintance"* ...

Anne begins to suspect she shares her inclinations with Miss Pickford regarding Miss Pickford's close friend, Miss Threlfall. Like Anne, her acquaintances Miss Pickford was an intellectual and somewhat masculine in effect. In further conversation, Anne makes coded references to subjects and authors to sound her out on sexual topics. Through conversation regarding the subject of gender, Miss Pickford spoke of the moon being made masculine by some nations, for instance, by the Germans... *Anne writes... "I smiled & said the moon had tried both sexes, like old Tiresias, but that one could not make such an observation to everyone"* ...

Tiresias was a well-known prophet for Apollo, he was blinded by Athena for having seen her naked, and for being transformed into a woman for seven years. However, Anne did not add that Tiresias had felt nine times more lust as a woman than as a man, though she realized that Miss Pickford would probably have known this fact. When Hera and Zeus were discussing whether males or females experienced more pleasure during sex. Hera said that it was the male, while Zeus said it was the female. They consulted with Tiresias, as he had been both male and female. Tiresias assured them that the answer without doubt was the female.

Miss Pickford has become "Pic" and the two of them became good friends calling upon each other and walking together on the moors, shopping and taking tea together. Pic tells Anne a story of... *"putting on regimentals and flirting with a lady under the assumed name of Captain Cowper"*... The lady was smitten and never discovered the deception she encountered.

Anne was wary about admitting her true feelings regarding her love of woman, it was not a subject that one spoke of without caution, though she could not deceive Miss Pickford, who appeared not believe all she said on the subject. In fact, Miss Pickford would have been aware of Anne's tendencies towards the female sex even though Anne attempted to dispel such impressions. She, on the other hand, was more open regarding her feelings. Anne confessed that... *"she liked her ten thousand times more for having told me. She was the character I had long wished to meet with, to clear up my doubts whether such a one really existed nowadays"* ...

In July, Anne is confident enough about the nature of Miss Pickford and Miss Threlfall's relationship that she asks directly if they are more than just good friends, and their relationship was confirmed, but she protests that she does not share her nature in turn. A few days later she has another talk with Miss Pickford and tells her about her own... *"particular friends"* ... *but* is still disingenuous regarding the sexual nature of their relationship. Anne kept up her deceit until Miss Pickford's departure...

"Now, said I the difference between you & me is, mine is theory, yours is practice. I am taught by books, you by friendship, perhaps few or none more so. My manners might mislead you, but I don't, in reality, go beyond the utmost verge of friendship. Here my feelings stop. If they did not, you see from my whole manner & sentiments, I should not care to own it. Now, do you believe me"? 'Yes, said she, 'I do'. "Alas, thought I to myself, you are at last deceived completely" ...

Francis Pickford an astute observer of character, did not it seems believe Anne, understanding that she did not speak the truth, her comments make this quite clear... *"She told me I said a great many things she did not at all believe"* ... *"Is this' said she, your philosophy? Does your conscience never smite you"?*...

Anne and Miss Pickford became close they... *"talked very unreservedly and we seemed to suit & like each other very well"* ... Miss Pickford thought gentlemen, in general, pleasanter than ladies. ... *"if she has as much nous on subjects, might let her into my real character towards ladies"* ... To Anne's disappointment, 'Frank Pickford', as Anne called her, was not a follower of fine fashion and cared little about style... *"I wish she would care more about dress. At least, not wear such an old-fashioned, short-waisted, fright of a brown habit – like Sarah Ponsonby, meaning a man's jacket with yellow metal buttons"* ...

At this time *in her life* Anne's finances had improved slightly so she could afford to be more extravagant in her dress; she had developed a greater sense of fashion and loved the quality of her own garments though she had not yet blossomed into the fine aristocratic looking person that she would eventually become. *She commented... "A lady's dress always strikes me, if good or bad"* ...

Anne loved to see women in fine clothes, with good cut and style, that accentuates the feminine figure. Frank Pickford's manner and dress sense was too masculine to be liked by Anne or to be admired by her; she would certainly prefer a pretty girl to flirt with. Though these two women, both clever and well able to get the measure of each other could have become even greater friends, it was not to be, Anne Lister did not seek friendship between equals. Anne admires her learning but *notes... "I am not an admirer of learned ladies. They are not the sweet interesting creatures I should love. But instead chose a much more feminine woman to pursue"* ...

Her meeting with Miss Pickford gave her a chance to observe the mannish, cross-dressing woman from without. We have no reason to suppose that Lister, for all her mannish characteristics, wished to be a man, apart from the occasional hypothetical comment, always made in the context of a seduction, as for example to Mrs. Barlow... *"Should have been in love with her if! had been a man'...*

Thursday 3rd July: Anne comments in her journal about sending for Mrs. Wood the leech woman to administer leeches to her back. The theory behind this practice was that blood and other bodily fluids were regarded as 'humours' that had to remain in proper balance to maintain health. Leeches were used to "treat" a wide range of diseases, becoming a standard treatment for almost every ailment, and was practiced prophylactically as well as therapeutically.

In the same evening at 7.40 Jane Rotheroe, Mrs Wood's daughter arrived to administer the twelve leeches to Anne's back which took 1 ¼ hours before the last leech took its fill.

Friday 5th July: Anne wrote of the effects of the leech treatment making her very tiered due to bites bleeding for several hours through the night. When her father and sister Marian call at Shibden, Anne did not tell them about the leech treatment.

Saturday 6th July: ... *"I could not walk.... on account (of) fridgeting the leech bites, which itched exceedingly all the while I was downstairs, sent for a blister today, at Suters"* ... Over the next couple of days Anne continues to suffer from the leech bites, she even baths her back with urine to sooth the skin.

'Leeching' the application of a living leech to the skin to initiate blood flow or deplete blood from a localized area of the body was frequently practiced in the 19th century in Europe and other parts of the world. The species of leech most used for this purpose is the European medical leech, *Hirudo medicinalis*, an aquatic segmented worm whose bloodsucking capabilities once made it a valuable commercial item.

Traditionally, the leech economy rested on the local knowledge of the rural 'leech gatherer', who were active across the United Kingdom in bogs and marshes throughout the 19th century. These collectors bared their legs as a lure and walked through ponds to capture the leeches. As the popularity of leech use grew, it was necessary to use even more obscure and cruel practises to collect the creatures. One alarming method was to use old horses, cut so they bled, driven slowly through leech ponds so that ever more numbers of leeches could be found to supply the growing trade. A downside for the host was that leeches would suck on the legs of the collector for 20 minutes or more, and even when they had finished the resultant wound continued to bleed for up to ten hours. Eventually, entrepreneurs recognised a gap in the market and set out to develop systematic methods of leech farming.

In April, Anne again went to York for a visit, mostly to get one of her horses trained for riding. Much socializing but not much in the way of romance. Back in Halifax, whilst observing Miss Pickford and Miss Threlfall made Anne depressed about her relationship with Mariana. Anne's optimism about their future wanes at each separation... *"Could not sleep last night. A violent longing for a female companion came over me. Never remembered feeling it so painfully before... It was absolute pain to me"* ...

In 1823 Anne wrote... *"I ought not to talk of being busy without giving some reasons for it. My average hour of getting up in a morning, is half past five. Dressing and (keep the secret, and do not laugh) going to look at my horse, take me an hour and a half; from 7 to 9, I read a little Greek and a little French; from 9-10, looking after the workmen; from 10-11, breakfast; from 11-12, out of doors looking one thing or other, workmen, etc.; from 2 to 3-3/4 walk out Isabella - ... from 4-1/2 to 6, at dinner, and sitting afterwards; from 6 to 6-1/2, dawdle, trifle, call it what you please, with Isabella; from 6-1/2 to 8, write letters or notes, or 'the book, at 8, go downstairs to coffee, and we all spend a sociable evening together till 10. Isabella retires about 1/2 hour after me, and my uncle and aunt sit up till 11. Such is the model of my present days...."*

Some ten volumes of language exercises and another nine volumes of *'Extracts from Books Read,'* are a partial testament of her daily labours to educate herself. Hardly a day goes by in the journal where she does not note the page numbers of the books, she has read that day. The extracts from classical works are punctuated by notes in code, most of which reveal her study of homosexuality or aspects of the female anatomy. The Sixth Satire of Juvenal, for example, was used as a way of communicating about same-sex desire in discussions with Miss Pickford. Lister was quite familiar with the so-called 'vice of the Greeks' and had read passages about tribades and the use of leather dildos.

An incident that occurred in August 1823 was the cause of a serious rift in the relationship between Anne and Mariana. Lister invited Lawton to stay at Shibden Hall. Anne, eager to see the woman she loved, set out on foot at around 7.30 that morning after taking a draught of water and three small biscuits for the journey to meet the coach. It was a wet and windy day and Lister had walked ten miles across the moor to reach Blackstone Edge, the paved road, which was a packhorse route at a point high, 472m above sea level on the Pennine hills, surrounded by moorland bordering Yorkshire with Lancashire. Anne's trek had taken her 3 hours 10 minutes.

On seeing the coach, she ran out to meet it...

"When I spied the carriage winding up the hill...It was a nameless thrill that banished every thought but of M-, and every feeling but fearful hope. Unconscious of any sensation but pleasure at the sight of M- who, with Lou had been dozing, one in each corner of the carriage, the astonished staring eyes of the man & maid behind, & the post boys walking passed the horses were lost to me &, in too hastily taking each step of the carriage & stretching over

the pile of dressing boxes, etc., that should have stopped such eager ingress, I unluckily seemed to M – to have taken three steps at once. I had still more unluckily exclaimed, while the petrified people were bungling about the steps, that I had walked all the way from Shibden. What with exclamation & with stride the shock so wrapped around M –'s heart it felt no avenue to any other feeling of joy that her friend, Miss Patterson was not there"...

Wet and dishevelled, witnessed also by Mariana's servant John who displayed a look of astonishment... *"the post boys, too; & how fast I talked! Thought to have met me at Halifax. Why did I come so far? Why walk?"* ...

Her lover was mortified by Anne's appearance and ungainly manner and failed to hide her obvious annoyance at Anne's impromptu appearance. Anne recorded... *"the awkwardness of the cut & curl of my hair'*... and the state of her wet clothes. Lawton called her a *"flight"*, and as Lister sadly related, she was greeted... *"not with any female weakness of sympathy but with the stronger mien of shocked astonishment. Why had I not come in the gig?' and had taken the three steps into the coach in one go, most unladylike"* ...

Anne wrote... *"The poisoned arrow had struck my heart and M – 's word of meeting welcome had fallen like some huge iceberg on my breast"* ...

Anne and Mariana had previously planned a trip to Scarborough, but when Anne attempted to discuss the details Mariana snapped... *"you are going to vex me. Hold your tongue"* ...

They appeared to have made up by the time they arrived in Leeds, but Anne felt unwell due to the hurt and obvious rejection she had suffered and when she brought up the late breakfast she had eaten on the way, Mariana blamed the milk... "It was not that, I said, it was the shock of the three steps" ...

Later Lawton must have felt some remorse at the severity of her reprimand because she wrote to Anne that she was only concerned that everyone should have a good opinion of Lister. Anne however, reading between the lines was not consoled, and interpreted her words as... *'[I am] ashamed for you for the fear of everyone's disparagement...'*

According to a diary entry for September 1823, Lawton persisted with her complaints, declaring that... *"people staring so ... made her feel quite low'* and *wishing Lister had a feminine figure" ...'She had just observed that I was getting mustaches & that when she first saw this it made her sick ..."*

It would be a long time before the incident was laid to rest, the memory of that day would trouble Anne for years to come. She later wrote... *"The 3 steps business haunts me like a spectre. I cannot throw it off my mind; it is my 1st thought in a morning & last at night"* ...

Mariana's concern over losing her reputation seemed to her like the... *"Paltry selfishness of coward fear"* ... One of the most poignant descriptions she wrote, was of the dying love Mariana Lawton had for her, which lies within the following words... *"Love scorned to leave the ruin desolate, & Time & he have shaded it so sweetly, my heart still lingers in its old abiding place..."* [20th August 1823] ...

In the light of Mariana's chronic venereal disease, Anne feared... *"knowing her had perhaps been the ruin of my health & happiness"* ... *"We have not much fellowship in feeling, yet I am attached to her. Alas I see more & more plainly for my own feeling, too deeply for my own happiness, were I to tell her of the effect of this 'three-step business' she could not comprehend it. It has taught me that, tho' she loves me, it is without that beautiful romance of sentiment that all my soul desires"* ...

It is during this period that Anne confides in her Aunt Anne about the venereal infection that she has; she has been decidedly unwell of late; she intends to seek medical help from a Mr Simmons in Manchester. Anne did not reveal from whom she had caught it, Aunt Ann blamed the Duffin family... *"This I denied (but) did not say how or where I had got it. Luckily, thinks the complaint very easily caught by going to the necessary, drinking out of the same glass, etc, etc"* ... Aunt Anne was concerned on discovering what she thought was an impostume or swelling containing puss forming on Anne's back, her worry was that it was scrofulous or something of great concern.

After going to Manchester to see a Mr. Simmons, who was hopeful that if she spent 2 or 3 weeks in Manchester in his care, he would be able to cure her. Her aunt was keen that she should go immediately to Manchester instead of going to Scarborough, but Anne was reluctant to miss the opportunity of seeing her lover Mariana.

Anne did go to Scarborough on the 12th of September 1823 to spend a week with Mariana and her sisters Louisa and Eli... *"the three steps business so in my mind"* ... Anne had limited funds with which to spend on fashionable clothes and realized that her code of dress and the quality of her garments embarrassed Mariana... *"When I have more money and a good establishment, I can do better, in the meanwhile I will not be much in M 's– way. ... is she ever conscious that she is at all ashamed of me?"* ...

At the sophisticated resort, Mariana saw her lover through new eyes... *"We touched on the subject of my figure. I asked her "taking me all together, would you have me changed? "Yes," said she, "To give you a feminine figure"* ...

Anne did not accompany her friends on many outings knowing that they felt uncomfortable in her presence. Her clothes were certainly inferior to their more expensive, feminine attire, it was her shabby dress and 'odd' choice of wearing black even for walking on the beach that caused Mariana a great deal of embarrassment. All the masculine traits which had fascinated, and excited Mariana for nine years now disturbed her. She found fault with everything and anything that Anne said or did, concerned that by association with Anne it would reflect on her own social standing.

During the time spent in Scarborough, the party met up with several other friends of Mariana's who Anne had met previously, on this occasion they were certainly less than courteous to Anne. A Miss Goodricke & Miss Morritt was introduced to Anne on Saturday but were less than friendly when they met the following day in the street... *"They passed us, too, this morning. It quite evident they particularly mean to avoid showing any civility to me..."*

Miss Fountaine of Bath had told them in 1814 that Anne was masculine and though she had previously been on good terms with them, their attitude had changed through this revelation. There were stares and whispering from strangers and altogether made for an extremely uncomfortable situation. Anne later wrote... *"I excuse them all &, tho' the thing mortified me"* ...

"It struck me, if we should not meet for years & then, when she expected being together, if I should be disappointed with her looks, etc, seen her grow old in the service of another, could I then cordially wish to realize the scheme of earlier days? If I should, by & by, meet with anyone who would quite suit me, could I refuse & still lose a substance to expect a shadow" ...

It is, for most of us, difficult to fully appreciate the hurt of rejection and prejudice that Anne had to endure throughout her life; remembering a few isolated incidents of our own can be devastating, but the fact that Anne suffered daily, something that only nature must answer for, testifies to Anne's courage and endurance.

At the end of the holiday, they had reconciled through their intimate connections. When alone in private, Mariana treated Anne in an adoring affectionate manner, the old, familiar affection could not have been more evident. Consequently, Anne's feelings for Mariana were once again loving... *"I am satisfied with M- yet unhappy here. I seem to have no proper dress. The people stare at me. My figure is striking. I am tired of being here. Even if I looked like other people, I should soon be weary of Saturday on the sands. I dawdle away my time & have no pleasure in it"* ...

On their return from Scarborough to York Anne stayed at the Norcliffe's townhouse, where she shared Isabella's room and bed, this at least went someway to alleviate the misery Anne was feeling. This visit resulted in Mariana's jealousy of their closeness, and so she visited for breakfast or dinner and accompanied them to the theatre, deliberately seating herself between them, revealing her own insecurity and perhaps guilt of her recent behaviour. On the 24th of September they were amongst the five-thousand-strong audience to hear Handel's Messiah, performed by four hundred musicians and choir in performing the Hallelujah Chorus which Cramer, the leader said... *"there would never be such a thing again during the life of this generation"* ...

Anne was later introduced to one of the soloists, world-famous Angelica Catalani, a singer she had heard sing many years before with Eliza.

Anne continued to suffer the pain she had felt during the Blackstone Edge and Scarborough business, she shed a great many tears over this. She found it difficult to reconcile herself to Mariana's evident feelings of shame and embarrassment at being seen in public with her. No matter how loving they when alone together, Anne recognized that something irreplaceable had gone from their relationship and it could never be quite the same again...

"Somehow I relapse too often into a feeling of imperfect satisfaction with her... she wants tenderness in her manner towards me. She is too commonplace. Her sensibility seems rather weakness of nerve than the strength of affection. She thinks a good deal of her appearance & dress & has not had time to think much of taking care of mine yet. She is subject to a feeling of shame about me, such as at Scarbro'. I fancy she would sometimes rather be without me. She too much makes me feel the necessity of cutting a good figure in society & that, if I was in the background, she would not be the one to help me forward. She is not exactly the woman of all hours for me. She suits me best at night. In bed she is excellent."
...

A message she received when she returned to Halifax from Isabella gave her great alarm... *"I have been unwell since last Friday & it has turned to the fluor albus (leucorrhea or 'the whites') & most violent"* ... There are many causes of leukorrhea, though Anne was sure it was sexually transmitted and immediately certain she had passed it on to Isabella. Anne wrote... *"All this struck me like a thunderbolt. My heart sank within me so unsuspected of having done her"* ...

How could this be unsuspected? Anne had been fully sexually active with Isabella for two years despite her concerns at the possibility she could infect poor unsuspecting Tib... *"Oh M- what have you done"?* *"Surely said I, I am more sorry for poor Isabella than you were for me"* ...

DIARIES OF 1824

In the early part of the year, Anne is much concerned with managing the property she shares with her aunt and uncle, taking over more of its control. Anne had three main aims in life, to re-enforce her landed gentry status, to improve the buildings and parkland of the family seat and to marry someone who would assist her in those improvements, someone she could share her life with, who belonged to her and who would love, cherish, comfort, and obey her, and to whom she in return could make happy.

In January 1824 Isabella arrived for a long visit to Shibden Hall. Her health was not good, and they talk over what has happened though Anne does not reveal that Isabella's condition almost certainly came via her... *"She never expects to be well of this complaint & it inconveniences her very much"* .... *"Poor Tib. I will, at any time, make up for it all I can by double attention & kindness. If she knew the truth, what would she think"* ...

When Mariana wrote to Anne it is clear from her letters and descriptions of her activities that she was finding her ascent into the higher-ranking status of society suited her, and had been making new friends, taking up new hobbies and interests, and generally becoming less emotionally dependent on Anne.

After a few weeks, Anne was wishing Tib's visit was over and was tired of her drinking, snuff-taking, and staying in bed till late in the day. After Isabella had left on 24th March Anne reviewed the situation in her diary. She complains that...

"she tells her stories much oftener over than she used to do, getting that she told us same again & again. She is growing gradually larger, due to alcohol and the ten hours a day spent in bed. How could I have loved her? Yes, how I adored her, had she had that temper & conduct which temperance & good sense might easily

have secured. But alas, it has not been so. God bless you Tib. Our interests are separated forever, but still, when I forget myself, I almost love thee. No, I do not love thee but love thy happiness" ...

Anne puts some effort into mending social ties with her Halifax neighbours who complain that she snubs them, especially when encountered elsewhere such as York. But Anne is also thinking more and more about traveling. There are no mentions of the sort of little flirtations recorded before, though in one entry in June she is reviewing her journals and comments on the account of her involvement to varying degrees with Anne Belcombe, Miss Vallance, and Miss Browne. As Anne's financial situation improves, she takes a far greater interest in her clothes, her taste becomes more sophisticated the quality of fabrics, cut and tailoring of her garments, she begins to look more like a landed gentlewoman though she still displays masculine undertones.

Throughout her life Lister had a good opinion of herself and was brimming with confidence. She records on Monday 10th May. During a visit to Mrs Kelly... *"On taking leave, I saluted her left cheek, which I believe I have not been in the habit of doing before. My manner was not quite so flirting this morning. I am well enough satisfied with it. We were talking of my dress. She said people thought I should look better in a bonnet. She contended I should not & said my whole style of dress suited myself & my manners was consistent & becoming to me. I walked differently from other people, more upright & better. Was more masculine, she said, she meant in understanding. I said I quite understood the thing & took it as she meant it. That I had tried all styles of dress but was left to do as I liked eight years ago. Had then adopted my present mode & meant to keep it"* ...

Anne appears to have been unhappy with some aspects of her female physiognomy. She carefully disguised her menstruation, which she called her *'cousin'*, from her lovers, even from her eventual life-companion, Anne Walker... *"No kiss. Had slept in cousin-linen with paper as usual, & white worsted stockings besides, which kept all very comfortable; A- never found out that I had cousin"* ...

During the 1800s' people began to think it unacceptable for women to simply bleed into their clothes. The method most women choose was the home made 'rags', pads/napkins, which could be washed for later use. Affluent women would perhaps stay home for the duration of their period. Menstruation was variously described as a 'monthly illness', 'catamenial derangement', a 'decline' and the 'breaking down and exfoliation of the decidua'. Gynaecology as an area of specialisation mushroomed in the 1850s. Yet, at the heart of this branch of medical expertise lay a fundamental paradox; essentially natural female reproductive functions were pathologized and collectively described as 'the diseases of women'. It wasn't until the late 1890's that mass produced sanatory napkins for ladies came onto the market when Johnson & Johnson made "Lister's Towels" (nothing to do with Anne Lister) disposable pads.

Physicians persisted in referring to menstruation as an unfortunate, unpleasant, and distasteful subject to address and certainly one from which women themselves should be spared. The menstruous woman was perceived as physically 'unwell' and psychologically vulnerable. Counselled to avoid the intellectual stimulus and physical activity for one-quarter of every month, women were thought to be biologically incapable of participating in society on an equal footing with men.

It was not until the early twentieth century that science began to fully understand menstruation. It is no coincidence that the mysteries of menstruation began to be dispelled as women entered the medical profession. Indeed, it was the pioneering work of Dr Mary Putnam Jacobi whose 1876 essay, "The Question of Rest for Women during Menstruation", won the Boylston Prize at Harvard University, and her intellectual heirs, Clelia Duel Mosher and Leta Stetter, who studied menstruation among college women from 1890 to 1920, who proved "menstrual incapacity" was wrong.

In late July, Anne and her aunt go on a tour of the lake district and the entries are all about travel, sights, and food. Anne drove her aunt in a gig to the Lake District. In Bowness on Lake Windermere, they dined on Soup, a beautifully dressed pike. A roasted forequarter of lamb, potatoes, and peas, 2 little sweet puddings, a tart & jellies. Although such a large amount of food may seem excessive to the low calorie, small portions, in pursuit of slenderness 'brigade' might consume today, but we should consider the daily calorie burning exercise people did at that time, not having any form of motorized mode of transport, they consequently took more exercise and burned off large amounts of calories, therefore able to comfortably eat more of the foods they loved without gaining unwelcome pounds.

During a trip in the gig, Anne saw the start of a footpath across the hills and she decided at once to take a two-day excursion despite the advice of their local guide.

In Rosthwaite, she hired James Coates, a cobbler who also worked as a guide to travel with her at a charge of 12 shillings. Anne arranged to meet her aunt the next day in Scale Hill in Loweswater. Their servant George Playforth would take Aunt Anne by road in the gig as a hike over the fatiguing terrain was physically beyond her aunt's capability. Anne intended to walk across the northern half of what is now the national park in one late afternoon. The ascent proved steeper and harder than Snowdon in Wales which she knew well. The path was barely secured, with loose stones costing her time and strength. After 14 miles they reached a farm, where she found the people very civil. The lady of the house told them that there was a good Inn at Gosforth just a short distance away. Anne, however, would have preferred to continue to Calder Bridge, another six miles away. Unfortunately, they lost their bearings and therefore they had no option but to stay the night at the Inn in Gosforth.

They had walked over twenty miles without rest or eaten anything since breakfast. At the Lion & Lamb Inn, Moses Sewell, Gosforth, Anne was parched but the proprietor had very limited supplies to offer them but brought a pint of gin & water of which Anne took 4 glasses but could have easily drank more as her thirst was so great. It was inevitable that her dehydrated body could not keep down the simple fare available that night and after retiring to her room and because of her concerns regarding the cleanliness of the bed linen she decided not to disrobe, instead she chose to lie in her sweat-soaked clothes. Anne, of course, blamed her guide for losing their way and gave no short measure in letting him know that fact. The next day, she walked along the valley to Calder Bridge, resting at the Stanley arms, where she was relieved to find that... *"they had horses, sent back my guide (who had offered forwards with me to Scale hill, thinking he could find his way by daylight, and agreed for a couple of horses for 10/ − (50 pence)"*... After a basin of boiled milk Anne continued on her travels in the direction where she had arranged to meet her aunt. The next part of the adventure after meeting up with Aunt Anne was Crummock lake where they took a boat to Buttermere their next point of interest — they returned to Crummock at 5, arriving at 5.50 and their next Inn at Scale Hill for dinner — *"roasted leg of mutton (good, but too fresh killed) peas and potatoes and gooseberry tart and cream — off from Scale hill at 7 ¼... we descended the hill upon Keswick about 9"*, retiring for the nights stay for a welcome rest. The next day they attended church before driving slowly... *"the lanes stony, & got to Pooley Bridge at 5 ¼. Off from Pooley Bridge at 7 stopt at Patterdale, a minute or 2 before 9 ¾, returned thro' the beautiful rich-looking vale of and pretty village of Lorton, and 4 miles from Scale hill got into the Cockermouth road, very good but very hilly — 12 miles"* ...

There was a visit in July from Mariana, and they were still passionate but disengaged. *Commenting on their passionate encounters, Anne writes... "Two last night. M− spoke in the very act. 'Ah,' said she, 'Can you ever love anyone else?' She knows how to heighten the pleasure of our intercourse. She often murmurs, 'Oh, how delicious,' just at the very moment. All her kisses are good ones"* ... After a brief return to Halifax in August, Anne travels to Paris in company with her maid Elizabeth Cordingley and stayed there for the rest of the year.

THE TRIP TO PARIS

Paris in 1824 was the perfect location for Anne. Paris was beginning to assume its role as the worlds scientific and cultural capital of the 19th century, and therefore a place of outstanding interest for Anne's insatiable appetite for knowledge. She intended to learn the language, immerse herself in the culture and, hopefully, meet a sophisticated, wealthy woman. Anne also intended to seek a cure for her venereal infection.

Foreign expats continued to be drawn to the more open society that existed in Paris due to the avant-garde, relaxed atmosphere which allowed those women with lesbian tendencies to become bolder and less discreet. Lesbians and bisexual women had an increased visibility during this period, which emboldened Anne to be more open with her own sexuality. She wasted no time in propositioning the other visitors at the guesthouse in 24 Place Vendome, but uppermost in her mind was to find someone who would dedicate their life in a commitment to be her life-partner.

It was there in the small pension where Anne met her next conquest. Mrs. Catherine Maria Barlow (née McCrea) (1786-1847) from Guernsey, the widow of a Lieutenant-Colonel Frederick Barlow of the 61st South Gloucestershires, who died at the Battle of Salamanca in 1812. Anne was attracted to this pleasant and pretty woman who it appears found Anne as equally appealing.

The small guest house was home to a group of women who were by no means unaware of the nature of Anne's sexuality. The licentious atmosphere which prevailed in that era, were by no means averse towards women's attraction to their own sex. The relaxed atmosphere inclined people to view with amused tolerance and acceptance what would later be condemned as unnatural and repugnant.

The predominant number of clienteles staying at this establishment were female, who for the main were looking for company, possible excitement, and romance. The lack of male presence would only encourage flirtatious interaction between the female guests.

From Anne's journal we learn that a great deal of seductive touching, holding of hands and kissing had taken place between the women staying at the pension but for Anne, idealistic and merely 'romantic' friendship between woman and woman was not enough. Her need for a woman companion to share her life included a strong sexual component. Anne was getting restless; she had been a guest at Place Vendome for six or seven weeks without any satisfying connections. Mlle de Sans, a young woman with delicate health, Mme de Boyve the proprietor of the guest house, and Mrs Barlow had all become objects of Anne's amorous regard. They were all aware that any relationship with her would go beyond the conventional platonic friendship but would be an all-consuming sexual correlation.

Mrs. Barlow was not exactly the titled demoiselle Anne had envisaged she would become involved with; her position in life was precarious, living as she did on a widow's pension of £80 a year and a government gratuity of £250 a year. The encouraging response which Mrs Barlow showed to Anne's flirtations, offered an opening for Anne's more predatory advances.

One evening after dinner the group of guests at 24 Place Vendome sat talking and with nothing better to do Anne took all their pulses. After several attempts to detect Mlle de Sans heartbeat, Anne passed her a note... *"When in my hand thy pulse is prest, I feel it alter mine, and draw another from my breast, in unison with thine ... Indeed said she, if you were a man I do not know what would be the end of all this, I think that Mme de Boyve would be right, I would be married before the years end"* ... This same young lady once remarked... *"I see you talk to her as you do me"* ... when she observed Anne flirting with Mrs Barlow. Anne managed to calm the obvious jealousy by replying... *"I am not the same to any two persons"* ... and added the following comment in her diary... *"She seems satisfied. Fancies me serious with herself and flirting, perhaps, with Mrs Barlow. They are all jealous of my attention"* ...

When this young Frenchwoman, Mlle de Sans, innocently kissed her goodbye on both cheeks, demonstrating the European custom, Anne pressed her lips straight on to hers... *"That is Yorkshire,"* ... she told her, triumphantly.

Anne succeeded in winning Maria's affections, though her social standing and financial worth did not meet Anne's aspirations. Mrs. Barlow had a daughter, 13-year-old Jane Maria Barlow (1811 b – 1880) who with a maid accompanied her mother whilst in Paris. Anne became fond of Jane and they spent a lot of happy times together. Jane herself began a journal at the age of 22. She later married Philip De Saumarez, R.N. Jane's published diary covers the years 1839-40.

Anne recorded that... "Mrs. Barlow *said I astonished Mme. Galvani at first, who once or twice said to the Mackenzies (fellow guests) she thought I was a man and the Mack's too had wondered. Mrs. Barlow herself had thought at first I wished to imitate the manners of a gentleman but now she knows me better, it was not put on"* ...

In early October 1824, as Anne is flirting with Mrs. Barlow, Miss Mackenzie, who was a companion in Paris to her mother, was seated in their company and undoubtedly Anne's match in the classics, passes her a confidential note...

"I have a question to ask you. Êtes-vous Achilles?' I laughed & said she made me blush. Brought Miss Mack into my room. Joked with her about her question. Said it was exceedingly well put. She said I was the only one in the house to whom she could have written it, because the only one who would have so soon understood it, that is, who would have understood the allusion to take it that way"...

What Miss Mackenzie was alluding to is the incident in which Achilles dresses as a girl in the court of Lycomedes to escape the oracle that says he is to die in the battle of Troy. The episode in the myth of Achilles, a Greek hero of the Trojan War became a popular topic in art and literature from Classical times until the middle of the 20th century and would certainly have appealed to the sophisticated, well educated, masculine woman.

A few days later, Mrs. Barlow, who was as profound in her thinking as Anne in such subjects began talking of that one of the things of which Marie Antoinette was accused of was being too fond of women...

"I, with perfect mastery of countenance, said I had never heard of it before and could not understand or believe it... I said I would not believe such a thing existed. Mrs. Barlow said it was mentioned in scripture, not in the New Testament not Deuteronomy, nor Leviticus. I said I believe that when reduced to the last extremity — I was going to mention the use of phalli but luckily Mrs. Barlow said, "You mean two men being fond of each other?' & I said 'Yes'. . . "I declared I was the most innocent person in the world concerning all I had seen & heard, for everybody told me things. She said she should not have mentioned it, but she knew she was not telling me anything I did not know before. I said I read of women being too fond of each other in the Latin parts of the works of Sir William Jones" . . . "In fact, she suspected me and she was fishing to find it out but I think I was too deep for her. . . We agreed it was a scandal invented by the men, who were bad enough for anything" ...

Although Anne tries to give an impression of naivety and unworldliness it is unlikely that she was deceiving Maria Barlow. Mrs. Barlow like Anne uses the same tact by also claiming to be inexperienced and naive, both women relish this coy seduction. Though the lead-up to their eventual sexual intimacy was a game of cat and mouse it is not clear who is the predator and who is the prey. When Anne spent some time in the company of the Paris pension proprietor Mme de Boyve, she was told that Mrs Barlow had had some gentleman callers before Anne had arrived, one in particular had been homosexual who had spent the night in her room. Perhaps these incidents were revealed in the hope that it might sour the regard Anne might have had for Mrs Barlow because of Mme's own feelings for Anne. But it did make Anne wary, knowing she would have to tread carefully with Maria Barlow.

The two women continued their flirtatious behaviour, Anne sensing that Mrs Barlow did not object to her amorous attention was sure that given time she would succumb to a more intimate relationship...

"I had kissed and pressed Mrs. Barlow on my knee till I had a complete fit of passion," ... one diary entry read... *"Got to tell her that the business of Thursday was exhausting beyond measure, as it always was to excite & then disappoint nature"* ...

"Mrs Barlow came to me & staid till 4—50. Sat talking for some time. It did me harm to sit on my knee. It was all for my sake she refused. At last she consented. Sapphic love was again mentioned. I spoke rather more plainly. [I] became rather excited. Felt her breasts & queer a little. Tried to put my hand up her petticoat but she prevented. Touched her flesh just above the knee twice. I kissed her warmly & held her strongly. She said what a state I was putting myself into. She got up to go away & went to the door. I followed. Finding she lingered a moment, pressed her closely & again tried to put my hand up her petticoats. Finding that she would not let me do this but still that she was a little excited, I became regularly so myself. I felt her grow warm & she let me grubble & press her tightly with my left hand whilst I held her against the door with the other, all the while putting my tongue into her mouth & kissing her so passionately as to excite her not a little, I am sure. When it was over, she put her handkerchief to her eyes & shedding a few tears, said, `You are used to these things. I am not.' I remonstrated against this, declaring I was not so bad as one thought me & injustice like this would make me miserable, etc. She blamed herself, saying she was a poor, weak creature" ...

"Asked her if she loved me a little bit. `You know I do,' said she. I still therefore pressed her to let me in tomorrow before she was up, when Mrs Page (Mrs Barlow ' s servant) was gone with Miss Barlow to school. She would not promise. Asked me what I would do. I said teach her to love me better. Insinuated we had now gone too far to retract & she might as well admit me. On leaving me her

face looked hot, her hair out of curl & herself languid, exactly as if after a connection had taken place" ...

By November Mrs. Barlow is much more responsive to Anne's advances and regularly sits on Anne's knee while Anne hugs and kisses her and rubs her through her petticoats until Anne's thighs shake and she experiences orgasm... *"She begins to stand closer to me. I might easily press queer to queer. Our liking each other is now mutually understood and acknowledged."* ...

Mrs. Barlow wanted Lister to dress as a man so they could have a legal wedding, but Lister refused. Lister wanted to marry a woman, as a woman. Anne's comments in her diary recorded her contemplating the suggestion that she remove her nightshift, she also said... *"If I wore men's clothes she would feel differently"* and, having joked that Lister... *had nothing to give, meaning I had no penis',* said that *'If I only wore breeches it would be enough"*...

The Christmas of 1824 finds Anne, along with her Ladies maid Elizabeth Wilkes Cordingley, is still in Paris. Anne's journal entry for Christmas day illustrates the difficulties of something which we now all take for granted–that of taking a bath.

Public bathhouses were for many people of that era the only place that they could bathe –at least for those who took baths at all! While in Paris, Anne frequented the Bains Chinois, a most famous public baths which drew a large clientele of well-heeled patrons and was recommended in travel guides to wealthy tourists.

The Chinese baths in the Boulevard des Italiens opened in 1787/88, so-called because of the style of architecture, the central pavilion in the style of a pagoda to its pseudo-ornaments in the oriental style. On Christmas day, having left it too late to book a time for her bath there, she decided to bathe in her room at the guest house.

This idea was not without problems. She first had to ask permission of Mme de Boyve, but as Anne and the proprietor where on such friendly terms it was unlikely that she would have refused. It was necessary to recruit Madame's maid and menservants to undertake the physical tasks necessary to accommodate Anne's ablutions, including, the lugging of the bath and many pails of hot water up several flights of stairs. Anne's room was 187 steps up from the ground floor! Anne writes... "Madame *de Boyve sent her maid to order me a bath here at 6 ... The bath being ready in Mrs Barlow's room (the men had tried in vain to get it into mine–the doorway too narrow), got into it at 6½, staid [sic] in just an hour and in 20 minutes had returned to my room & got into bed & had my dinner– my soup & a little fish-pâte & a little French plum-pudding having been kept warm for me on my hearth."* ...

Baths were an integral part of the cure that had been prescribed for Anne's venereal disease by the top medical man in Paris, Baron G Dupuytren. Anne's first consultation with M. Dupuytren 29th November 1824 was a recommendation by Mrs Barlow. Anne had confided in Mrs Barlow about her condition though Mrs Barlow claimed she had already suspected there was a problem. Those pimples lately on Anne's face and the tendency to sore throats warned her what might be a possibility.

When seeing M. Dupuytren the intention was to pass herself off as a respectable married woman by using Mariana's marital and medical history in an attempt at discretion; to admit to her single status would have been quite shameful under the circumstances. Explaining to him that she had first become ill three years previously. Asked what it was and how it was caused she went on to explain about the discharge and that she knew it was a 'case demonari'. Telling him about Charles Lawton who had scares in his groin. Asked if she had seen his linen? *"No, he would not allow this"*. Did he have much intercourse with her? *"No, never since she was ill, not in the last three years"*. Was he gay with others? *"Yes, at first with house servants, but no, not now"*. The man who prescribed Charles Lawton all his medications said he was malformed. How so? *"Because he has only one testicle"*. Did he have difficulty when you were first married? *"Yes, it was a fortnight before he could manage it"*. How old are you? *"Thirty-two"* (Anne was in fact thirty-three). How old is he? *"Fifty-two"*. How long have you been married? *"Eight or nine years"*. Do you sleep together? *"Yes"*. Does he have erections? *"No"* ...

M. Dupuytren then said he must examine Anne which was precisely what she had been hoping to avoid, she naturally expected him to discover that she was a virgin and that all she had told him was a lie.

After the examination, when probably for the first time Anne experienced penetration, her imagination grew curious about what sex was like with a penis, the examination certainly had not been pleasurable, but it set her mind to wonder what the difference might be between her own method to gain sexual pleasure and that achieved by a penis, though she certainly had no intension of experimentation with a male partner...

"Inserted the middle finger of my right hand as high as I could. It gave me no sensation. But in trying to, what he [Dr. Dupuytren] calls, embrace it by pushing myself internally backwards and forwards, which is done with little or no external movement, in five minutes I had felt probably all the pleasure of coition and my finger told me how to guess the sensation that must be experienced by a penis and how much art there may be on the woman's [part]... After the five minutes spent in the experiment, with my finger kept my hand there resting as many minutes. The[n] in as many more incurred a cross my own way and think it far the longer and pleasanter of the two. That dawdling about more on the surface and keeping nearer to the front gives a keener sensation; all pleasure with no trace of anything like pain or too great exertion. Hence I can understand why I give [Mariana] so much delight and why I might please any married woman who did not like the ladies" ...

Between November 1824 and her departure for England at the end of March 1825, Anne paid several visits to M. Dupuytren. He recommended she abstained from the vaginal douches of sulphate of zinc solution she was already using but advised her to take regular warm baths. He gave her a prescription for pearl barley and nitrate to dissolve in liquid and prescribed mercury. Despite his reputation he failed to cure Anne of her complaint.

There was a great deal of ignorance and confusion about venereal disease throughout the years and was not solved until after the Second World War. Syphilis and gonorrhoea were often classed as two different stages of the same condition. Discharges in women, such as that suffered by Anne and Mariana was likely to be Trichomoniasis which is the most common condition that can be transmitted during lesbian sexual activity. Syphilis is virtually non-existent amongst lesbians due to the absence of penile penetration.

Mrs. Barlow began to regularly allow Anne to 'grubble' her 'queer' with her hand through a thin layer of petticoat while they lie in bed together and Anne presses herself against her and experiences spontaneous orgasm...

"We had tea a little before 10. Very soon after she came, she lay on the bed. This rather starved me for I would have my arms out to .... this. She got in and I had my arms around her, she lying ... with her back to me, my right leg under and left leg over, her. I got a hand towards her queer by degrees. She so turned round that my left hand got to her very comfortably and by degrees I got to feel and handle her. I got her gown up and tried to raise her petticoats also but, finding that this would not do (one of her hands prevented it), I was contented that my naked left thigh should rest upon her naked left thigh and thus she let me grubble her over her petticoats. All the while I was pressing her between my thighs. Now and then I held my hand still and felt her pulsation, let her rise towards my hand two or three times and gradually open her thighs, and felt her as well as .....as it was possible to do over her petticoats, and felt that she was excited. I continued for, I daresay, quarter-hour more then, after being quiet a while, she half-sighed and said, "Oh, I think I could do anything for you" ...

Though Anne's dearest wish was to have full sexual contact, her infection would prevent this...

"Were we gone to 'Italy' it would be different but in my present state we were both quite safe. I loved her far too well not to be quite sure we were both secure" ...

At the beginning of January Anne writes... *"I soon took up her petticoats so as to feel her naked thighs next to mine. Then after kissing with my tongue in her mouth, got the middle finger of my right hand up her & grubbled her longer & better than ever, she seemed rather more at ease than before & taking it with more emotion & apparent pleasure, which made me keep dawdling there a long time. She seemed more moist than before but really very nice. She hides her face on my shoulder & we lay a good while silent & as if half dozing"* ...

As Maria becomes more relaxed with Anne's sexual advances, she was not only willing but facilitated Anne's love making... *"I began to handle her & look at her – Licked a little bit of her queer, opened her with my finger and slavered into her"*...

Always eager to experiment to perfect her lovemaking technique to please her partner... *"Trying last night to get the middle right finger up myself to see which manner of doing answered best, that I might practise this on Mrs. B. [Barlow] But it gave me no pleasure at all. Rather, hurt me, and I left off and incurred a cross in my own way. That is, by rubbing the top part of queer"* ...

During the Christmas/New Year holiday they lie together naked and Anne is permitted to insert her finger and 'dawdle' Mrs. Barlow until they both achieve orgasm.

Anne and Maria were aware of the gossip other patrons of their pension indulged in regarding the special closeness they were cultivating, which made them consider finding alternative accommodation. They were it seems constantly under the other guest's scrutiny, ever watchful of their movements and behaviour.

In January of 1825 they found an apartment and moved in together, out of the way from prying eyes. After searching the vacancies, they decided upon 15, Quai Voltaire where they set up home together, but always in the background was the knowledge that Anne still held such strong feelings for Mariana. The constant reminders that Mariana still played a huge part in Anne's emotions had a considerable effect on their relationship. The feeling of insecurity resulted in tearful episodes from Mrs Barlow, which soured the smooth running of their affair.

During this tense atmosphere it became clear that Mrs Barlow was suffering much distress from a deep, profound gilt not only because the affair was with another woman, but that it was outside of marriage, a socially damnatory act and in effect, she was no more than a mistress. On the other hand, Anne did not suffer the same torment, in fact it was an accepted and common practise for those males in a higher social class to keep a mistress, but Mrs Barlow's pride and self-esteem would not allow her to be anything other than a wife.

Anne with some degree of confidence was sure Mrs Barlow loved her... *"I begin to be persuaded she really does love me & feel I cannot bear to give her uneasiness. My heart half ached for her"* ... *"It was too late now but she would always think herself wicked for having so yielded to me. Agreed we should forgive each other... but still, she could never think so well of herself again. Said I, Circumstances alter. As we cannot go & be married, what should we do?" Oh, said she, telling me she quoted from Cowper, it is pairing time anticipated"* ... (William Cowper (pronounced Cooper) (November 1731 – 25 April 1800) was an English poet and hymnodist, one of the most popular poets of his time... *"Misses, the tale that I relate, this lesson seems to carry, Choose not alone a proper mate, but proper time to marry"*...

In her subconscious Anne continually compared Mariana and Mrs Barlow and although she had become very fond of Maria, she had a great many reservations regarding her suitability as a life partner. Mrs Barlow not being a woman of wealth, having little money of her own, no assets or future inheritance to attain was not a suitable partner to become a wife. she noted that... "she *lets me see too much that she considers me too much as a woman. She talks to me about being unwell (Menstruating). I have aired napkins before her. She feels me, etc. All which I like not. Mariana never seems to know or notice these things"* ...

Mrs Barlow had become increasingly aware of the depth of feeling Anne still held for Mariana and the past sexual intimacy that Anne and Mariana shared. She was continually reminded in news and intimate letters that Anne regularly received, and her name continually mentioned in conversation, which caused so much jealousy and heartache that would eventually have insurmountable consequences...

"Said it made me quite wretched to see her unhappy (and indeed a pang of remorse really did lie heavy at my heart). I would do anything in the world for her, etc., & on this, the tears really ran down my face too. "Ah, said she, perhaps shall get over it in time, but never, never can I think so well of myself again" ...

As the weeks passed the intimacy between them was gradually replaced with a kind of formality and reserve. *Anne suggested* that they should become merely friends and no tears from Mrs Barlow could change this very painful decision.

With thoughts of returning home to Shibden, Anne purchased a pendula with a bronze figure of Minerva for Mrs Barlow, costing three hundred & twenty-five franks. On leaving Mrs Barlow... *"She clung round me at the last & when I wanted to go, saying staying did no good, 'Oh, no, said she, stay till the last minute". ... "I leave Paris, said I to myself, with sentiments how different from those with which I arrived. My eye was accustomed to all it saw – it was no longer a stranger nor found fault as before with all that differed from that it left at home. "Imperfectly as I speak the language, I felt almost at home in Paris & seemed to feel so in France. I thought over my whole acquaintance with Mrs Barlow. I was sorry to leave her but yet, somehow my sorrow was not so deep as I expected. She does not satisfy me in several little things & and the connection would be imprudent. Besides she lets me see too much she considers me to much as a woman...... somehow my heart is not so deep in this business as it ought to be & I scarce know why I have gone on & led and been led on. Very strangely, it seems like a dream to me"* ...

However, the relationship between Maria Barlow and Anne did not end there, in fact they remained essentially friends for many years. On Wednesday, the 20th April 1825 after arriving back in Halifax Anne received a letter from Mrs Barlow which made it clear that she was unable to accept that their relationship had ended. She referred to other interests from suiters, one from a Mr William Bell, who had asked her to consider him as her future husband, but because of her deep feelings for Anne she could not consider his proposal... *"You have taught me much untaught before & surely I must strangely learn that hardest science – to forget – ere I can associate another with these sentiments which you have chastened & refined"* ... Maria tells her how much she has suffered since Anne left her, how sick she has been, and how much misery she has endured because of Anne's rejection. Anne too is suffering, her longing for a female companion is overwhelming knowing that a future with Mariana is unobtainable. The prospects of being alone for the rest of her life was a constant worry, the difficulty in finding someone whom she can love as much or more, visits her every thought. Perhaps Mrs Barlow came near, but Anne has concerns that she knew little of her background and she was conceded that her lack of breeding and status is too insurmountable to seriously consider her as a wife.

THE DEATH OF JAMES LISTER

It was 9.30 on the morning of 26th January 1826 when Elizabeth Cordingley who was at that time working as Housekeeper rapped at Anne's bedroom door to ask Anne to go immediately downstairs because her uncle James Lister had fallen and was lying on the floor. Anne's aunt standing in the hall was almost in hysterics not knowing what to do. She had seen him fall most probably from a heart attack, but there was nothing Anne could do, it was too late he was dead. Anne had her father and sister Marian brought from Northgate House and began to organise funeral arrangements fitting for the head of the family.

Following the death of her uncle, James Lister, Anne inherited Shibden Hall and its estate, achieving her lifelong ambition to be the head of the Lister legacy. Her net income from the estate fluctuated just on either side of £1,000 p.a. When James died the inventory of his belongings listed the farming stock at Shibden Hall. This included: two heifers, five milk cows, two draught horses, a hackney horse, a quantity of hay and manure, a plough and two pairs of harrows, three shovels, three muck forks, two pails, two wheelbarrows, and an old carriage.

On the day of his death, the family gathered to hear his last will and testament read out by Anne. James had left his entire estate to his niece Anne, but she had to share the annual income with her Aunt Anne, his brother Jeremy and his niece Marian, they all had a right to live at Shibden for the rest of their lives. So, Marian and Jeremy left Market Weighton to take up residency at Shibden.

The challenge of managing the estate in such a way that it would both maximise her income and be passed on to her heirs in an improved condition was one that Anne took very seriously. Her entrepreneurial flair, her acquired knowledge over the years again through participation in estate matters, of mathematics, geology and engineering and her sharp negotiating skills with her male business rivals, made her a formidable businesswoman in the newly emerging world of industrialisation...

Christopher Rawson magistrate, banker, landowner, and industrialist and one of the most influential men in Halifax knew Anne from a young age took delight in obstructing her business dealings and political influences. They crossed swords on many aspects of business particularly on the extraction of coal and trespassing beneath her land to steal her coal... *"Mr Rawson said he was never beaten by ladies & I had beaten him. Said I gravely, 'It is the intellectual part of us that makes a bargain & that has no sex, or ought to have none."* ...

TRAVELLER AND ADVENTURER

Being an avid traveller Anne visited major sites around the world, her enquiring mind propelled her to seek destinations not usually on tourist's itinerary. During these adventures she would often visit sites such as orphanages, factories, prisons, and mines. She found it necessary on occasion to stay in unconventional accommodation, from grand hotels and private mansions to roadside inns, monasteries, mountain huts, and on occasion it was her carriage that was the only place she could lay her head.

The trips abroad often found her in inconvenient locations, she was in Spain in 1839 during the Carlist Civil War 'The Embrace of Bergara' which put an end to war in the Basque districts. Aunt Anne was in Paris during the July revolution of 1830. *Trois Glorieuses* in French ("Three Glorious Days"), led to the overthrow of King Charles X the French Bourbon monarch.

In 1827. Once again Anne returned to Paris this time staying in an apartment at 6 Rue de Mondovi, accompanied by her Aunt Anne. Anne felt at home in the French capital and had hoped to rekindle old relationships. Though Anne did renew her affair with Mrs Barlow, she was more of a convenience than a true partner. Anne toured Switzerland and northern Italy with Maria Barlow and her daughter Jane, leaving her aunt in Paris, but it was becoming perfectly clear to Maria just how powerful the connection between Anne and Mariana was, which obviously caused many emotional and jealous scenes.

Maria must have realized that she was simply a distraction and a substitute. However, there they both were together, so Maria made every effort to try to win Anne's affections, her willingness to continue their intimate relations even though Anne's participation appears to have been less than enthusiastic, with occasional flushes of passion, which failed to dissipate Anne's all-consuming love for Mariana... *"I this morning looked at her kissed the top hair with my mouth and letting fall a little saliva. This excited her again. The bed both yesterday and this morning was a good deal wet"...*

This trip only convinced Anne that she and Maria Barlow were not fully compatible, whilst they pleasured each other in the bedroom there remained a fear that Anne's feelings for Maria did not go deep enough, and this made the act of separation easier to manage, their return to Paris was a welcome relief and they parted company once again.

During the winter of 1827-8 while still in Paris she found a new proposition, a young and pretty Parisian widow Madame de Rosny. It was not long before Anne moved into her house as a lodger to the obvious astonishment of her aunt Anne_and the Barlow's. Anne was smitten with her new fancy but the fact that the Madame had friends who were aristocrats, people who were favourites of the French Royal family and frequented as guests at the King's social gatherings, helped to gain Anne's interest... *"Sucked each breast a few seconds, and afterwards, between three and four she sat on my knee and I had right middle finger up, she evidently liking it and feeling some little. Elle est plus mouillée n'est ce pas ces. She was more moist"* ... A new affair then began between Anne and Madame de Rosny, though Anne first appeared enraptured by her new love interest, her feelings gradually faded before she made her way back to England and home.

As the year's past, Anne had become more critical and less easily swayed by her emotions and thus more in control of her life. Although Anne and Mariana remained friends the intensity of past years had gone. Anne however, still loyal offered a place of refuge at Shibden should Mariana's marriage become too difficult to withstand or if she should be left a widow. Mariana did once leave Charles but returned to him after a short period at Shibden.

Anne had reluctantly come to terms with the knowledge that the affair with Mariana was all but over, deep in her heart she had known for some time, she had accepted, though reluctantly that the situation between them would not change. Anne had spent most of her adult life chasing a dream, passionately pursuing a selfish woman who had always put herself first. Anne had been there as a safety net should she be left a widow without financial support, a devoted lover, and sex provider. Mariana had been the truest love of Anne's life, and never again would she invest in any relationship with the same ardour she had felt for Mariana.

Anne left for the continent in 1829 and although it was unusual for a lady to travel alone with only her servants to accompany her, showed a strong personality and self-assurance. In 1830 With Paris as her base, she visited Belgium and Germany before heading south to the Pyrenees.

In 1830 Anne in the company of Lady Elizabeth Margaret, Stuart de Rothesay, (1789-1867) wife of Charles Stuart, 1st Baron Stuart de Rothesay, British Ambassador in Paris, her two daughters and several attendants, left Paris to visit the Pyrenees. Whilst there she took on the challenge of climbing Mount Perdu, an astonishing achievement for an amateur climber. She filled her time there by hiking as well as crossing the border into Spain. Anne had always been a hardy walker and a visit to Switzerland in 1827 had whetted her appetite for mountain expeditions, although her intention to climb Mont Blanc had remained unfulfilled.

SIBELLA MACLEAN

Sometimes Lister's relationships became the topic of open discussion between her acquaintances. Once when Charles Lawton was drunk, he came home and told Mariana what was said about Anne, and Mariana relayed this to Lister... *"She told me how much had been said in York about my friendship for Miss Maclean. Mr. Lally had been visiting at Moreton last September & said he would as soon turn a man loose in his house as me". As for Miss Norcliffe, whom he suggested two Jacks would not suit together & he did not blame there but Miss Maclean's was a last resource & therefore she took me"* .... "Mariana had turned it off gravely saying *I had been brought up by my brothers. Had a masculine mind - more sense than most people & therefore people said these things"* ...

Through her friendship with the Norcliffe's Anne had been introduced in 1820 to Sibella Maclean, (1784-1830), daughter of Lieutenant Colonel Alexander Ruadh Maclean 15th laird of Coll and Catherine (Cameron) Maclean of the Isle of Coll in Argyllshire, Scotland. Sibella was baptized in the Parish of Tyree and Coll, Argyllshire on June 20, 1784. She had seven siblings. The two formed a close friendship which was continued throughout the 1820s. Much of Sibella's appeal for Anne lay in her good breeding as a member of an ancient Scottish family and the opportunity she offered Anne for social advancement.

It was Sibella Maclean, who introduced Anne to people who belonged to the English and Scottish aristocracy, thus gaining entry for a time into higher social circles. Sibella cancelled an invitation she made to Anne in 1825, having heard gossip about her, it wasn't until 1828 when Anne's earnest courtship of Sibella began to soften her feelings towards Anne, and they started to exchange financial confidences in preparation for living together.

On Lister's tour with Sibella through Scotland in 1828, Lister recorded each place they visited with intricate detail, obviously delighted with the scenery around one of the most spectacular locations in Great Britain. The two became lovers and Anne began to hope that Sibella would become her life partner. Lister had confided in her diary as early as 1822 *"I would rather spend my life with Miss Maclean than anyone"*. During the time she was courting Sibella Maclean, she was eager to present herself as eminently respectable. Sibella had quite openly told Anne that she thought her *"odd, very odd."* Anne replied, *"Perhaps you are right - I am an enigma even to myself and do excite my own curiosity. But this, at least, is comprehensible. There is something (but it breathes not of dishonour) that parts me from the world I meet with...Do not mistake me. The freedom I venerate, will never offend you. The independence I feel and practise, will never shock even the gentlest of thoughts like yours. I always supplicate assistance to enable me to do my duty in that state of life into which it has pleased God to call me, and, humbly trusting in that mercy which endureth forever, I cheerfully look for the things which are to come"* ...

Anne might be described as a social and sexual butterfly but always in her heart was a powerful desire to find someone who she could share her life with, and if the following months proved successful, then surely it would lead to a permanent arrangement. Their adventure began in late May 1828. The two friends shared a room, a normal thing for ladies who travelled together did. Their intension was to travel throughout Scotland staying over in suitable locations taking in as many points of interest as possible. Anne's behaviour was beyond reproach, but her companion, when they were alone together, gave off signals according to Lister, that she was happy to be close to her, which caused Anne to record in her diary... *"Incurred a cross just before getting up after she left me. Having been foolish on Saturday night made a point of being better last night and hardly touched but she lies close to me always"* ...

June 1st, 1828, after arriving in Callander, situated on the River Teith, west of Stirling Anne writes ... *"Had a little room and bed to myself the first time since being with Miss MacL. Said I was in a foolish humour from the whiskey punch. It was better not to run any risk of being too foolish. In fact, I am afraid of sleeping with her on account of her cough and care not to make love too far. I do quite enough. She looks oldish in the face yet takes all very well tho' properly enough. Yet I see that if I seriously pushed the matter I might succeed, but I forever now talk of having M- if anything happens to C-[Charles]."*

It was obvious to Anne that Sibella was not in robust health, she had a nasty cough and that coupled with what Anne called 'The whites', a vaginal discharge that caused Sibella discomfort and embarrassment. This was something which Anne was all too familiar with, so it did cause her to be cautious... *"She told me the whites had come on Thursday night and she was quite alarmed. It was six years since she had had them when doctor Belcombe cured her. Lays all to walking up the hill at Inverary. Feared I should now hate her. Only sorry for my disappointment. Would have me when she was able. Wished I had known her twenty years, she should then have been better worth my trouble. Said I would be prudent for a night or two but assured her I should not love her less but if possible, better"* ...

Their first sexual intimacy happened on the 4[th of] June with some reluctance from Sibella... *"At last sucked her right breast. She resisting, but not preventing and not being angry, merely saying it was not fair as I endeavoured to get my hand down to her moustaches. Said she was not like other people, cold etc. She denied being cold but said it was not right, she had scruples, two females ought not. She could do all I wished if it was right"* ... Anne appears not to have pushed the matter further, telling Sibella that she respected her scruples and her feelings... They discussed Sibella's previous romance... *"It was her brothers friend Colonel Hepburn of the guards whom she felt the only inclination she ever did feel to love but they mistook each other. She had not seen him of sixteen years and did not care for him now, she had never loved anyone half so well as me"* ...

However, another day brought new opportunities...
"Awake at eight. Took no notice of scruples, began again. Got my hand down, she putting it off. At last I begged her to leave me alone. To my surprise she said nothing but did so and we lay till after ten and I had my right middle finger moderately up twice. She evidently struggling not to shew did not dislike and I persuading her I could not find out whether she liked me or not,

that she was cold to me etc. However, she lay very quietly with my legs twined round her" ...

On the 6th of June Anne Records... *"Two last night one this morning after having had right middle finger up. Better than she was. Better last night and this morning than before, but still hardly moist. I really had a kiss this morning and my moisture did do a little at hers. Breakfast at 9 35/60."*

The seriousness of the relationship with Sibella Maclean is attested to by the fact that Anne persuaded Sibella to buy her a ring at a jeweller's in Glasgow and recorded in a coded passage in her diary on 11th June... *"Called at a jeweller's shop. Some time choosing a guard ring for Miss McL- to give me."*

Alone together Anne records... *"About an hour playing and trifling, right middle finger up but no kiss just getting her excited with my finger, having looked at and kissed her queer when the woman came to say it was ten o clock"*...

"Miss MacLean put on my finger the little guard ring". A Guard or perhaps Anne is referring to a 'Regard' ring, popular since around 1820. These precious little pieces signified romance, pre-engagement, or a betrothal or just to say, "I have regards for you". Georgian and early Victorian jewellery was made in high carat gold before 1854. Precious rings were created with 22k or 18k yellow/rose gold (75% pure gold alloyed with copper, silver, nickel, or a mixture of these metals) after 1854 a lower carat of gold became available which made the item less expensive. Another precious metal used in jewellery was silver. Popular gemstones of this early period include, table cut or rose cut diamonds, amethysts, bloodstone, chalcedony, garnets, emeralds, onyx, moss agate, ruby, smoky quartz and organic gems such as coral, ivory, tortoise shell, and seed pearls. The Georgians and Victorians were great romantics and loved the use of hidden messages in jewellery. Regard rings were usually pretty and of a delicate design often set with a variety of mixed cut stones, the first letter of each gemstone name spelling out the word 'Regard': Ruby, Emerald, Garnet, Amethyst, Ruby, and Diamond. The ring that Anne later purchased for Anne Walker had a black onyx gemstone.

During their tour, Anne and Sibella had visited many of the usual tourist spots in the vicinity of Glasgow, including the Trossachs and Loch Lomond, and around Tayside. They also made use of the new steamboat services to travel around the East coast, visiting St Andrews, Elgin, and Inverness, and visit the Highland forts and the Western Isles. The two became so close that Sibella asked Anne if she had ever received a proposal of marriage. Anne told her she had had six offers during her life. *"In my mind, I meant from Anne Belcombe & Louisa Belcombe & Mrs. Henrietta Milne, Miss Valiance, Mrs. Barlow & Madame de Rosny".*

Anne continued to add daily in her journal instances of their love making, recording the number of connections and if they were successful and satisfying... *"Two very good ones last night and two still better this morning, for told her of running away, just when that was coming that ought to come, so she remained as long as I wished the last time and we wet the bed."*

Monday 16th June 1828. Yet another hotel, this time... *"A double-bedded room. On going to wish her good night and saying I would go to her for a while, she said I must go to my own bed for some nights. It seemed her cousin was come so kissed and went away. Moved my bed from the wall and thus made a nice dressing place. Quarter hour this morning on the pott. No use. Then again in vain just before setting off. Lastly after breakfast, after straining, had a tolerable motion, rather lumpy and slightly tinged with blood at one end of one of the pieces."*

Friday 27th June 1828. *"Had a motion in quarter hour then went to Miss MacL to say we would stay here today. Got into bed to her and staid till eleven not daring to go near her but with my right middle finger up and handling her well. She said she thought we should have quarrelled last night. She would have been obliged to do so. Unjust suspicions bad to bear"* ... Was Anne's suspicions regarding the discharge? had she perhaps alluded to other connections Sibella must have had? *"Rallied her out of this and made her more easy with me than ever, she yielding as if she had no dislike"* ...

Anne was frank in her conversations with Sibella, probably more so than she had been with many of her other lovers... *"Staid talking to her in her room till near one. Told of Mr Simmons of Manchester examining me. Hint as if an operation might have been performed which might enable me to give more satisfaction to those with whom I had connection. Then the account of my first visit to Dupuytren.* [The Parisian doctor, Baron Guillaume Dupuytren a French anatomist, and military surgeon. He had gained much esteem for treating Napoleon Bonaparte's haemorrhoids]. *saying I had mentioned myself as tho I had been Marianna so that I could not forget my story. Told the queer questions he asked me but not owning to his having examined me, tho said Mr Simmons had. Then told of being near a man and woman in copulation (Mr Duffin and Miss Marsh, they thought me asleep). Asked if she loved me. Yes, too well. On leaving her got into my own bed for twenty and incurred a cross thinkg of her"...*

However, Anne was always secretive about revealing that she was menstruating, and this situation did not change here, even though the two women had become so familiar... *"Dawdling over 1 thing or another. Having worn one napkin with papers since Tuesday morning, that is two days and as many nights, sent it to the wash determined to wear nothing. This is the first time in my life of trying this plan. I shall be ready for Miss MacL as soon as she will be so for me"* ... *"When the clothes came from wash would get hold of them slyly. Got them and withdrew the one napkin I sent, telling Miss MacL I suspected her shamming Abraham not to have me at night so would see it came out"* ... It appears that Sibella was also a little bashful regarding her monthly period... *"She bought a yard of flannel at Glasgow (I asked at the time wh[a]t for and she said it was for the poor people at home) and cut it into four having no napkins with her. Good idea".* (Shamming Abraham, is a phrase which means to tell a lie to avoid or gain something).

As their travels take them closer to Sibella's home, the entries Anne makes in her diary reporting... *"Still no kiss"* ... begin to take prominence in her entries. Finally, on 30th July they arrive at the McLean family home, Breachacha Mansion House, built in the mid-1700s by the McLean clan, on the same site as Breachacha castle, situated on the beautiful, west coast of Scotland in Coll, an Island west of the Isle of Mull in the Inner Hebrides.

Lister tried to persuade Sibella's parents that Sibella should go and live with her in Paris, it would be beneficial for her health... *"Sat talking in the breakfast room to Mr & Mrs McLean & Albane about their going abroad, the expense &c. Then talking to Miss MacLean. Beg her speaking to her brother about money to go with to Paris"* ... After dinner that evening Anne again brings up the subject of Paris... *"Afterwards sat up talking to Miss MacLean. No money to be had but she might take of her five hundred. I then asked what her father had. Three hundred a year for himself. Very well ask your father"*...

Friday 1st August 1828. Lister's final day with Sibella... *"Two kisses last night, neither of them good to her and I cared not for them but thought it best to try the last night. All her nervousness gone up and quite brisk. Delighted to go to Paris. Tell her and fold the rest she ought to be off on the first September"* ... Lister then travelled alone on her homeward journey to Yorkshire, taking in more tourist sites in the Scottish borders, and arriving back at Shibden on 15th August. Sibella's health was in decline for many years, suffering from consumption, she finally died two years later November 16, 1830 in London, England, aged 46 years.

(Source information gathered from the website: The Real Anne Lister by Leigh Mitchinson (@annelisteruncut) https://iknowmyownheart.co.uk)

FURTHERING AN EDUCATION

Anne's reading for the 1820s and 1830s turned more and more frequently to publications such as the Royal Institutional Journal, Fleming's '*The Philosophy of Zoology*', and Dr. John Ayrton Paris, MD. (1785-1856) '*A Syllabus of a Course of Lectures on Pharmaceutic Chemistry*'. She also read the work of Marie Jean Pierre Flourens (1794–1867) a French physician, famous for various significant discoveries relating to the nervous system. Known for experimental brain science and a pioneer in anaesthesia who was the first to prove that the mind was in the brain and not in the heart. Flourens was an opponent of Darwin's theories and authored '*Examen du livre du M. Darwin sur l'Origine des Espèces*'.

In 1830 Anne's education continued in Paris, her 56-year-old Aunt Anne was her travel companion; they choose 39 Rue Godot de Mauroy as their base. Anne was determined to pursue her ambition of studying science. Along with other ladies, she took presentations in the Lady's gallery, listening to various thrice-weekly lectures at the Jardin du Roi and the Royal Institute. M. Desfontaine lectured on botany; Langier lectured on chemistry; Bronguiart on mineralogy; Cordier and Pelletier on geology and M. Geoffrey St. Hilaire on the natural history of mammals. For this course, she had a tutor in anatomy, M. JuiMart, who came to her rooms each Saturday to give lessons in dissection.

Anne had taken a separate apartment for this purpose at no. 7 Rue St. Victor. Amongst the subject matter Anne learned to dissect was a deceased rabbit, a severed human hand, a disembodied ear, a woman's head, and a baby. She preserved the parts in rectified spirits and kept them in a cabinet she obtained especially in which to keep her specimens, which also contained a skeleton and several skulls.

Not everything ran to plan, the body of the deceased child that Mr. Julliart had acquired for Anne to work on began to rot. The cover that contained the little body had burst open revealing the contents in a state of putrefaction. Anne comments... *"the luting had not been good enough the spirit had evaporated and the foetus was swollen up like a drowned man a sad pity we must try and manage better in future"* ...

In England it was not until 1862 before the first woman, Elizabeth Garrett Anderson graduated from medical school after overcoming many obstacles all aimed at thwarting her ambitions to qualify as a physician and surgeon. It was June 1868, when the University of London's Senate voted to admit women to sit the General Examination, so becoming the world's first university to accept women. However, unlike their male peers, on passing the General Examination successful women did not receive a degree but a "Certificate of Proficiency". It would be another decade before women were admitted to the university's degree programme.

The lecturer in Paris who she most admired was Georges Cuvier, a major figure in natural sciences research in the early 19th century to whom Anne had written in 1819, asking for help with her studies in natural history.

 The Halifax archives contain three volumes of Cuvier lecture notes which she took between 1830-1831. She noted in 1830 that *"Cuvier's 25th lecture brought us down to the sixteenth-century from which time to now he will divide the subject into five branches, anatomy, and physiology, zoology, botany, mineralogy and chemistry."*

Perhaps one of the reasons why she was able to continue with her scholarship, despite the potential risk to her social standing, was because of her reluctance to publish anything. In fact, it was difficult for a woman to gain approval for their work and to have anything published. Female authors tended to use male pseudonyms in order that their work was accepted for publication. Lister did fantasise of achieving greatness through literature: *'Thinking as I dressed of the Literary & philosophical society just established at Halifax. I have thought of it repeatedly since hearing of it - building castles*

in the air about the part I myself may take in furthering it" ...
(Liddington, 1998: 45).

In 1821, she wrote... *'The idea of publishing at some time or other has often come across me & I have mused on what subject to fix; ... one might give a few useful essays on these matters, such for instance, as politics, religion, etc., & each essay 36 containing a sort of digest of its subject"* ('The Secret Diaries of Miss Anne Lister' Whitbread, 1988: 168).

Even though Anne's attention was primarily focused on study, she continued to hope for making the acquaintance of a love interest... *"incurred a cross last night thinking how nice it would be if I could have some nice girl at my little apartment near the Jardin du Roi"*

VERE HOBART

After her extended tour of the continent Anne returned to Shibden Hall in 1831. She found life with her father Jeremy and sister Marian so uncomfortable with constant quibbling, and irritations. Lister described sister Marian who irritated Anne constantly and after several arguments, as the 'cock of the dung hill'. (Gentleman Jack: The Real Ann Lister by Anne Chroma & Sally Wainwright). Anne almost immediately left with her friend Mariana Lawton for a trip to the continent. All in all, between 1826 and 1832, she only spent a few weeks at Shibden Hall, with travels around Britain and Europe allowing her to avoid her family at home.

By the time she was in her 30's, Anne was travelling around Europe and mingling in high society, meeting cosmopolitan and aristocratic women such as Vera Hobart, a lady whom Anne desperately desired though they never had intimate sexual relations.

It was through her relationship with Sibella Maclean, that she became friends with Lady Louisa Stuart, (12 August 1757 - 4 August 1851) of Richmond Park, daughter of John, Earl of Bute, Prime Minister to George III. She had often discussed Sibella Maclean with Lady Stuart when visiting the embassy, and Sibella's failing health, suffering from consumption was a frequent topic in the letters she and Lady Stuart exchanged.

Anne had spent a fruitful winter in Paris in 1829-30 socialising with her aristocratic friends and formed a special friendship with Lady Louisa Stuart's great-niece, Vere Catherine Louisa Hobart, (1803-1888) sister of the 5th Earl of Buckinghamshire who was also the niece of Sibella Maclean. With her eye on climbing the social ladder and forming a good connection, Anne had begun a tentative flirtation with Vere who was 28 years old, Anne was 40.

After returning together to Hastings they made plans to travel again to the continent but were prevented after an outbreak of cholera, so they arranged to spend the winter together instead in Hastings. Anne and Vere spent 5 months in St Leonards in 1831-32. The Asiatic cholera pandemic reached Great Britain in December 1831. Between 1831 and 1834 it had caused 60,000 deaths in the population of 14 million. Anne believed Vere had become increasingly aware of her sexual interest and would in time reciprocate her romantic overtures.

Anne had convinced herself that she may have at long last found a woman who held all the necessary qualities which Anne had so long been searching for. Aristocratic Vere Hobart represented everything Anne Lister desired in a partner. She was sophisticated, educated, and elegant, with enviable connections to the high society circles in which Anne aspired to move. But convincing Vere to give herself to Anne was a challenge too far to end in success. It was a fraught winter. At times, it seemed to Anne that she was making progress in her softly, softly approach; in November, she wrote... *"I think the idea of being with me eventually is somehow getting more familiar to her mind. She begins to flirt a little with me and looked very pretty when playing this evening. Well, strange things happen – she may like me after all."*

Anne Lister and Vere Hobart often spoke of their finances and made plans for their future as if they were a heterosexual couple, and Vere certainly was heterosexual. One evening after dinner they had a rather oblique discussion about their relationship:

"[I] talked of having a right to provide for the person who lived with me if I married and [that] I had a right to do so none would dispute". Said she innocently, *"but I don't think you have a right to marry",* meaning I was too unlike a woman for that. *"This spo[k]e volume. [sic] I said well, but I have apparently a right the world must suppose I have. In fact, her manner is much more what it would be to a lover than a mere friend"* ...

There was certainly some flirtatious behaviour and light-hearted banter on Vere's part and perhaps that came easily to ladies who fell under the spell of Anne Lister. It was certainly acceptable that should the two ladies live and travel together, their financial arrangements would mirror those of heterosexual marriages...

"In walking home joked and said I should have seven hundred a year from her and leave her three". She thought four would be enough as much as she should cost me... Then joked with Miss H. that our match would be off on account of pecuniary matters and we both laughed and called each other mercenary. She afterwards laughed and said she would have all I had for her life. Well, said I, I have no objection to leave all I have for one life to the person who may be with me. She laughed and said, oh that ought really to be known. I see she knows quite well what she is about as I do" ...

Vere had other plans a foot after meeting Donald Cameron of Lochiel, 23rd Chief of Clan Cameron, son of Donald Cameron of Lochiel, 22nd Chief of Clan Cameron and Hon. Anne Abercromby. It appears that Vere kept her new relationship with Donald Cameron secret and continued to flirt with Anne until he asked her to marry him. This was a cruel and bitter blow for Anne who had grown increasingly positive about her relationship with Vere.

After Anne's devastating discovery she wrote three full, very emotional pages almost entirely in code. They are full of revealing sentiment, such as... *"I neither want her pity nor her ridicule both which I might count upon"*... She confined herself to her room and tried to hide her swollen eyes and will herself out of having a broken heart. She thought of a previous suitor of Vere's, a Henry Yorke, who had given her up... *"he may marry more happily and so may I too"*...

Anne resolved to go back to Halifax and Shibden and – for the first time in years – stay there... *"I have been an Icarus – but shall full less fatally, for I can still live and be happy,"* ... she wrote... *"Here I am at forty-one, with a heart to seek. What will be the end of it?"* ... Letters discovered in a Highland archive have since revealed that she did indeed stay in touch with Vere throughout her life. After the wedding which Anne decided not to attend, she wrote affectionately... *"My dearest Vere, I am quite happy for your sake,*

and know not that I have one wish concerning you unsatisfied." ...
She thanked Vere for... *"her discretion"* and for staying faithful to
"her own very self." ...

DIARIES OF 1832

In 1832, for the first time in many years, she had accepted that Mariana would never be hers alone, and the engagement was well and truly over. Anne needed someone else to fill the void in her heart and began thinking of whom to approach who might be suitable with the necessary wealth, status and breeding that was so important for a contender with which to win Anne's affections... *"The thought struck me of going from Croft to Edinburgh to see the Mackenzies. Lady Eliza [...?] Thackeray and Miss Hall to try first. First for Miss Mack. Thought of Miss Freeman and Miss Walker of Lidgate as people here. Louisa Belcombe and Miss Price in York besides Miss Salmon, Surely I shall get some sort of companion by & by"*

May 1832: After the disaster of a failed bid to win Vere Hobart's heart, Anne Lister made her forlorn way back home to Halifax, to her dispiriting family: her elderly father, aunt, and her inconvenient sister... *"And back to ancient Shibden Hall,"* ... which she now found old-fashioned and shabby.

Aged forty-one, Anne Lister knew her romantic youth was over. So many of her female friends had married and settled. Anne had longed to find a loving female partner and to settle down for most of her adult life, but all her plans of matrimonial bliss had been thwarted and once again she was alone to dwell on what might have been.

Later in May, Anne wrote... *"The thought of exile from poor Shibden always makes me melancholy. Come what may, I've been happier here than anywhere else... Providence ordains all things wisely... I'm attached to my own people-they are accustomed to my oddities, are kind, are civilised to me... But... A great deal will, and must, depend on that someone known or unknown, whom I still hope for as the comfort of my evening hour"* ...

Anne was concerned with the failing health of her Aunt Anne; the rheumatism had got worse as time went by, resulting in her being housebound, her increasing health deterioration requiring frequent attention from her physician, causing Anne a great deal of worry.

Shibden Hall, hidden from view by the steep hillside above bustling Halifax, provided a quiet, safe, rural space. In July 1832, a chance re-acquaintance with neighbouring heiress Ann Walker of Crow Nest estate in rural Lightcliffe changed Anne Lister's life forever.

By the autumn of 1832, Anne had written 20,000 words in only 5 weeks! Her usual method was to jot down memoranda and then write up her journal later that day or the following day.

Marriage offered a powerful metaphor for the kind of lasting sexual and emotional bond Lister craved for, but it must be with a woman for a relationship with a man would be abhorrent to Anne. Her philandering with, among others, the Belcombe sisters, Isabella Norcliffe with her fellow Parisian pensionnée, Mme de Boyve, Maria Barlow, and at the Norcliffe's house-party, with Mary Vallance, were well and truly apart of her past. She describes her... "violent *longing for a female companion*" ...

FIRST MODERN LESBIAN

Anne's generic euphemism for lesbianism is *'connection with the ladies'*, and her euphemism for a full sexual connection involving full commitment is *'going to Italy'*. Anne's pleasure results from spontaneous orgasm, that is her excitement peaks to climax while making love to another woman.

Anne's use of the word 'queer' to denote the female pudendum is nowhere else recorded. Wikipedia suggests that the word entered the English language in the 16th century, and originally meant "strange", "odd", "peculiar", or "eccentric." The exact origin is obscure, though it virtually always means inferior and often used as an insult. It has no demonstrable link to the slang 'quim' 'cunt', literally 'cleft' or any of the 60 plus words recognised as slang terms for female genitalia. Perhaps Anne's application of the term literally to the 'nether regions' is the original meaning of the word.

In sexual affairs, Anne prefers not to be treated overtly as a woman. Anne does not like it when Mrs. Barlow touches her queer... *"I started back"*. *'that is because you are a pucelle [Maid, virgin]. I must undo that. I can give you relief, do to you as you do to me'*... Mrs Barlow was obviously concerned with the concept of a spontaneous orgasm being able to fully satisfy Anne's insatiable sexual appetite. Anne realized that it was bemusing for Maria to interpret her physical reaction regarding her role in the sex act.

Anne did not like to be reminded of her womanliness; her lover Mariana referred to her as "Fred". Yet we gain no impression from Anne's journals that she wanted to be a man or to pass as one. As she told one lover... *"as a man I should have been shut out from ladies' society"* ... After all, a young bachelor could not have flirted so openly, or have been as familiar with ladies, kissed ladies on the lips, been alone with ladies in closed drawing rooms, sitting them on his knee, or spend time alone in their bedrooms as Anne Lister often did with her lovers.

It is not difficult to decipher the sexual act covered by Anne's euphemism *'kiss'* a familiar word in Anne Lister's diaries... *"No Kiss"*, (which like the French *baiser* meaning 'Kiss' but can also mean 'fuck' depending on the accompanying words in the sentence. Apparently *baiser* gained the sexual meaning in the 16th century). Menstruation is sometimes mentioned as a reason not to 'kiss'... *"Two good kisses at once last night & three this morning, after eight'...* Presumably, these are multiple orgasms... *'Three of four all at once last night & one more, a good one, at four this morning."* ... *"Mariana had a very good kiss last night; mine was not quite so good but I had a very nice one this morning,"* ... *"Tried for a kiss a considerable time last night but Isabella was as dry as a stick & could not succeed . . . [she] fidgeted herself exceedingly at our want of success"* ...

Lister uses X or the word 'cross', indicating sexual self-stimulation (masturbation) or, sometimes, spontaneous orgasm... *'incurred a cross sitting on my chair it somehow came on suddenly not thinking particularly of anyone till lastly"* ... Another highly expressive term Lister uses is 'grubble', meaning to grope with sexual intent or to sexually stimulate, a northern dialect word for 'poke about'. 'On the amoroso' describes her lovers' eagerness to engage in sexual activity.

Anne's apparent outward appearance indicated that she had masculine traits, when in Paris Anne walked into a Parisian salon in fashionable petticoats, ribbons, and ringlets in her hair and even such ladylike apparel did not fully conceal her masculine body language as she was mistaken for a man.

Through her detailed accounts in her journals, we discover that there is a tradition of lesbian lovers exchanging pubic hair with one another, just as heterosexual lovers exchanged locks of hair. Anne has a collection of these love tokens in her cabinet of curiosities, which she shows to Mariana, even asking her to guess who they once belonged too, but it is unlikely that she would have revealed that one such keep-sake came from Mariana's own sister Anne, taken in a celebration to their reunion…

Mariana put me on a new watch riband & then cut the hair from her own queer & I that from mine, which she put each into each of the little lockets we got at Bright's this morning, twelve shillings each, for us always to wear under our clothes in mutual remembrance. We both of us kissed each bit of hair before it was put into the locket" …

During one visit to York, Anne Lister's friend, Isabella Norcliffe, jokingly accused Anne of being a *"tuft-hunter"*. Isabella died in 1846 she was sixty-one years old, having outlived Anne by six years.

Around 1670, "tuft" became a slang term to describe the golden tassels which ornamented an academic mortarboard of titled undergraduates. The less exotic dictionary definition of tuft is "a bunch or cluster of small, usually soft and flexible parts, such as feathers or hairs attached or fixed closely together at the base and loose at the upper ends". Isabella's accusation, however, had nothing to do with gold tassels or tufts of fur. The definition is much more closely related to Anne's fetish for collecting locks of hair from the women she seduced, and was likely retained as a type of trophy, spoils of love so to speak, recording her seduction successes, or to remind her of love once shared…*"Just after we got home from the walk I went into her room & asked Miss V- for two locks of her hair in such a way that I am sure she knew what I wanted & I durst say no more"*… Mariana said Mrs Milne had told her *"I was become a tuft-hunter"*…

Anne's masculine thinking suggests that she was more likely to respect a woman if she showed some restraint and reluctance to be sexual at the beginning of their relationship. She never, in any part of her four-million-word journal recorded an instance where a woman took the first active overtures of seduction and made love to her.

In the act of sex Anne prefers a recognized gender division between giver and receiver, with herself as giver. Today we might classify her as a 'stone butch', / 'stone femme' a recognized term to describe a lesbian identity who displays female butchness or traditional masculinity and sexual behaviour. The title first used and popularized by Leslie Feinberg in her 1993 novel 'Stone Butch Blues'.

Stone butches usually do not like to be sexually touched genitally by their partners or do not want to be penetrated during sex, or have certain areas touched during sex or everyday life, such as breasts or inner thighs. However, they still provide their partners with sexual gratification and experience pleasure themselves in doing so. Anne's record of her orgasm is always one of spontaneous stimulation. Generally, like Anne, they do not identify themselves as a lesbian. Anne Lister considered herself natural and unique.

Anne realized she was different from a young age though this did not appear to alarm her but rather excite and fascinate her. She went to great lengths to understand the nature of her sexuality. She undertook extensive study to interpret her nature and she appears to be in full knowledge of her own situation. To Mrs. Barlow ... *"Said how it was all nature. Had it not been genuine the thing would have been different. I said I had thought much, studied anatomy, etc. Could not find it out. Could not understand myself. It was all the effect of the mind. No exterior formation accounted for it. Alluded to their being an internal correspondence or likeness of some of the male or female organs of generation. Alluded to the stones not slipping thro' the ring till after birth, etc.".* (Stones was a middle English word for testicles.)

Anne is offering her understanding of anatomy which she has derived both from classical works and nineteenth century anatomists. In the 18th and early 19th century it was thought that female and male bodies were the same except that the female genitalia were male genitals turned inside out. Anatomists saw the vagina as an interior penis, the labia as foreskin, the uterus as scrotum, and the ovaries as testicles. They support the claim that the female organs were analogous, though inferior to the male organs. It was accepted that woman have testes with accompanying seminal ducts very much like men's, one on each side of the uterus whereas the males are contained in the scrotum. Even in 1819 The London Medical Dictionary is rather muddled in its nomenclature.

Anne is aware of but rejects as deficient, the early proto-sexological literature regarding lesbians as hermaphrodites. Lister was familiar with theories of hermaphroditism. While she described her sexual attraction to women as 'all nature' and pondered that it was also *'all the effect of the mind,"* she considered physiological causes but found no apparent evidence: Although she did consult anatomical works (including Latin works), she is the instigator of her own attempt to understand herself.

She already has a powerful sense of identity but is nevertheless endeavouring to understand its true nature... Whilst Anne is daydreaming about seducing a coquette, she fantasizes about having a penis: *"Fancying I had a penis & was intriguing with her in the downstairs water-closet at Langton before breakfast, to which she would have made no objection."* ... Although Anne occasionally fantasizes about seducing young women from the lower classes, she dared not give way to lustful liaisons with commoners, as any possible disclosures could lead to disastrous consequences for her reputation and social standing.

Anne is both secret and blatant, like many lesbians and homosexuals until relatively recent times. In female company she openly assumes the liberties and manners of the opposite sex, her flirting with women is so open and gentleman-like that several women of her acquaintance wonder if she is a man in disguise.

She is aware that her sexuality is an object of discussion among some of her friends and acquaintances, and Mrs. Barlow asks what her maidservant thinks of her behaviour... *"Oh, merely, that I have my own particular ways. "I happened to say that my aunt often said I was the oddest person she ever knew. Mrs. Barlow said, "But she knows all about it, does she not? Oh, said I, she & my friends are all in a mist about it."*...

Anne's reply suggests concealment rather than naivety, she cannot be under any illusion that her behaviour with other woman would escape her family's notice or their suspicions. In fact, they obviously had accepted fully Anne's sexuality and wished only for her happiness.

Sexual pleasure and desire were considered beyond heterosexual marriage and therefore labelled deviant and considered to be sinful and sinister. Discussion of sexual encounters and matters were met with ignorance, embarrassment, and fear. Public opinion of women's sexual desires was that they were not very troubled by sexual urges. Eminent Biologists at this time had extraordinarily little knowledge of reproduction and of what governed the production of an egg. By saying that conception was not related to orgasm, sexual pleasure for women seemed to lose importance. Women were thought of as passionless and drew no enjoyment of sex. Later in more enlightened times Sigmund Freud uses the analogy of the clitoris as "pine shavings [used to] set a log of hard wood on fire!

In middle and high-class society obsessed with virginity, girls were encouraged to have female romantic friendships and share beds as protection against marauding males. Indeed, up into the mid-20th century, it was considered quite normal for ladies to share a bed without the suspicion that anything improper was occurring. There were no laws in Britain against women cross-dressing or having sexual relations with other women as there were on the European continent, where marriage imitations between women were criminal and the penetration of one woman by another with an object was a serious offence.

Lister may have been familiar with the trials in Holland in the 1790s of tribades for sodomy or 'dirty acts'. One such case that came before the courts were the arrest in 1798 of Anna Schreuder and Maria Smit for their own protection from a marauding mob. Neighbours had suspected Schreuder and Smit of unspecified activities and spied on them through a hole from a neighbouring room while they were engaging in sex.

The two had lain together with their lower bodies naked, had kissed and caressed each other 'like a man is used to do to a woman', had moved up and down on each other, and finally one had lifted her leg over the other's shoulder who had then performed oral sex on her.

178

The peeping went on for several hours, with other neighbours being invited to watch, then neighbours assembled a mob outside the house until the constables arrived and made the arrests.

In Britain, women who married women were charged under a motley collection of laws, including financial fraud and vagrancy. Two cases reported in the Gentleman's Magazine in the 1770s: a young cross-dressing woman charged with financial fraud for marrying an older, richer woman, and a woman sentenced to the pillory and six months in jail for marrying three women under a fictitious name.

Fielding's pamphlet The Female Husband (1746) fictionalized an account of the life of Mary Hamilton, who was arrested in 1746 and accused of posing as a physician and marrying Mary Price under false pretences. She was charged under the vagrancy act and sentenced to four public whippings and six months of hard labour. The pamphlet was reissued in 1813 as an anonymous chapbook and may have been known to Lister.

Anne demonstrates some anxiety about the possibility of transgressing legal as well as social laws when she expresses relief that Miss Pickford, *"seemed persuaded I never had any criminal connection with any of [close women friends]"*. Lister held Enlightenment views about the expression of sexual feelings as 'natural' and 'instinctive', she was aware that this sexual tolerance did not extend to homosexuality.

It required constant vigilance to negotiate the narrow path between society's acceptance and opprobrium. In October 1819, when she was under threat from a persistent stalker, Anne examined the strains occasioned by fear of homophobic attack and exhorted herself to physical and emotional resistance: *"I will never fear. Be firm. Learn to have nerve to protect myself & make the best of things. He is but a little fellow & I think I could knock him down if he should touch me. I should try. If not, whatever he said I would make no answer. Never fear. Pray against this & for God's protection & blessing, & then face the days undaunted. It is always a relief to me to write down what I feel"* ...

It is evident that Anne did have real concerns of the consequences of being different, *'Learn to have nerve & make the best of things'* together with calculations about *'knocking down'* her pursuer show just how concerned she was and how closely she monitored her responses. She tried to construct an emotional defence through earnest self-counselling. The repeated self-assurance to 'never fear' and the implications of that sinister *'if he should touch me'* reveal real anxiety, for she had, as this diary entry reveals, already been touched with fear.

An economic analysis of the situation that Lesbian women faced in the period which Anne Lister lived reveals mainly that financial independence allowed Anne to follow her instincts. Capitalism facilitates rather than inhibits lesbian relations. The rise of capitalism increased mobility, more tolerance of unconventional behaviour for those whose status is achieved through wealth rather than birth, greater independence through inheritance of moderate but adequate wealth without the necessity of marital or family alliances.

Anne always knew that she could live respectably with her lover as a lesbian couple incognito since it was accepted by society for two single women to live together as friends and companions. Anne who as a young woman drew quite a reasonable income from her aunt and uncle and discussed her affairs with them, comparing the different merits of her potential female partners.

If she did not openly reveal the sexual connections with these women, they were likely to have guessed the truth and perfectly aware of Anne's propensity with females. In fact, the realization by her uncle that Anne was unlikely to marry a man must have played a part in his leaving Shibden to his niece. Like caring custodians, they accepted their charge's maverick lifestyle; they looked forward to the time when she would fix upon a suitable companion to live with her and at last settle down.

Anne took lovers from beneath and above her social class but when looking for a long-term partner/wife, she looked for someone with more wealth or/and a higher social status than her own. Economic considerations were as important for Anne and her lovers as for heterosexual couples. The affair with Mrs. Barlow eventually failed partly because Anne realized that she could never feel as much regard for her as she did for Mariana, and that she would not be accepted by Anne's aristocratic friends and therefore she was not an asset to Anne's aspirations. Like Anne, Mariana had sort to better her standing in society by marrying into a wealthy family and the reason why she had rejected Anne's modest income for an opulent lifestyle.

Anne regretted what she had termed Mariana's *'legal prostitution'* she had once encouraged the marriage because of its obvious financial prudence; Charles broke off friendly relations with Anne when he discovers that she and his wife had hoped for his early death so they could live together and use his wealth to sustain their lifestyle; After their long forced separation Mariana reinstated her relationship with Anne when she realized that she was unlikely to have a child by her husband, and that he had not put her into his will, though she signed her income over to him as was the law (coverture) in that period, which means she would be destitute after his death. Eventually, Charles reconciles himself with Anne and resigns himself to her affair with his wife, facilitating their travelling together and feigning indifference when they sleep together even in his own house.

Lawton and Lister remained friends until Lister's death in 1840 and their love affair continued sporadically until Lister chose Anne Walker as her life-companion. Lawton's New Year letters refer to the past joys of love and continue a narrative of loss and resignation triggered by what Lister, perhaps unsurprisingly, interpreted as Mariana's betrayal in marrying Lawton.

Lister copied the letters, presumably verbatim, into her diary, and then offered a commentary on them. The following extract is from Lawton's New Year letter of January 1832...

"As far as present appearances go [Charles Lawton] may live these twenty years, as Mr. Ford [the apothecary] told

him last night tho he does bother me sadly ... I often think of what you told me in the coach from Peterborough that I was so used to Mr. L[awton] 's odd ways that I should probably feel his loss more than I suspected & really my Fred [Lister' s pet-name] it would be so & since I find that no unreasonable conduct would justify my leaving him I think I have made up my mind.., to make the best of it C[harles] will never change"

THE WALKER FAMILY OF LIGHTCLIFFE

Ann Walker's grandfather, William Walker (1713 – 1786), was a wealthy Halifax worsted manufacturer who was instrumental in the building of St Matthew's Church Lightcliffe. In 1775 he had travelled to the Baltic to buy timber. This was the wood used on the roof of St Matthew's old church. William Walker also used the timber to rebuild his family home, Crow Nest, and then to build a new home Cliffe Hill, to the designs of Thomas Bradley, in 1788, on the family estate in the village of Lightcliffe, situated in the West Riding of Yorkshire.

He and daughter Ann gave generously to the poor and he and some of the fellow benefactors are named on the board which is now stored in the Church tower. St Mathew's church was replaced in 1880 and demolished in the early 1970s. The 'Friends of St Mathews Church' Wakefield Road, Lightcliffe, rescued the memorials that were on the walls of the church and these are also stored in the tower. The Walker family would have worshipped at St Matthew's Church and, of course, had family pews.

The unmarried daughters of William Walker, Mary Walker (baptised at Lightcliffe on 17th September 1747) lived with her sister, another Ann Walker (baptised at Lightcliffe on 2nd September 1757), they were sisters of John Walker and so the aunts of Elizabeth and Ann Walker. Another aunt, Elizabeth Walker (baptised at Lightcliffe on 31st January 1750) had married a John Priestley on 17th September 1776. These interlinked families – the Walkers, the Edwards, the Priestley's and then the Rawson's – get many mentions in the diaries of Anne Lister.

When granddaughter Ann became the 'wife' of Anne Lister, Lister bought a pew and had it refurbished in green velvet so that they could worship together (and, most likely to avoid the gossip from the potentially more hostile environment at Halifax Parish Church).

John Walker, son of William of Crow Nest & Cliffe Hill, Halifax, was born in 1753, he married Mary Edwards, born in 1763 on 18th June 1794. They produced five children, William (1798-1798), Mary Walker. (1799-1815), Elizabeth Walker. (1801-1844], Ann Walker. (Born 20th May 1803, Died 4th March 1854), John Walker. (1804-1830)

In 1830 Ann Walker and her sister Elizabeth were the last remaining children of John and Mary Walker who had both died in 1823. Their two daughters eventually inherited the enormous Lightcliffe estate situated close by that of Lister's land. After the death of their parents and brother following an unhappy childhood with an abusive father who had been once described in 1822 to Anne Lister as a 'madman' by William Priestley. Elder sister Elizabeth had married on the 29th of October 1828 and moved to Scotland, Ann remained single, living alone at Lightcliffe with few interests other than the family estate to occupy her time.

Elizabeth married Captain George Mackay Sutherland of Udale, after they met at a ball at the Walker's Lightcliffe home, Cliffe Hill. George MacKay Sutherland was born on 10th November 1798 at Uppat House, Sutherland, Scotland the son of George Sackville Sutherland and his wife Jean (nee MacKay). George MacKay Sutherland is recorded as being a Captain in the 92nd Highlanders.

Elizabeth and George Sutherland lived in Scotland for most of their early married life and so this was probably where all their children were born; Mary on 27th September 1829, George Sackville on 1st March 1831, Elisabeth on 21st October 1832, John Walker on 16th September 1834, Evan Charles on 12th October 1835 and Ann Walker Sutherland on 17th October 1837. Although George Sackville Sutherland was baptised at St Matthew's Church on 19th April 1831 when his parents' abode was Crow Nest.

ANN WALKER

Little is known about Ann Walker's early years and education. According to a memorial plate in Old St. Matthew's Church, Ann Walker was born the 20th of May in 1803. She was the youngest daughter of merchant John Walker (1753-1823) and his wife Mary, née Edwards (1763-1823) from Pye Nest. The father was indeed successful with his business and the family became one of the most important within that area. The Walker family owned and lived at the Crow Nest Mansion. The Latin motto of the Walker family was *Iustum perficito nihil timeto* meaning 'do what is right and fear nothing'.

Aged just six, Ann Walker moved into Crow Nest with her parents, older sisters, Mary and Elizabeth, and younger brother, John. Her parents had named their first-born William, but he died at just 21 days old on the 26th of April 1798. Completing the family, second son John Walker was born in 1804 dying in 1830.

In her teens, Ann's mental problems begun to surface, and she suffered all her life from depression. It has been said that the consequences of her abusive father may have played a part in her mental state. As an adult, she was shy and somewhat withdrawn. Her extended family thought of Ann as delicate, vulnerable and invalid and with an eye on her considerable wealth, that she needed protection against fortune hunters, which did nothing for Ann's psychological resilience.

Teenaged sister Mary Walker died on 1st February 1815 and was buried on 8th February 1815. Mary, Elizabeth, and Ann were family names. The Rev. Robert Wilkinson conducted the funerals of John and Mary Walker, Ann's parents, in 1823. By the age of nineteen, Ann Walker had lost a sister and then her parents, the latter within a few months of each other. Ann Walker's younger brother John then inherited the Crow Nest estate, but their father had made ample financial provision for his daughters Elizabeth and Ann.

In 1829 younger brother John Walker married Frances Esther Penfold on 28th July in Steyning, Sussex. Fanny, as she was known, was one of the large family of Reverend John Penfold and his wife Charlotte Jane Penfold (nee Brooks). Born on 26th August 1803 Fanny was baptised on 14th October 1803 in Steyning. At least two of her younger brothers were given the middle name Rawson. This suggests that the Penfolds might have been related to the Rawson's and hence Priestley families and therefore the Walker family of Lightcliffe.

This may well explain how Fanny became the companion of Aunt Ann Walker at Cliffe Hill which was presumably how she met John Walker. After the wedding John and Fanny set off for a honeymoon in Naples, Italy. But on 19th January 1830 twenty-five-year-old John Walker died on his honeymoon. He was buried at the old Protestant cemetery, Corso Garibaldi, Naples.

It took a long time for this news to reach the Walker family and for a pregnant Fanny to return to England. Ann Walker went down to Dover to meet her, the Walker family being fearful that a child would inherit everything. But later in 1830, at her parents' home, she gave birth to a stillborn son. With no heir and no will – John Walker died intestate – matters were complicated. There were much reading and rereading of his father and grandfather's wills. The result was that the sisters Elizabeth Sutherland and Ann Walker became very wealthy coheiresses. Anne Lister's diaries record that an initial settlement of £25,000 was made to Fanny, approx. £2.8 million today.

The Walkers were certainly a wealthy family. The properties they owned covered a wide area – Honley Lindley, Golcar, Crimble, Scammonden, Greetland, Mixenden, Ovenden, Northowram, Southowram, Saddleworth, Halifax and Hipperholme. The total income from the estate was over £20,000, (approx. £2.3 million) today.

After her brother's death Ann Walker moved out of imposing Crow Nest into Lidgate, a smaller, far less grand house on the estate.

The first impression we might gain of Ann Walker is that she was introverted, inhibited, and impotent. This is very wide of the mark. Ann had been successfully running her jointly owned estate for several years, an estate much larger than Lister's own. The wealth that she had accrued was not entirely made up of inheritance but from investments and acquisitions. Ann Walker independently owned property in Ovenden and Stainland. There was a valuation of Listerwick Colliery amongst Ann's papers for £377 per annum (approx. £41,000 today). Samuel Washington was still collecting rents after Ann's death which were transferred to Evan Charles Sutherland Walker.

COURTSHIP & MARRIAGE

Ann Walker was twenty-nine to Lister's forty-one when Anne Lister began to court her. They had met previously when Ann Walker was just fourteen years old when she had been involved in a carriage accident on Shibden land and had been given a drink at the manor.

Their paths crossed again when she was eighteen after the death of her parents. Anne Lister had made quite an impression on young Ann who was smitten from the moment they first met but she, in turn, had made little impression on Anne Lister. The first time they met, Anne Lister was twenty-six so she would have considered Ann at just fourteen, a child. Four years later Anne Lister thought her dull and awkward writing in her diary... *"a stupid, vulgar girl indeed,"*

On Tuesday 12ᵗʰ June 1821... *"In the afternoon at 5 ¼, walked along the new road and got past Pump when Miss Ann Walker of Crow Nest overlook me, having run herself almost out of breath. Walked with her as far as the Lidgate entrance to their own grounds & got home at 6.40. Made myself, as I fancied, very agreeable & was particularly civil & attentive in my manner. I really think the girl is flattered by it & likes me. She wished me to drink tea with them. I hope for another walk to Giles House & the readiness she expressed showed that my proposition was by no means unwelcome. She obviously has no aversion to my conversation & company. After parting I could not help smiling to myself & saying the flirting with this girl has done me good. It is heavy work to do without women's society & I would far rather while away an hour with this girl, who has nothing in the world to boast but good humour, than not flirt at all".*

It was after Anne's return from Hastings when the two women's paths crossed again – this time it was different. On 6ᵗʰ July 1832

188

Miss Walker paid a social call to Shibden Hall after hearing that Anne had returned from her extended travels and with encouragement from her relatives to meet such a fascinating, well-travelled neighbour. Ann Walker had developed into a pleasant-looking and good-natured young lady, though subject to nervous or depressive debility, unattached, and above all wealthy. Anne said of her... "She has pretty flaxen hair".

Miss Walker along with her relatives Mr & Mrs Atkinson made a social call upon the Lister's. During that visit whilst making polite but flirtatious conversation, Anne joked with her about traveling to Europe together. It was during this visit that Anne wondered if it might be entertaining to pursue Ann Walker in a romantic sense, after all she was without any other romantic interests and she had observed that her subject appeared to be quite enamoured with her and would surely welcome the attention.

A week after the visit Anne Lister returned a curtesy call to Miss Walker; as they got to know each other over the next few weeks, they found that they got on well together. Anne Walker was seen by Anne to be attentive and docile and surely biddable. Lister's revealing remark in her diary...

" Miss W & I got on very well ... If she was fond of me & manageable, I think I could be comfortable enough with her".

"It seems she had observed and felt my manner of sitting by her when she called with her uncle and aunt Atkinson – I said that was done because I really could not help it, or I should have sat by Mrs Atkinson".

After Ann Walker's pre-planned holiday in the Lake district, accompanied by her cousin Catherine Rawson... "She said she had thought of me every day at West Water and could not help thinking now of the very great anxiety she somehow felt to get home again. She had always an idea that her thirtieth year would be a very important one".

Friday 10th August 1832 Anne Lister put her thoughts in writing about the possibility of courting Ann Walker... *"Thought I, as I have several times done of late, shall I try & make up to her?"*

Clearly, Anne's intentions towards Ann Walker were strategically inclined. Anne's income at that time was between £830 and £840 per annum. She was working within a frame set by her heterosexual peers: for the middle and upper classes in the nineteenth century, a 'good match' was a marriage that made financial sense, with love a secondary consideration.

"The object of my choice has perhaps three thousand a year or near it probably two-thirds at her own disposal. (£345,000) No bad pisaiier even if I liked her less. A better take than Lady Gordon or even perhaps than Vere either. Well now I will be steady and constant and make the poor girl as happy as I can so that she shall have no reason to repent .... perhaps after all she will make me really happier than any of my former flames. At all rates we shall have money enough".

"Awake at five and from then to getting up, lay thinking of Miss W-; at nine incurred the cross – I really am getting much more in love than I expected to be again – in fact, she likes [me], it is evident, and I think we shall be very happy together".

Deft courtship by Anne Lister was extremely flattering, it also proved enthralling, interest from an educated, well-travelled, sophisticated, and agreeable companion, one who had made such a profound impression upon Ann Walker from a young age must have seemed like a gift from heaven to the reserved and isolated Ann. Seduction soon followed, the newly built, secluded little moss-house or thatched *chaumière,* built near the goldfish pond on Shibden estate provided a conveniently intimate and comfortable space to meet and get better acquainted without being disturbed. In such intimate surroundings their talk was of their travels to the continent together. Ann Walker was especially keen on this idea as it would be her first experience of travelling abroad and what better opportunity than in the company of a sophisticated, knowledgeable, and adventurous companion. They also spoke of a kind of marriage, in Anne Lister's eyes an essential element of a lasting, respectable relationship, which appeared to be enthusiastically welcomed by Walker...

"We laughed at the talk our going abroad together would [create?]". She said, "it would be as good as a marriage". "Yes said [I] quite as good or better. She falls into my views of things admirably. I believe I shall succeed with her. If I do I will really try to make her happy and I shall be thankful to heaven for the mercy of bringing me home having first saved me from Vere, rid me of M [Mariana] and set me at liberty. We shall have money enough. She will look up to me and soon feel attached and I after all my turmoil's shall be steady and if God wills it happy, I can gently mould Miss W{Walker} to my wishes and may we not be happy? How strange the fate of things if after all my companion for life should be Miss Walker.... How little my aunt or anyone suspects what I am about nor shall it be surmised 'til all is settled."

After dinner at Lidgate one Saturday evening the two women sat talking of how happy they would be together...

"She said yes she had often looked at all her things and said what was the use of having them with nobody to enjoy them with her. She said it all seemed now like a dream to her.... I begged her to take up her French and sketching again and we already begin to feel at home together and very much (however little she may understand it) like engaged lovers ".

It certainly appears that Ann Walker did not find fault with Anne's style of dress nor did she appear to be uncomfortable with her androgynous traits but seems to have been wholly infatuated by Anne. However, though they were discreet about their true alliance particularly in the early days of their courtship, there is one passage in Anne's diary which provides some evidence that other women in the local gentry were in fact aware of the sexual aspects of their relationship.

One afternoon during their courtship, Lister and Walker were engaged in a great deal of passionate intimacy on the sofa at Lidgate when Mrs. Priestley unexpectedly called... She was ushered to the drawing room where she discovered the pair so wrapped up in their intimacy that they had not heard the approaching company but had quickly reacted to the room door being thrown open and jumped to their feet, a second or two later would have found them in a somewhat compromising position.

"I had jumped in time and was standing by the fire, but Ann looked red and I pale, and Mrs. P. must see we were not particularly expecting company. She looked vexed, jealous and annoyed and in bitter satire asked if I had [been] where I was ever since she left me there. No said I, only ought to have been. My aunt had been in a host of miseries Mrs. P. said as if turning it all on this, Yes, she was quite vexed with me. I laughed and said I really did not intend doing so again. 'Yes' she replied 'you will do the same the very next time the temptation occurs.' Plain proof thought I of what you think and that you smoke a little [sic]. I parried all with good humour saying I really must stay all night She only stayed a few minutes and went off in suppressed rage probably giving me far more credit than deserved for plotting the visit of yesterday and being there all today and having refused breakfasting with her not to go to Stonyroyde but be with Miss W. Mrs. P. probably believes her confidence insecure me insincere and the lord knows what...

"Miss W. laughed and said we were well matched. We soon got to kissing again on the sofa. She said I looked ill. I denied then said if I did look so I knew what would cure me. She would know what. Said I really would not could not tell her. At last I got my right hand up her petticoats and after much fumbling got thro' the opening of her drawers and touched (first time) the hair and skin of queer. She never offered the least resistance in any way and certainly shewed no sign of its being disagreeable. However, having not uttered before I now fell upon her neck seemed sickish just whispered that I could not stand it and stood leaning my hand off her shoulder till apparently composed. Then entreated her forgiveness in general terms saying she behaved beautifully. No she said she knew she led me on. I would deny this tho' owning that I was of course sure she cared for me. Oh yes said she or should we go on as we do. [?] In fact she likes my attentions and the first night of my being there will give me all I am able to take. When dusk she asked (I had said I was at no time likely to marry. How far she understood me I could not quite make out) 'if you never had any attachment who taught you to kiss?' I laughed and said how nicely that was said. Then answered that nature taught me. I could have

replied, and who taught you? She told me as she had done yesterday that she had always a fancy for me and thought how much she should like to know me better" ...

No doubt this shocking discovery by Mrs Priestley would have reached the ears of other local residents, most of them relatives of Ann Walker's. It was the practise for ladies to make visits and call upon their social equals, when news, and on occasion, titbits of gossip would be disclosed. This occurrence was just the sort of revelation that would have stirred the assembled groups gathered in drawing rooms and parlours.

*One evening o*n leaving the dining table and cosily seated on the sofa together. *"We were so affectionate – we let the lamp go out – long continued (mumbling moist) kissing, I pressed her bosom – then finding no resistance and the lamp being out – let my hand wander lower down, gently getting to queer – still no resistance – so I whispered, surely she could care for me so little? – yes – then gently whispered she would break my heart if she left me – she then said I should think her very cold (how the devil could I?) and it came out: how that her affections had been engaged to one of the best men – that they could not be transferred so soon for he had only been dead just three months – and she got crying. I begged a thousand pardons etc – declared it was only through ignorance that I had ever been so sanguine etc – and thinking a scene would then come beautifully from me, seemed in a paroxysm of stupid tho' deeply sighing grief and stifled tears – and declared myself hopeless – said my conduct (or rather, my hoping) was madness and she had no longer any reason to fear my preparation for myself – nothing but disappointment. All this as very prettily done".*

Ann Walker revealed that her previous suitor, an Andrew Fraser, had died in July 1832; she also hinted at other romances in the past and attentiveness from a Reverend Thomas Ainsworth from Cheshire, who apparently had taught Ann to kiss though she said they had not gone further than she had with Anne, but she emphasised that she had not reciprocated his interest.

Whilst past confessions were being revealed it is unlikely that Anne Lister would have disclosed her own past intimate connections.

Anne had cause to make comments in her journal regarding later intimacies between them as there were obviously occasions when love making didn't prove as satisfactory as it might have been... *"Grubbled her a little. Did not do it well enough or she was not much in humour for it. So, lay still. She thought me asleep, but I was not. About two turned round and grubbed her again rather better than before but still not well. She said it had not been so agreeable to her the last few times. She thought I was nervous, and she said she did not think it right. Wished we could do without it".*

Ann Walker's apparent disappointments caused Anne Lister to suffer doubts about her abilities as a lover. Not being a man, Anne must have felt that all her love making capabilities where not enough when it came to sexually satisfying Ann Walker. This combined with Ann Walker's sense of guilt about their intimacy give Anne a great deal of doubt about their future happiness.

Ann Walker continued to express scruples about their sexual interaction... Miss Walker sent a note later saying that her... *"convictions as to its being right and against my duty remain. I think we had better not meet again'* *"Poor girl. What a miserable state of mind. All for nothing"...*

Nevertheless, they continued to meet and continued their sexual connection though Miss Walker seemed to change her mind frequently about whether she wanted to continue the relationship or not...

"She thinks me over head and ears with her. She is mistaken. Her mumbling kisses have cured me of that It has struck me more than once she is a deepish hand. She took me up to her room. I kissed her and she pushed herself so to me I rather felt and might have

done it as much as I pleased. She is man keen enough. If I stay all night, it will be my own fault if I do not have all of her I can. I really [think] she wishes to try the metal I am made of and I begin to fear not being able to do enough and doubt whether even fun will be amusing or safe. ...My real and romantic care for her is set at rest and all I shall now feel for her will not get the better of me. Shall I or shall I not give in to fun with her? Stay all night and do my best without caring for the result... .at all rates I may handle her as I like if I choose to venture it. How changed my mind. Respect so staggered yesterday is gone today. I care not for her tho' her money would suit...I am cured" ...

Tormented between her feelings for Anne and the moral significance of shared intimate sexual knowledge of another woman filled Ann Walker with trepidations. Anne Lister on the other hand tired of the wavering, and had little respect for Miss Walker, partly since she had shown no resistance previously to the intimate touching and had been too willing too quickly to allow Anne to go further, preferring instead that Ann to have been modest and chaste before allowing herself the pleasure of more intimate sexual freedom.

Although Anne felt that Miss Walker would eventually submit to a full sexual relationship, for the time being she agreed that they should abstain from all intimate sexual contact and that she would honour Ann's wishes.

A few days later Lister was surprised to find Ann Walker passionately returning her kisses and even inviting her to spend the night, though this latter event was delayed through mutual coquetry related to sexual respectability. Anne was anxious about how she would perform with a full sexual experience the first night she spent with Miss Walker, believing that if she did well then Miss Walker was certain to give up her own residence and agree to her proposal to live at Shibden.

6th December... *"Talking last night till two.... She excited as she lay on me & I pretended great difficulty in keeping my word. I felt her over her chemise & this all but did the job for her. She owned she could not help it & that now she had got into the way of it & did not know how she should do without it...Yet still, she talked of her suffering because she thought it wrong to have this connection with me....She will not do for me"...* At breakfast I referred to her scruples and wishes and said I would try not to care for her in that particular way and promised her that if I once seriously tried I would succeed but I was not quite sure whether we should be the happier for my success or not. Sat talking all the morning combatting her scruples and really thought I had made some impression and done her good till on going away and asking her to write and tell me how she was tomorrow she said oh no she should be no better and burst into tears and I left her thinking I never saw such a hopeless person in my life. How miserable said I to myself. Thank God my own mind is not like hers. What could I do with her"?*

Even though Lister felt that Anne Walker's resistance coming before her eager submissions were tiring and frustrating, Ann Walker, however, still managed to have a powerful attraction for Lister... *"I don't know how it is,"* Lister laments at one point, *"but whenever I see the girl, she always manages to unhinge me."*

Anne's semblance of romantic despair and Miss Walker's insistence that she had not yet said 'no' to the proposal of marriage gave her some sustenance to continue their association... Anne Lister recorded the first time she put her *"right middle finger"* inside Ann Walker, some weeks after their first kiss, and recorded Miss Walker's lack of resistance. Anne felt sure that Miss Walker had had some previous experience...

"taking it altogether as if she had learnt her lesson before in this way too as well as in kissing. She whispered that she loved me then afterwards said her mind was quite unmade up and bade me not be sanguine".

The next time they met when the kissing continued to a more physical encounter Miss Walker pushed Anne's hand away, saying that she had suffered from the previous occasion when they had made love, that she was *"very tender there"* Anne talked to her soothingly and said how gentle she would be and expressed anxiety for her health. On that occasion Anne recorded that she used only one finger, but Walker still complained that she was still tender...

" I think she was more intact and virgin than I had latterly surmised she whispered to me how gentle and kind I was to her and faintly said she loved me or else how can you think said she I should let you do as you do".

On Thursday 27th September, Anne Lister confided in her diary that Ann Walker had always been told by relatives like the Rawson's that...

"I was not to be depended on ~ I successfully parried this - & she believes me.... I now really believe she will go [abroad] with me! She seems to take all I say for gospel... [She] said she was sure people [cousins] never meant us to get together - that Mrs. Stansfield Rawson looked odd at finding me [at Lidgate] ... "We shall have money enough. She will look up to me... I can gently mould Miss W- to my wishes... How strange the fate of things! If after all, my companion for life should be Miss Walker - she was nine-and-twenty a little while ago! How little my aunt or anyone suspects what I am about!" ...

As the courtship progressed rapidly, the conditions Lister attached to the match become clear. On 28th September 1832, she wrote... *"Bordering on love-making in the hut ... Our liaison is now established.'* Significantly, she added... *"Jam provided [for] & the object of my choice have perhaps three thousand a year or near it - probably two-thirds at her own disposal'.* The arrangement she envisaged, was, like marriage, to combine a sexual connection with economic exchange.

Miss Walker told Anne they had to *"give up their fondling"*. In her diary, Anne expressed a certain degree of sexual insecurity and certainly frustration because of this...

"She did not think she should have suffered so much If she was really married it would be different. Would be easier" ... *"Oh, thought I to myself I see how it is. My difficulty in getting to her on Monday night and my being able to do so little was not what she expected or relished. I combated her idea that she would suffer less with a man. Thought her mistaken unless she spoke from experience which she denied explained. why! thought her mistaken thinking she would bear a man more easily than me. Explained the sizes of men. How Caesar was biliber [sic], as big as two books. Mentioned some women taking even an ass and the woman in Paris with a dog to be seen for ten franks etc. all which she listened to with interest and composure"* ...

Lister's courtship of Anne Walker took her into the dangerous territory of local family relationships. The Walkers had married into other elite Halifax families ~ so Ann had an inconvenient number of cousins. Many of them ~ such as the Rawson's ~ knew Anne Lister of old. They had no polite language for Anne's Lister's predatory reputation with which to alert gullible Ann Walker. Ann Walker received some anonymous letters warning her of Anne Lister's unnatural tendencies which Anne Lister believed must have come from a one of Ann's relatives.

Ann Walker was torn between complying with her suitor and her own family and her religious torments. Anne Lister, staunchly Anglican, had no doubts that her sexuality was natural, she could not change anything, it was how she was even from childhood; it was God-given. Ann Walker shared this Anglican faith but was wracked by torturing scruples. Anne Lister was blessed with confidence, self-assurance, assertiveness, independent and self-reliance with a good opinion of herself. How would the courtship develop? They proceeded in their courtship in much the same manner as a heterosexual couple of their class would. They exchanged financial confidences, Miss Walker consulted Anne Lister about estate business, asking her advice about the legal technicalities of things such as tenant rights and work around her estate.

A formal meeting was arranged between Miss Walker and Aunt Anne Lister once her new status was established. Anne had previously discussed with her aunt and sister Marian regarding her intentions concerning Miss Walker, both had given their approval to this match ...

"My aunt not to appear to know anything about it even to Miss W [Walker]. seemed pleased at my choice and prospects. I said she had three thousand a year or very near it... She thought my father would be pleased if he knew and so would both my uncles."

To the old-fashioned and Conservative Tory Listers, the Walker family were upcomers, new money with no real pedigree or heraldic family history. However, the Walkers were successful manufacturers and accomplished businesspeople, Ann Walker had inherited 50 percent of the prestigious family property and sizable estate. Compared to the well-bred, high society, landed gentry Anne Lister, with a significant historical past, but with limited finances, young miss Walker had little pedigree but was indeed an extraordinarily rich young lady.

Lister often makes notes in code about Ann's health, who would spend many days in apathy, resting on the sofa, doing nothing. Ann had a recurring problem with her spine suffering pain and discomfort the cause diagnosed by Dr Belcombe was nervous hysteria. Her depressions also included symptoms of religious mania and possible anorexia. Decreased self-esteem is associated with mental illness, a vulnerability to depression and some physical illnesses. Ann's description of herself was as being weak and delicate, not surprising then, in part, aided by the way she was perceived and treated by those around her. Dr Belcombe often remarked that if she were less wealthy then she would most likely not suffer in the way that she did.

Both women at this stage had reservations regarding their relationship: Ann Walker about saying yes to Anne's proposal of marriage, and Anne Lister about whether marrying Ann Walker was the good plan it had originally seemed to be in the heady, early days of their courtship. The complications that they both had to consider meant that by the end of 1832 the relationship was uncertain, though certainly intense.

After eighteen months of on-and-off courtship, Anne was still unsure about whether there could be permanent relationship between them. According to Lister, Walker was equally concerned that their union should carry the same weight as a marriage: Lister tried to reassure Ann of a happy future but still, doubts prevailed...

"Said I expected to have ultimately two thousand a year. She told me it was more than expected from my manner of speaking before. I then asked if she thought she could be happy enough with me to give up all thought of ever leaving me. This led her into explaining that she had said she would never marry but that as she had once felt an inclination not to keep to this, she could not yet so positively say she should never feel the same inclination again. She should not like to deceive me. Begged not to answer just now. I said she was quite right. Praised her judiciousness. That my esteem and admiration were only heightened by it, that no feelings of selfishness should make me even wish my happiness rather than hers. That I would give her six months 'til my next birthday to make up her mind in and should only hope that as we saw more of each other my reasons for despair would not increase......on the plea of feeling her pulse I took her hand and held it some time to which she had no objection. We both probably felt more like lovers than friends. I wanted to hint at the propriety of her leaving me for a minute or two on our getting to Lidgate, but she was too modest to seem to understand me at all. I see there is evidently coming on all the shyness usual in such cases. Well, I shall like her all the better for it and am already fairly in love myself, thought I she is in for it if ever girl was and so am I" ...

Even with all Lister's tender words and showing a great deal of enduring patience, Lister records that Anne Walker was not entirely happy with her requirements, perhaps wary that her considerable wealth may have played a part in the attraction that Lister had for her. The idea of marriage was something Ann Walker began to show little enthusiasm for... and probably she would have been happy to have continued with their affair, discreetly and indefinitely, without any outward signs of romantic connections to avoid the scandal and shame that such a love match would generate.

... *"[she] got into the old story of [how] she felt she was not doing right morally, could not consent, had determined to say no'. 'But she portrays herself as ruthlessly managing the situation, and 'laughing it all off' so successfully that Walker apologised and 'let me grubble [grope] her this morning gladly enough"* ...

When Lister pressed for a promise, suggesting that... *"our present intercourse without any tie between us must be as wrong as any other transient connection"* ...

Ann Walker had always been close to her elder sister Elizabeth and decided to gain her opinion so she wrote to ask for her approval to setting up home and making a life with Anne Lister, declaring that if Elizabeth thought it right, then she would say 'yes'.

It was a difficult letter to phrase, she did not wish to reveal the precise details of her relationship with Anne Lister, she could not confess the true circumstances of their association, so she chose her words carefully but dithered a great deal so that the business dragged on much to Anne Lister's frustration. In any event by not divulging the true circumstances of their association how could she be given a true approval or rejection of their situation... *"I never saw such a hopeless person in my life. How miserable, said I to myself, Thank God my own mind's not like hers"* ...

The long-awaited reply arrived from Elizabeth advising Ann to take lodgings in York for the winter, so that she could see Dr Belcombe, then go up to Scotland for the summer then if they are both in the same mind, a tour of the continent together and then make up her mind as to the future. Elizabeth also added that she believed Anne Lister would never marry. Anne wrote in her journal... *"How little Mrs. Sutherland guesses the real truth & how coolly she plans for us"* ...

The reply did little to ease Ann Walker's mind however, her mental torment grew steadily worse over the coming weeks. In her tortured mind Thanatophobia took control of the night-time hours, she was unable to sleep, racked with fear and foreboding, crying out that she would suffer everlasting torment and Hellfire. The threatening voices she believed she could hear came from the large clock standing in the passageway next to her bedroom filled her with terror. Anne who had stayed with her in her room removed the weights so that the clock stopped ticking but really this did little to ease her torment. Ann's friend Catherine Rawson on hearing of Ann's plight, took it upon herself to stay with her and keep her company. But Ann's mental misery frightened her friend as it was impossible to know what to do to help her. Although Ann had refused to commit to Anne Lister and their romance practically over, nevertheless Anne spent a great deal of time with Ann, staying overnight as she was quite unfit to be alone and Catherine appreciated Anne's willing support as the night-time hours saw the worst of her torments. It was these acts of care and kindness which changed Catherine's opinion of Anne Lister. Witnessing for herself the concern and tender care Anne had shown, made her realize that the venomous gossip that she had so willingly believed previously, was unfounded and cruel, making her weep for the injustice at her own naivety in believing what had been said of Anne.

Ann Walker was quite incapable of over-seas travel at that time, she decided not to go on their planned continental adventure. As their romantic relationship was practically at an end, Anne was keen to be off on her travels to lick her wounds and try to forget the past months of disappointment and disastrous endings. Knowing that poor Ann was in no fit state to be left alone, she contacted Elizabeth Sutherland suggesting that Ann might be better under her care in Scotland.

Writing to Steph Belcombe on 6th January 1833: ...
"I never exactly understood before what nervousness meant and God grant that I may know no more of it in any case which concerns me much... it is dreary to combat sickness without disease, and misery without reason" ...

In February 1833 after a particularly bad bout of depression Ann was escorted to Scotland by brother-in-law Captain Sutherland and his mother. Before they left for Scotland Mrs. Sutherland senior enquired of Anne who had stayed over the previous night, if any love affair was on Ann's mind. After Anne had said... 'no'... Mrs. Sutherland went on to say that a relative had once proposed but Ann had declined his proposal. She then revealed that his handling of money was poor and that he had huge debts and dependants to support but under the circumstances, he might make a suitable husband for Ann. Anne Lister was horrified at such a suggestion... and replied... *"Surely Captain [S] would take care that proper[marriage] settlements".* *"Poor girl, they want her for some of the kin, if they get her"* ...

After their carriage left Lidgate for Scotland, Anne walked home, she felt a great deal of sadness at their parting, believing that their relationship was totally at an end, and perhaps they would not meet again. But her feelings were mixed, there was some degree of relief that Ann Walker was now someone else's responsibility... *"Heaven be praised, said I to myself as I walked homewards, that they are off & that I have got rid of her & am once more free"* ... Though deep in her heart it is doubtful that these sentiments rang true, she must have suffered regrets and a huge sense of loss.

Though Anne wished to know of Ann Walker's condition, she decided that all correspondences should come via Elizabeth. In June of that year, Anne Lister went on a long trip to the continent. During that tour whilst staying in Paris Anne received a perplexing letter from Elizabeth Sutherland who reported that Ann was... *'better in bodily health, at least fatter, but still no better in spirits"*

... Elizabeth added flatteringly that her sister had... *"repeatedly stated that there is no individual living by whom she would be so much influenced"*, and Elizabeth hoped for Anne's continued *"kind interference and influence... as at present, she is certainly unable to judge for herself"* ...

Anne wrote in her journal... *"How extraordinarily things happen! Incurred a cross just before getting into bed thinking of Miss Walker"* ...

Anne promptly wrote back to Elizabeth, suggesting that Ann be discreetly placed under the care of Dr Belcombe as Ann trusted him and had great faith in his expertise It seems that Ann had not received the care of any medical practitioner whilst in Scotland. Captain Sutherland strongly disagreed with this proposal and refused this course of action. Anne also revealed that she would be soon leaving France for Copenhagen, therefore further correspondence should be sent to her address there.

Anne Lister eventually reached Copenhagen where she enjoyed the company of Lady Harriet de Hagemann, half-sister of Vere Hobart, Countess de Blucher, and many other minor aristocratic women. Through her host's contacts, she found herself presented at the Danish court dressed in... *"black satin gown my thinnest black silk stockings & silk shoes"*, ...

Surrounded by so much finery, Anne was conscious of her own provincial attire, she confided in her journal... *"it was a great gaucherie...I shell learn in time"*.

Writing to her aunt Anne wrote: ...

"I go out a great deal in the evening. Since writing to you last, I have been presented at Court, to the King and Queen, and the rest, had separate audiences of the queen, and the five princesses, and was at the queen's ball on her birth night, and at the ball the other night at Prince Christian's. Prince Christian is heir presumptive to the throne; and his princess is one of the handsomest and most dignified women I have ever seen. She is clever, too, and most graciously agreeable. The queen is a very superior person a woman of great tact and talent, and still preserving her good

figure, and good style of dress. You would be pleased to see how well I am received here. I am invited everywhere. At a ball the other night at the Swedish Minister's I think one of the princesses stood talking to me at least ten minutes" ...

Not hearing more from Elizabeth Sutherland, she assumed that things in Scotland were as before but the concern and strong feelings that she held for Ann Walker ensured that she was constantly on her mind.

In late November she received alarming news from Dr Kenny and Marian informing her that Aunt Anne was very poorly; they feared she might not have long to live. Anne and her servants, Thomas Beech and Eugenie Pierre left Copenhagen immediately cutting short their stay, travelling for several days on the road through Germany. The vessel Anne boarded for her last leg of her journey home was the 400 tone, cargo ship 'Columbine' a wooden three Mast Barque sailing ship (whose eventual destiny was to be wrecked on Maplin Sands, Essex on the 12th of January 1849.)

The dangerous journey back to England was long and arduous due to the time of year with atrocious weather and rough seas which put all their lives at risk. Anne wrote in her journal... *"five nights, from Copenhagen to Hamburg without taking my clothes off, and ten nights from Hamburg".*

Eventually tired, weary, and desperate to be home she arrived in the port of Gravesend in northwest Kent on Sunday 15th December 1833.

After returning to Shibden on the evening of the 19th of December Anne found her Aunt recovering well and very much better than she had expected to find her, considering the alarm Dr Kenny's letter had caused. Aunt Anne was joyful at Anne's return but scolded Dr Kenny and Marian for making the fuss that had brought Anne's adventure to such an abrupt end. The crisis over for the time being and feeling restless Anne visited York for Christmas, then went onto Langton to stay with Isabella and her family.

It was there that she received a letter the 27[th of] December from Anne Walker; it conveyed that she was no longer in Scotland but had returned to Lidgate on Christmas eve, just a few days after Anne herself had arrived home. She had known nothing of Anne's whereabouts thinking she was still in Copenhagen and not knowing her address after it had curiously gone missing during Walker's time in Scotland, she went to Shibden, where she spoke to Anne's aunt and father to learn_of Anne's whereabouts. Ann immediately wrote to Anne offering to accommodate her, *"Whilst you are in England, I hope you will consider my little cottage [Lidgate] as your own. I have plenty of accommodation for your servants, and 2 rooms entirely at your disposal"* ... She also asked if she would meet her in York to visit Dr Belcombe.

Anne's reply was affectionate though somewhat formal. She offered to help manage Ann's life for her and suggested that instead of meeting in York, they should meet first at home in Halifax and then decide what would be the best course of action. Anne Lister left Langton for Halifax in January 1834 first calling at York where she went to see Dr Belcombe to talk about a consultation and treatment, and to decide where Ann would stay in York.

Back to Shibden and with John Booth to carry her bag, she walked to Lidgate at 9.10 arriving at 9.35. Ann was, of course, overjoyed to see her. Lister wrote... *"looking certainly better in spirits than when I saw her last, but probably this improvement is merely the result of the present pleasure and excitement on seeing me. Dinner (a mutton steak) then tea and coffee – and went upstairs at 11.40"* ... their courtship resumed.

January 1834: Ann said that...

"she repented having left me- longed to go to Copenhagen. Had had Mr. Ainsworth writing and offering again etc. once thought she ought to marry_ lastly refused him. Her sister told him she [Ann Walker] was not able to judge for herself _but [Ainsworth said] he did not mind this_ so both Captain and Mrs. Sutherland got annoyed at him, I suppose saw thro' him. Miss W_ talks as if she would be glad to take me_ then if I say anything decisive, she hesitates. I tell her it is all her money which is in the way. The fact

206

is, she is as she was before, but was determined to get away from the Sutherlands and feels the want of me. But [I need to] take someone with more mind and less money. Steph [Belcombe] is right: she would be a great pother. Have nothing serious to say to her- she wants better manning than I can manage- I touched her a little but she soon said it exhausted her. I had my draws on and never tried to get near, knowing that I could not do it well enough. I am weak about her. Oh, that I may get well rid of her" ...

However, the renewed intimacy was confirmed by formal family visits, and by their sudden changes to their inheritance plans. Anne writes of their intimacies, Wednesday 8th January 1834... *"Goodish touching and pressing last night- she much and long on the amoroso and I had a good kiss as possible with draws on"* ...

The two ladies left for York on Monday 13th first to the Black Swan for dinner and a night's stay before going to meet Dr Belcombe who had arranged some discreet lodgings at Heworth Grange, a mile outside of York where his patient, Ann Walker would stay. They visited a Mr. Bewly's out of Monk bar to inspect the rooms, where Ann was to stay for the duration of her treatment, finding the owners... *"Good, homely people, Miss Walker well enough [pleased]with the 3 rooms and terms:2 guineas a week"* ...

23rd Thursday 1834: Anne left Ann Walker in the lodgings and returned to Shibden after first visiting Aunt Ann of Cliff-hill to reassure her about her niece's remaining in York. After considering Ann Walker's education and finding it lacking, Anne decided that it would be beneficial for Ann to further her education and occupy her mind all relevant to her full recovery. Anne planed that Ann was to study French, life drawing, which she already had shown some ability, and reading, this coupled with a daily walk would occupy and expand her mind to benefit her wellbeing. Plans were made to organise tutors for when Ann returned home. However, the other relatives were perturbed by Ann's stay in York and treated Anne Lister's part with suspicion and concern...
"Poor girl indeed! They are all against the only plan likely to answer – I shall be much talked of & blamed for all the good I have tried to do. I shall by & by be scared from attempting more – and once off again, perhaps I shell not return in a hurry" ...

Thursday 27 February 1834:

"No drawers on last night first time and first attempt to get really near her. Did not succeed very well but she seemed tolerably satisfied" ...

Anne made several visits to York to see Ann during the months she underwent her treatment...

"Breakfast at 9 ¾. A little French. I ½ asleep over it. Off to Langton at 12 50. Damp rainy disagreeable day. She was poorly and tired tho she had got up so well in the morning. I saw there was much nervousness about going to Langton but took no notice. I asked her to buy the gold wedding ring I wore and lent her six pence to pay me for it. She would not give it me immediately but wore it till we entered the village of Langton and then put it on my left third finger in token of our union, which is now understood to be confirmed forever tho little or nothing was said" ...

The two women arrived at the Norcliffe's at Langton, there they met Mrs. Norcliffe and Charlotte who were surprised but happy to see them...

"Our visit went off very well – all sides sufficiently pleased apparently – came away at 7.20 and home at 9.3/4 – coffee – sat talking till 11.3/4 Glad we went – the Norcliffe's very civil to her – shyness went off and she seemed much pleased with her visit" ...

Their stay together in York whilst Ann Walker continued with her treatment with Dr Belcome, lasted three more days, Anne then returned to Shibden leaving Ann in York. They wrote regular letters to each other, though Anne records in her diary that Ann was still expressing doubts about living at Shibden Hall. Anne experienced great concern about this, realizing that it was still possible for Ann to change her mind, and wondered if she was being deceived, which naturally caused her a great deal of worry. However, a month after the ring exchange the church 'ceremony' took place.

Ann Walker appears at long last to have put past guilt behind her and even though it meant disapproval and even repulsion from her relatives she was at long last ready to accept fully, a partnership with the woman she loved.

That same month they planned for Ann Walker to move into Shibden Hall after her return from York.

Easter Sunday 30th March 1834 Wedding Day – Anne Lister wrote in her diary... *"Three xxx's better to her than to me. Very fine morning. F 49° at 8 ½ a.m"*. Confirming their union in York at Holy Trinity Church ... Anne Lister and Anne Walker performed the second act of their symbolic union with the escort of servant Thomas Beech.

... *"At Goodramgate church at 10.35: Miss W-and I and Thomas Ann's servant stayed (for) the sacrament... The first time I ever joined Miss W- in my prayers-I had prayed that our union might be happy-she had not thought of doing as much for me"* ...

Anne Lister is referring here to the significance of the two women taking holy communion together. She believed that it confirmed their union, or marriage, in the sight of God.

Thursday 17th April: Anne received a letter from her ex-lover Mariana Lawton... *"Dearest Fred, I have received your letter – the die is cast and Mary (Lawton) must abide by the throw. You at last will be happy... Ever yours, Mariana"*.

Anne gave the letter to Ann Walker to read, though Anne had never told Ann Walker about their true former connection. Ann asked questions about their relationship detecting from the letter that there is more to their friendship than she had been led to believe, but Anne manages to talk off the true nature of their past association, giving her the impression that it had all been a chaste, platonic friendship like that of herself and her cousin Catherine Rawson; after all, Mariana was a married woman!

Friday 18th... *"As last night but not quite so good – she woke me up by a scream in the night, for I was biting her lip through. She got up and put sprit of wine [on it] – good laughter"* ...

The deteriorating health of Anne Lister senior, caused Anne great anguish, realizing that her aunt's days are numbered and their time together short... *"My poor aunt suffers a martyrdom and may still survive some months. It was her arms that 1st held me – hers was like a mother's care, and to her liberal kindness were owing half the comforts of my early life – I see her sinking slowly and painfully into the grave"* ...

Ann Walker spent a further short visit at Heworth Grange for treatment with Dr Belcombe and seems much improved. Anne continues to take care of her business affairs and to the plans for improvement to Shibden and while in the past she had relied almost totally on Samuel Washington her steward, she now became more adept at running her estate and less dependent on employees.

Tuesday 6th: Anne receives a 3-page letter from Mariana,

... *"Your having taken another to your bosom has not left vacant your place in Mary's heart... If the sunshine of love has illuminated our youth, the moonlight of friendship may at last console our decline, ever affectionately Mariana"* ...

Both in their courtship and later 'marriage' Lister and Walker's relationship was intricately connected to financial exchanges, as was common for their class in heterosexual marriages. When both she and Ann Walker were wavering over whether to commit to each other, Lister had commented privately... *"I know she would like to keep me on so as to have the benefit of my intimacy without any real joint concern"* ... Yet after they were 'married' Lister wrote... *"I am anxious that Ann's concerns should never appear to have interested me less than my own."* ...

In June 1834, the two ladies visited France and Switzerland, this time for their honeymoon. It was the first time Ann Walker had been abroad. Lister's pet name for Ann was 'Adney' who wrote cheery letters to her aunt reassuring her that she was a happy traveller. However, Anne Lister's journal tells a slightly different story... *"Never in my life saw such a fidget in a carriage – she was in all postures & places till at last she luckily fell asleep for about an hour. She had too much Roussillon wine which made her feverish without being tipsy"* ...

SHIBDEN HALL

In a letter to her aunt Anne 12th October 1820, Anne Lister wrote...

"You know that as far as place is concerned, every ambition and every wish of my heart are in the welfare of Shibden where in so long a series of generations, we have lived with that unblemished respectability which I cannot think of without a feeling of honest pride, nor ever remember without a sentiment of deep and heartfelt gratitude to my uncle who has done so much towards its support. I am daily more and more sensible of this, and more and more anxious to shew that his kindness to, and confidence in myself, are neither unappreciated not undeserved" ...

Hanging on the wall of the main hall or house body are eight oil portraits. Anne wearing black adorns the central position painted sometime after her death by Joshua Horner, with Anne Lister senior on the left, painted by Thomas Binns, it is a front facing portrait which is referenced in Anne Lister's diaries as being sat for by her Aunt in 1833. It is said to be a good likeness. On the right hangs the portrait of Uncle James Lister painted by Joshua Horner also painted after his death in 1826. Anne intended to commission a portrait of her sister Marian, but Marian refused to undertake the sitting, so Anne commissioned instead a view of Shibden Valley, which she titled Marian's View, it was painted by John Horner.

Although Anne came to love Shibden, she recognised the shortcomings of the "comfortless house" her greatest wish after her desperate desire to find a wife, was to develop Shibden into a far grander and more imposing property.

With her indomitable will, she soon renewed her energies. She would turn herself from the old Anne Lister into the new. She would remodel herself from traveller and high society philander into commanding landowner of Shibden Hall's ancient acres.

Like most old buildings Shibden could be very cold and draughty place to live... "Wrote *all this journal of today, feeling not at all too hot in my pelisse, plaid wrap fourfold round my loins, & 2 greatcoats put on over all, besides my leather knee-caps on & my thick dressing gown thrown across my knees overcoats and everything. A large high green baize, fold screen on my right to exclude the air from the door. The curtains drawn so as only just to admit light enough, to keep out air from the window. Yet, still, in spite of all this & my towel-horse with a large green baize thrown over it to keep the air from my legs next to the window, an air always does come thro'...*

Anne set herself a program of self-education so that she could manage her estate. At the time she took charge, the estate had some 400 acres but was to expand in the years following her ownership.

She financed the upkeep of Shibden and her lifestyle with revenues from agricultural rents and investments in properties in and around Halifax and the surrounding area, the coal deposits and stone quarries, canal, water and timber investments, turnpike road trusts. Though comparatively small sums, Pew rents came in twice-yearly all helped to provide a comfortable income.

Anne became an astute businesswoman in a male-dominated society. A once important major income for the estate was its reserves of coal. Shibden Hall being situated just on the edge of the extensive West Riding (primarily soft bed) coalfield. Messrs. Oates, Green, Walsh and Hinchcliffe leased areas in which they were able to extract the coal. In 1826 they paid £240 to lease the coals, in 1827, £187.6/9, and 1828, £324.2/9.

However, the single largest source of Anne Lister's income from 1826-1828 was from canal shares. In 1826 the Navigation dividends paid to her a total of £325.1/10, almost a third of the total estate income.

Samuel Freeman's payment of £100 a year for stone was also significant. The old Wakefield and Halifax Turnpike Road, by contrast, had for several years been paying the comparatively small sum of £10 per annum. It was, however, the stable income, which rents from the farms and cottages on the estate generated, that this amounted to a firm base from which Anne could branch out into riskier investments. The Lister Family owned 48 properties most of them farms but also Inns and ale Houses in and around Shibden Hall and properties in other parts of Halifax.

Once she had full control of Shibden in 1836 following the deaths of her Aunt Anne and her father Jeremy Lister and marriage to Ann Walker, she set about creating the splendid residence that she had long dreamed it might be. With her architect John Harper they planned for a commanding structure and parkland that would rival many grand homes in the county. Anne would probably not recognise the building as we know it today because work was only in progress when she set out for Russia in 1839. The main changes which came about were the terracing of the south lawn, the opening of the low ceiling in the body of the house, a Norman-style tower at the west end with water closet, and in the park, a cascade through a wilderness, an ornamental lake, and a carriage drive to Godley with gatehouse.

Even before her marriage to Ann Walker, she had begun to make improvements to her ancestral home. First, she would re-shape the landscape of her estate, moulding nature to her powerful desires. Inspired by her travels and by her readings, she was determined Shibden would look elegant.

Anne began by re-designing the section of the estate immediately visible from the Hall: the removal of trees opened the vista giving a view of the parkland beyond, a patchwork of pocket-handkerchief fields sloping down 400 yards to a small brook. The land was boggy, Red Beck was liable to flooding it must have adequate drainage or be redesigned into a wetland feature. Shibden must have charm and character and become the landscape of her desires. She would have new walkways made, with a *chaumiere* or 'moss house' to sit or shelter. Sadly, the original, little, cosy thatched building is no longer standing, it was re-constructed for filming of the drama 'Gentleman Jack', during the summer of 2018, but was demolished afterwards.

Once married and with more funds available to her Anne began the tidying up of the crooked timbers of the old Tudor house by installing a new Victorian, mock-Tudor fireplace, and panelling in the main room. She removed the Tudor ceiling and adding a gallery, creating the effect of an open medieval manor hall. It was also reflected in the Lister lions – the family symbol – featured in the main body of the house, two intricately carved lions in wood and a large stone example in the grounds, carved from Millstone grit for Anne Lister in 1830.

Anne had cellars and tunnels dug under the building. This was part of a contemporary trend, ensuring that owners would not be disturbed by the comings and goings of their servants when moving around the property undertaking their daily duties.

New timber bay windows replaced the sash ones; the east side was rebuilt creating new kitchens and servant's quarters; on the west, a three-story Gothic tower was constructed to house Anne's library, a project which had long been a dream of Anne's, but one which she would not live to see completed. Sadly, her vast collection of books was sold after her death with just a few remaining examples now on display in the hall. On the 12th of May 1836, Anne began clearing out the upper rooms before the floor was taken out: this would open up the main body of the house to the eaves, with a new grand staircase and gallery installed and decorated in the "Jacobethan" revival style that was highly popular in England from the late 1820s.

In the grounds, the layout constructed in the 1830's was by a Mr Gray of York, incorporating designs by the architect John Harper (1809–1842) who had worked for many eminent aristocrats of the 19th century. Amongst his clients were the Duke of Devonshire and Lord Londesborough. Harper's plans recommended extravagant improvement, which would see the Hall transformed into a grand residence, though some of his designs were too ambitious and beyond Anne's budget.

Anne made a park, which included a cascade through a wilderness (Cunnery Wood) and dammed the Red Beck to make an ornamental lake. A carriage drive was built to the new road from Halifax to

Leeds and a gatehouse built alongside it. On the plans being adopted Shibden was given over to the builders for four years whilst a south terrace was constructed providing Shibden with an elevated platform. Joshua Major (1786–1866) an English landscape gardener and designer and his Son Henry designed the layout for the main terrace in 1855, the construction work was undertaken by William Berry of Halifax, who also laid out the lake in the park.

Today, Cunnery Wood is a Local Nature Reserve. Calderdale Council holds regular free 'Practical Days' at the Woods, where volunteers can help to look after the Reserve. Other events such as Easter Egg Hunts take place in the Woods throughout the year.

The wood panelling visible at the south front of the Hall today was also restored under Anne's instruction. The initial alterations were complete by 1839. Anne's death was followed in 1842 by that of John Harper her architect, and all other planned work ceased.

At Shibden Hall you can view some of Anne's possessions, such as her travel writing case, music book with signature, three portraits of Anne and her funeral hatchment. Much of the oak furniture at Shibden was there during Anne's time, the Lister collection of carriages including, the Lister Chaise built in 1700 /1725, one of the oldest carriages surviving in the world which can be viewed in the barn and the Lowther State Chariot just two of the wonderful old artefacts on display. Also on display is The Apothecary's shop, The Basket-maker's shop, The Blacksmith's shop, The Brewhouse, The Dairy, these are just some of the features the visitor can enjoy.

The Hall is set in 32 hectares of informal park and woodland, which have won the Green Heritage Award. Exploring the beautifully restored historic grounds where Anne walked is an absolute joy, the superb cascades, pools, tunnels, terraced and fruit gardens and "Paisley Shawl" lawn and flower beds, inspired Victorian bedding designs by Joshua Major offers a truly tranquil experience.

Shibden Hall has been a Grade 11 listed building since 3rd November 1954. In 1996 the huge stone Lion sculpture was stolen

216

but was tracked down to Sotheby's auction house in Sussex and brought back to Shibden. The restored Lion was unveiled by the Duke of Kent on 8th May 2008, marking the completion of the Shibden Park Restoration Project. The park and gardens were restored between 2007 and 2008 with almost £3.9 million from the Heritage Lottery Fund and £1.2 million from Calderdale Council. The gardens were listed Grade II on 27 June 2000.

Hidden within the depths of Shibden Park southwest of Shibden Hall is a small, wooded area known as Cunnery Wood. This Local Nature Reserve is on the footprint of Anne Lister's kitchen garden, fishpond, top-up of the cascade and rabbit warren (hence the name Cunnery from Coney-rabbit).

The area is rich in wildlife from stunning displays of bluebells under English oak in mid-April to late May. Majestic English elm with sprawling foliage with dark fissured bark and imposing, tall slender birch trees with their attractive bark and light canopy, a multitude of songbirds, a healthy butterfly, and moth populations, and home to numerous small mammals.

Shibden park a gateway to Beacon Hill and beyond, boasts one of the best places to escape to for peace and tranquillity. A short tunnel under Shibden Hall Road takes you from Cunnery Wood to the grounds of Shibden Estate and Shibden Hall.

ANNE'S RELATIONSHIP WITH STAFF AND TENANTS

The management of an estate involves the staff who work both on the land and in the main house. The conduct of the staff can have a direct effect on the reputation of the whole establishment. In her relationships with tenants and servants, their respectability reflected upon hers. It was not a case of each individual acting for themselves, but rather a community where one's behaviour reflected on the respectability of the highest person in the hierarchy.

Any misdemeanours however trivial could cause a great deal of embarrassment to the whole ménage. It is crucial in any large household that the rules of employment have adhered too, for a servant's misbehaviour could cause widespread gossip and effect the morel of the whole estate. Anne's perception was that morality was a women's concern, so that morality was the woman's sphere of influence over the entire establishment.

Anne's authoritarianism was also moderated by a class identity that included concepts of patronage and charity. For instance, when she had tickets to concerts in Halifax, she sent one along to her steward's widow, Mrs. Briggs, as an act of kindness in appreciation of her late husband's service to the estate.

When one of her older tenants needed help mowing his acre field, she sent two of her workmen over to help... "He did not ask me and seemed much obliged by my offering. Behaved very well about it. Pleased when the people behave handsomely" ...

Wages for the working classes were low, therefore "gifts" to servants were small enhancements given to reinforce the hierarchical relationship. Anne Lister's neighbour Mrs. Priestley paid her housemaid twelve guineas and her cook fifteen guineas a year but the place, she said, was worth twenty pounds... *"She and Mr. P. each*

gave the cook a pound at the fair at midsummer. She thinks my
giving my maid, a thoroughly good one, sixteen pounds a year and
a pound on New Year's Day enough with all my cast-off clothes"...

As Lister was one of the major subscribers to the new Philosophical
Society natural history museum in Halifax, she had access to
tickets; she made sure a couple of them were given to her servants
'Odd & Cookson.' The gifts were a display of gentle paternalism,
they reflected self-interest more than philanthropy. When
Cookson's sister died suddenly, Lister gave her leave to go home for
Morality. However, Anne Lister preferred it, if someone other than
she was perceived as the merciful charitable one, and usually left
such matters to Ann Walker.

Anne Lister preferred her partner to be seen showing a softer, more
feminine nature supposedly to avoid the implication of any fragility
in herself. Giving things away was simply not seen as good business,
but it was a practice that had to be repeated occasionally to again
reinforce the gentry class identification. A related theme can be
found in the practice of pronouncing judgement upon the sexual
behaviour of both tenants and servants. The concern for
respectability is where the discourses of class and gender most
obviously overlap.

The employment of servants was a major cultural signal about class
and status. It distinguished the employers of servants from the non-
wealthy quite markedly. As the century wore on, domestic service
grew to be the single greatest category of female employment.
Servants were to appear in public with clean hands and clothes and
act appropriately deferential. Their behaviour bolstered the display
of class power which any serviced woman could wield.

When planning on setting up an establishment in York with Ann
Walker, to socialize there, they were to... *"take plate and linen and*
have a good handsome lodging and to call James by his surname
and make him powder..."A new Lister manservant had for his
livery an Oxford mixture jacket and waistcoat and plush breeches
and plain yellow buttons...."

This conspicuous display added to respectability. No upper-class woman would go about anywhere without her servants. Servants presented and helped to define the boundaries of class and respectability. It was therefore important that servants displayed a degree of refinement and manners. Upon giving George Playforth a raise in wages in June of 1830, to £20 a year, in honour of his ten years' service, she told him she only... "*wished him to be a little more tidy about his work, and be as particular as possible about his dress and appearance and keeping his hands and nails clean - Poor fellow! he is [a] good-hearted and attached, but sadly illiterate, vulgar servant - whom I cannot keep eventually.*"

If the servants were ill, Anne Lister and Ann Walker paid for doctors to come to see them and if, as happened in 1835, one of them was so ill they could no longer work, they promised to send money while the woman went home to recover. Anne told Mary 'gently and kindly'... "*I thought she had better go home. Consoled and cheered her. She would not want for money. That I as well as Miss Walker should be very glad to do anything for her.*"...

Anne Lister's servants did not often engage in behaviour which could be the cause of dismissal. However, on one occasion the senior female servant, Susan Oddy, came to the library to inform Anne Lister that two other servants, Eugenie, her ladies' maid, whom Anne had engaged in 1832 on the recommendation of Mariana Lawton, and Matthew a fellow servant, were..."*too intimate...more her fault than his...hoped she would pluck up spirit to keep Matthew out of the room...she thinks Eugenie would have him if she could get him.*"...

Making further inquiries Anne was told that Matthew 'walked out' (romantically involved) with Eugenie and 'plays cards' with her after all the rest of the servants have gone to bed. Oddy reported them once again to Anne claiming that... "*they sit on each other's knee in the kitchen*" ... Anne decided that she must gain evidence herself before taking any disciplinary action.

It took Anne two weeks to establish that what had been said was truthful. When she found them together "*in the hut,*" she was determined to act. She immediately sent for Eugenie and asked if she had any intention of marrying Matthew, *"No, Madame!"* she replied. Lister then told her she was... *"at liberty this day"* ... Eugenie tried to excuse herself, but Anne was firm and replied... *"I have nothing more to say"* ... Matthew went to try and appease Anne telling her that they did intended to marry, as a result of which, she retracted her dismissal to give them a second chance.

A few months later, yet another household scene involving Eugenie accusing John Clarke of swearing at her, and an accusation accusing Eugenie and Matthew of stealing. Two days later, Eugenie and Matthew, had their bags and boxes packed and they were sent on their way. This distressing tale ends with Eugenie's sister sending a concerned letter to Lister at the end of October, worried that she had not had any communication from Eugenie for some time and did not know her whereabouts. Anne replied back to Eugenie's sister saying that she could not... *"in conscience vouch for her being a well-conducted person. Conclude she is already married & in want of no other protection than that of her husband"* ...

Towards the end of November Eugenie's sister wrote Lister a 3-page letter, saying Eugenie was in lodgings in Doncaster, ill, with not enough money to return to her family. *"Repents having ever known Matthew. Not married."*... Lister again wrote back, saying that Eugenie and Matthew had spent 3 or 4 days at a little Inn four or five miles away from Shibden and she had merely *"concluded"* that she was married... *"It is not my intention to keep any servant who acknowledges I am very sincerely sorry that I am not the person who can conscientiously give it"*...

The day after Anne Lister's lady's maid, Eugenie, left in disgrace, Lister was obliged to dress herself, though Ann Walker did Lister's hair. Lister records this situation in her journal though she chose to hide the details in code. Ann Walker took on new duties, though not all by herself. In the absence of Eugenie, both ladies were obliged to do other household chores.

She employed servants who would add to, not detract from her prestige. Anne Lister's did not record any instructions or general routine conversations with servants, except when she spoke to them for reasons of discipline, or when they were entering or leaving service. Because of their place in the hierarchy, they only occasionally are mentioned in the written record even though she had daily interactions with them.

George Playforth was Anne Lister's manservant from June 19, 1820, until his sudden death in June 1st1832 from an accidental gunshot wound to the head whilst he was up a tree scaring crows at Langton Hall... Anne was returning from her futile attempt to win Vere's heart consoled herself by visiting Isabella at Langton Hall when this misadventure happened.

"The half-hour bell had just rung at 3.1/2 when a man was seen returning up to the house ...come for a ladder – the keeper had shot a man in a tree – all in alarm – soon learned it was George – shot in the head – was dying – prepared for the worst. He soon brought up and laid on a bed in the dressing room downstairs ... by 4 ¾ Mr (Dr) Cobb & his son arrived...no wound of any consequence but for one gram of shot that had entered the socket of the left [eye] small shot - at the distance of about 30 yards – in the top high tree near a carrion crows' nest – the keeper shooting the old birds – this one must have pierced the socket, from the stupor and insensibility, & the catching convulsive cloths-pricking motions of the hand & arms – this always take place in cases of apoplexy and any pressure on the brain from extravasated blood or otherwise"...

Anne was determined to get the best treatment for George and asked if the doctor could stay all night if necessary, sadly George died 3 days later. Anne attended the post-mortem carried out by Dr Cobb and from their findings it was evident that the shot had passed deep into the brain and so would have been impossible for him to have survived.

Anne and George had had a long history together. Once when they were in Paris in 1829 her carriage was late. She was annoyed and told George it was up to him to look after these matters...

"He answered that it was not his fault in a manner I did not quite like, tho' it was not exactly impertinent I pothered over this in my own mind and meant to speak to him about it afterwards but happened to hear Henry do quite as bad to Lady S[tuart] so

determined to say nothing to George but merely give him less opportunity in future. The more, thought I, he speaks to me, the less I will speak to him. Hardly uttered at dinner. The less one speaks to servants the better" ...

ANN WALKER GOES TO LIVE AT SHIBDEN HALL

Their homecoming back to Shibden was controversial with hostilities from Ann Walker's kin who made it abundantly clear that they did not approve of the cohabiting arrangements. After encountering Ann Walker's aunt who scolded her niece severely, it must have been a tremendous relief for Lister to witness Ann's adamant attitude, and refusal to be dissuaded from their plans of togetherness. Aunt Ann Walker continued to scold Ann whenever they met and complain to anyone who would listen about how her niece had fallen into Anne Lister's clutches, which would eventually lead to Ann's social isolation, the rest of the tribe Priestley's, Edwards and Rawson's choose to snub Anne Lister at every opportunity.

When Mariana Lawton finally realized that Anne was deeply involved with Ann Walker and was pressing ahead with her plans to move Ann into Shibden, Mariana had evinced a fit of considerable jealousy especially after Lister's Marriage to Ann.

Mariana had refused to visit Shibden Hall. She told Lister she was sure she would like Walker during the daytime...

"but could not bear her at night. Could not bear to see her go to bed with me. I kindly parried all this.... [I] spoke highly of Ann's high principle & honourable feeling & that even in any case if it cost me life itself, I would not willingly give her uneasiness. She trusted me & she was right"...

In a later letter, Mariana had written...

"Fred if it is destined that another should take my place, I will wish for your every happiness but do not ask my friendship for more than yourself, above all do not ask to see me again....How much of

224

all this feeling is still hanging 'round my heart, and yet we have met, and Adney (Ann) sends me her kind regards, and I am on the point of returning them. She hopes to see me some of these days - yes, some of these days perhaps we shall all meet, but we wait a little, wait till sorrows are rather more forgotten. Now they are consoled rather than unremembered" ...

Anne wrote in her diary... "And all these sorrows were her own forcing on!" ...

It was decided to rent out Lidgate House in 1834 Ann Walker's former home to a young newly married couple, Lamplugh & Frances (nee Hird) Wickham. They secured a 10-year occupancy at £100 per annum. In the 1840's after the Wickham's had vacated Lidgate, Ann failed to find suitable tenants. It would then become the home of Samuel Washington and his family.
(Source: Friends of Saint Mathews Church Lightcliffe)

Monday 8th... *"A - & I off to ...Cliff-hill and brought A – away at 5.35 – no shaking hands with her aunt who had been crosser than ever. How tiresome! Gets upon poor A-'s nerves and undoes all good. Surely, she will cease to care for such senseless scolding by and by – all sorts of bitterness against me – I am said to have said in York I would have nothing to do with her 'troublesome friends' – and indeed her friends, said Mrs. A W-, would not trouble her (A) much at Shibden. The poor old woman's head is crammed full of pother and untruths"* ...

Anne Lister attempted to place herself in the protective, authoritative, responsible, and financial role of the husband in so far as it was possible to do, but this mirroring of heterosexual arrangements was not supported by the legal and class structures in which they were embedded. Their financial lives became inextricably intermingled. Lister herself paid the steam engine engineer some of the money due on an engine that Walker had bought for her Water Lane Mill. Ann Walker reciprocated by giving several sums of money to Lister and when Ann Walker received her moiety from the division of her family's estate, most of the money, some £1187.10/0, was loaned to Anne Lister at 4 p.c. The two ladies jointly bought a field belonging to their joint steward Samuel Washington, and this was added to the Shibden Hall estate.

The land belonging to Shibden was rich in resources, coal was one of them. Throughout the history of coal mining in Britain, landowners often leased the coals to others to extract. Anne Lister went in the other direction: from an emphasis on leasing, she decided that the most profitable undertaking was to sink her own pits and get her own coal. Anne's agent or digging contractor dealt with the excavation work and employing the miners.

In 1834, John Mann and brother Joseph won the bid to work the new Walker pit, named Walker in recognition of Anne's partner. The auction to carry out the work was held at the Stag's Head public house, Mytholm. The pit was sunk in 1835 by the men employed by Mr. Mann who was later known as Anne Lister's **Master miner.** In 1836, Christopher Rawson Anne's nemesis had his men burned dung to smoke Joseph Mann out of the pit. The ornate ventilation shaft is still standing alongside the path from Shibden Hall to the top of Beacon Hill.

Anne's contractor paid his men 2/. (10 pence) a day for a 12-hour day and that when the men worked two shifts, the first was from 4 a.m. to noon, and the second from noon to 8 p.m. The coal market in the 1830's in the Halifax coal fields grew fast, as cut-throat competition made a rough, tough industry to participate in. It was a system of competing private landowners and tenants, but because the coal beds did not respect surface boundaries, each of the contenders had to negotiate rights of way through other people's land, which on occasion caused friction between the two neighbouring parties. What each of them did in terms of leasing coal or draining water or letting shafts fill up again, had the potential for affecting someone else and on occasion to catastrophic consequences.

By 1835 with Holt as agent, and Hinscliffe advising, they succeeded in the bottoming of the Walker pit and the opening of the Listerwick pit. In all these activities Anne demonstrated her mastery of engineering and geological capability learned through extensive study and reliable advice and a stubborn ruthlessness that destabilized traditional categories of gender. Two partnerships were bidding for Anne Lister's coal in 1832, Hinscliffe & Co. and the Rawson's, both competing for a larger share of the market for soft bed coal in the town of Halifax.

The Rawson's were already mining with a pithead near Law Hill, technically under the Shibden Hall estate. Anne became convinced by her advisers that the Rawson's were *"stealing her hard bed."* Anne's knowledge of geology surprised her rivals, but it was her mathematical skills enabled her to calculate what she could ask in rent. By calculating labour costs, the price achieved for the coal and how much profit they would make and therefore estimate what was a fair price she could charge. Her conversations with other colliery owners paid off, and she learned an enormous amount about her business.

16th October: Talking to Marian... *"It seems She had made up her mind to marry Mr. Abbot...*

Anne was not in favour of Marian marrying Mr. Abbott and made this perfectly clear to her...

"I promist not to name it to anyone – said I would not advise against it, but I did not think it would answer so well as she might think. She knows what & how she was – to mind how she gave up that till pretty sure of being [gaining?] better. She did not know the mortification of giving up her own family, meaning (and explaining) myself and Shibden. But the best thing [if they did marry] would be to get him to settle as far off as she could. Agreed she would not live happily alone, but to mind not to leap out of the frying pan into the fire. If she sold Skelfer [Market Weighton estate], might sink [invest] the over-plus [surplus] money, if she could get ten percent for the four or five thousand – it would make her income comfortable with the stay [visits] she would have here. Said I would help her – she said she could not get ten percent – I told her not to despair of that but did not say further - tho' thought I would give it [the money] myself". ......She said she had not

determined on taking M Abbott- did not know that she should do it".

To Anne, Marian's forthcoming marriage represented a betrayal of her family heritage. John Abbott came from 'Trade' which socially was inferior to that of the landed Lister status, and by marrying someone from a lower class, would discredit the Lister family name and importantly dilute the bloodline. Of course, Ann Walker also descended from 'Trade or New Money' but being a woman, it was impossible for them to produce descendants, unlike a marriage between a man and her sister Marian. Crucially would any sons from their marriage have more claim on Shibden than Anne herself? She had concerns about Abbott's motifs; and would he be willing to marry Marian without a dowry?

On the 1st of December Anne has a long conversation with Marian...

"She has made up her mind to marry Mr. Abbott – can make out his having two thousand a year out of trade, I merely said she knew [what] I should think and what I should do. I only made one request – that she should not marry from here, and that she herself would send the news to the papers (Halifax, Leeds and York), styling herself Marian daughter of Jeremy L. Esq of Skelfler House in this county. She said she had meant to do it in this way- I said there would be no impropriety in her marrying six months after my father's death...not to stay long here after his death and not to announce to me her marriage – it would be enough to see it in the papers. Whatever I did, I should do nothing from caprice or without reason – that I sincerely wished her happy – that her best friend would probably [be] that person who mentions me to be seldomest – and that, as for A- and myself, her (Marian's) name would not pass our lips any more. Marian was almost in tears- I could have been but would not. Spoke calmly and kindly- said I should probably not tell my aunt as she would be much hurt and, as many things happened between the cup and the lip, perhaps the match might not take place- one of the parties might die" ...

Friday 19th Mr. Abbott came to see Marian...

"[I] had told Mr. Abbott she (Marian) had nothing to expect from here [inheritance] he merely said she might not want it. But she says they are not engaged, tho' she having made a proposal, could not now in honour be off – old enough for one side to be bound and not the other" ...

Ann Walker, probably prodded into action by Anne Lister, made efforts to take control over her own half of the Walker Estate. Captain Sutherland being an astute and ambitious man was keen to gain control of all his wife's family seat. With an eye on the future, he may have preferred to continue the business in the same way thus avoiding the likelihood of Anne Lister getting her hands on any of the Walker assets.

Sunday 21st A letter arrived with Ann's aunt at Cliff-hill from Ann's sister in Scotland, Mrs. Elizabeth Sutherland who appeared to be against the proposal of a division of the Walker property and eager to know if Ann was quite able to act for herself, alluding to her mental state. Obviously fearing that Anne Lister would be instigator and manipulating the division.

Thursday 18th: Letter from Mariana, 3 pages and ends... *"she now wishes to see me, and so earnestly asks me to go over to Lawton before the end of this month that I cannot refuse"* ...

At the end of 1834, only a few months after Ann Walker moved to Shibden Hall, Anne Lister spent Christmas at Lawton Hall with Mariana, who was visibly distressed at the final ending of their 'engagement,' which had been a constant theme in both their lives since 1815. Though it appears strange to us that Lister would visit her ex-lover at this point on the calendar we see from the evidence available in her journals that Christmas at Shibden Hall, was a sober affair with attendance at church on Christmas day the focal point of the whole period. Virtually nothing is recorded by Anne about anything remotely festive.

Mariana was keen to know the financial status of their relationship. Anne told her that their fortunes were equal... *"I was thankful things were as they were, for I was determined to have [someone] and certainly could not have done better"* ... Anne assured Mariana that she was fond of Ann and was comfortable with her, money played no part in her feelings.

Lister wrote when she first arrived at Lawton Hall... *"I never felt less in love's danger"*... and surely must have intended to be faithful to Ann Walker, but she found it impossible to over-come her deep-seated feelings for this woman who had meant so much for so long, by the end of her visit the two women had participated in an adulterous liaison...*"She says she is glad to see me but talks of the difference there is when my interest is hung on another peg.... but she would lead me astray if she could."*...

When they were alone together, Mariana was inconsolable...

"So low she could not stand it. Drank cold water, sobbed, was almost in hysterics. Then asked if I loved her. Yes, said I you know I do. We then kissed our lips seeming glewed [sic] together and somehow tongues meeting she sobbed & said it is hard very hard to be a friend for one who has been a wife. I was attendrie. We both cried our eyes nearly when we were obliged to go down to tea after nine....it occurs to me that I inadvertently kissed her rather too warmly just after dinner. Was it this that upset her...? It is very Sad I am very sorry, but my own indifference makes me safer than she thinks" ...

The following day was Christmas Day. Lister and Lawton began kissing again... though in Lister's mind it appears that she puts herself as the innocent party in Lawton's predatory advances, it is clear from a diary entry that she participated willingly without reserve.

"wandered to queer outside till she took up her petticoats & put it to her & I gave her a thorough grubbing.... what is the meaning of all this? Can this be the conduct of a pure minded virtuous woman! I despise it. She has tried all ways to upset me. I have done what I

have done but she shall never gain more nor ever I hope a repetition even of this. I could have done without it but somehow, I thought gratify her passion by one parting grubble. It ought not to have been...My respect is gone. She sends Ann a little pocketbook, yet she will try to lead me astray from her! But she shall do no worse & I hope & trust the scene of tonight cannot recur. Is this the chaste & quiet Mariana" ...

Anne it seems was incapable of refusing an opportunity of a passionate connection but was determined that she would not make the mistake of renewing the love affair that had given her so much heartache for most of her adult life.

Friday 26th Mariana and Anne went to Middlewich to see Mrs. Lamb the worm-quack... *"I looked at all her phials full of worms – tape & all sorts, & catechised [questioned] her pretty severely -her secret is in the solvent mixture (vegetable alkali) Said I should be lastingly obliged if she did my friend good"* ...

Anne does not reveal the reason why Mariana is making this visit, whether she was suffering from a worm infection or because she would like to lose weight with the popular method of tapeworm ingestion.

The tapeworm craze was an aid to losing weight, a popular treatment administered by quacks in the 1800s. The beef tapeworm cysts were added to chalk to form tablets and were consumed by the patient. When hatched the worm eats a large quantity of the food that is meant to be digested by the patient, so preventing them from gaining weight. This treatment could result in brain inflammation, seizures, and an 80-foot-long (25meters) tapeworm that could live for three decades in the body. Once a person reached their desired weight, they then took an anti-parasitic pill which, they 'hoped', would kill off the tapeworms. The dieter would then have to excrete the tapeworm, which could cause abdominal and rectal complications.

That evening Anne Lister returned to Shibden arriving at 10.55 finding everyone had gone to bed. Cordingley and John Booth came down to welcome her. Ann Walker rushed downstairs and was so delighted to see her, meeting her wearing her dressing gown & cloak saying that she had almost given her up and who knows what had passed through her mind considering where Anne had been staying. The two ladies sat talking and drinking tea, Ann Lister, telling her she... *"was astonished how little I had thought of Mariana either going or returning. Very glad to be back again. Mentioned how I had offered her the use of Shibden in the event of Charles' death etc ..."* That evening she and Ann had sex, recording in the prosaic style usual to such occasions, *"One very good kiss after getting into bed & not long after this another not quite so good but very fair"* ...

DIARIES OF 1835

January 1835, just after the election in which Lister's Tory candidate bested the Whigs...

"Washington took coffee with us, and with some humming and ahing, pulled out of his pocket today's Leeds's Mercury-containing among the marriages of Wednesday last: 'Same day, at the parish Church H-; Captain Tom Lister of Shibden Hall to Miss Anne Walker, late of Lidget, near the same place'. I smiled and said it was very good - read it aloud to A- who also smiled and then took up the paper and read the skit to my aunt, and on returning the paper to W- begged him to give it to us when he had done with it - he said he would and seemed agreeably surprised to find what was probably meant to annoy, taken so quietly and with such mere amusement" ...

The incident was followed two days later by the receipt of 'an anonymous letter ... from H-; directed to *'Captain Lister, Shibden Hall, Halifax',* containing the extract from the Leeds's Mercury ... and concluding..."*We beg to congratulate the parties on their happy connection. Probably meant to annoy, but, if so, a failure'*... The announcement was repeated in the Halifax Guardian and the York Chronicle, and two months later, on 15 March, the post brought an anonymous letter of 3 pages long with promise of another to Anne Walker...*"extreme abuse of me - pity for A-; sure, she is unhappy & the writer will do all to aid her getting away from me & Shibden"*...

This was not the first time that harassment via newspapers and anonymous letters had accosted Anne Lister. In 1819, when she was 28, she had received several letters written under the pseudonym, William Townsend: *'As I understand you advertised in the Leeds Mercury for a husband ...'* She was later physically assaulted by a young man she believed to be the letter-writer and took the matter to a solicitor (Whitbread, 1988: 113-5).

This latest cruel assault alluded not only to Lister's sexual identity but included Anne Walker's too, ensuring that they could not fail to appreciate the public nature of the announcement and would also experience a direct personal threat. The sobriquet, 'Captain Tom Lister' gave reference to Anne's masculine appearance and to the eighteenth-century slang word for lesbian, 'Tommy'. Other implications of a sexual relationship were made with the use of words such as 'Marriage' and 'happy connection', and 'sweetheart'.

Although Anne claimed not to be upset or annoyed by the latest attack, she must have suffered extreme distress by this very public announcement, which would have certainly affected not only both the two women but caused distress to their close friends and relations not to mention the amusement for some of their staff, neighbours, and acquaintances.

Anne Lister had ambitious plans for her business ventures and home improvements, which alone was beyond her financial capabilities. It appears that Ann Walker was not asked to simply hand over funds to finance her renovation projects, but instead was asked to make her substantial loans to do the renovations at Shibden and sink her new pit.

By this time Anne Lister had become more actively involved in the management of Ann Walker's estate and took care of her investments and interests it was clear that a joint ownership of the Walker estate with Elizabeth, Ann's sister, was not in Ann's or her own interests.

There seemed no other way but to divide up the estate and to draw lots as to which pieces of land should belong to whom. But It would be a complicated business to divide it up to everyone's satisfaction, more so because of the suspicions of the extended Walker family regarding Lister's involvement.

The Sutherland's and Walker families feared that Anne Lister would play a considerable part to manipulate Ann's interest. They feared that Ann Walker had given over her assets to Lister and therefore it would be Lister who ultimately would benefit from gaining the most valuable assets.

Friday 13th The two ladies went to the Old Bank then on to Mr. Parker's office Anne's solicitor, where Anne explained Ann Walker's intention to divide up the property. They set a time level to be completed in six months. Anne thought it prudent to employ another lawyer recommended by Mr. Parker, someone out of the area so that no one could accuse them of getting an advantage by having Mr. Parker Anne Lister's lawyer acting on Ann's behalf. Mr. Parker approved the idea of division of the land by lots providing it was done fairly to both parties. However, regarding employing someone else to draw up the deal, Mr. Parker felt that this idea would be risky and awfully expensive, coupled with the trouble in sending off the deeds to a stranger.

Friday 20th: ... *"No kiss. Had slept in cousin linen with paper as usual, & white worsted stockings besides, which kept all very comfortable; A-never found out that I had cousin"* ...

Wednesday 25th... *"Pretty good one last night, but she said I had half killed her and she would have no more, and she woke me two or three times in the night to tell me she could not sleep"* ...

Wednesday, April 1st... *"Talking to Marian till near 12.... told me she had made herself the talk of the town by passing Mrs. Abbott's every time in going to & returning from Miss Watkinson's school with Miss S Inman & calling to enquire after Mrs. A(bbott) -each time, Poor Marian. What want to good judgement she perpetually shews!"* ...

Friday 3rd: Ann Walker finally received the expected reply from her sister Elizabeth which amounted to a 'civil put-off' commenting on tenants' rent arrears and colliery accounts, and general dissatisfaction regarding the running of the business. It was void of any sisterly affection but rather like a letter that a lawyer would compose and have all the hallmarks of Captain Sutherland's influence. Although having reservations as to Anne Lister's influence on Ann and fearing that they could lose out due to Anne

Lister's business know-how skills, it might be expected that they would tread warily regarding the division of assets.

Udale House 31st March 1835.

My dearest Ann
I fear you have thought me long in replying to your kind letters, but I have in various ways been prevented doing so.... I think the division of the Estates very fair so far as appears on paper, and I doubt not Mr S. Washington has paid the greatest attention to the subject. I am most anxious that the division should be made in such a way as to leave no room for after-reflections; consequently I think it an act of justice to you and to myself that (Captain) Sutherland should see each farm and compare it with the value put upon it by Mr S. Washington....We are as anxious as you to occasion no unnecessary delay, and unless something very unforeseen occurs Sutherland will be in Yorkshire in July for this purpose...when the land of course will be seen to the best advantage. I shall be very glad to give every facility to you taking any Land which you may wish as being contiguous to your property...

April 1835 Wednesday 8th: Mr. Parker called to see the two ladies...

"Ann got on from little to more(conversation) till she talked over all about her sister's signing away (by a sort of deed of sale) all her unentailed property. Mr. Parker explained & quite acquitted himself of all blame-it appears Mrs. Sutherland was quite aware of the consequences of what she did & cut out Ann without any scruple. A- explained the Sutherland condition [situation] during her last visit at Udale – said she had in fact been ill-used altogether & mentioned Mrs. S-'s letter to me at Paris & its purpose. Mr. Parker astonished thought it well A- had got away safe. All this explanation had arisen out of A-'s speaking of the division of the joint property & naming her intention of employing someone (lawyer) at a distance, on which Mr. P – behaved very handsomely. Allusion was made to reports circulated here against A- & myself-my tricking or getting out of her all she had- all (of) which Mr. P- had heard. Explained Mr. P- thought people were

already beginning to think very differently- the right would come out at last" ...

One of Anne Lister's major estate projects at this time was the conversion of her uncle's former residence at Northgate after extensive refurbishment she hoped would become a prosperous Inn. The work for such an improvement, was expected to be £5,000 the equivalent of approx. £640,000 today. Also, in the plans was to be an adjoining casino, and when the first stone of the casino was being laid there was a public ceremony at which Anne Lister and Ann Walker officiated.

They arrived in Halifax in their carriage with two footmen in livery behind them. They put a time capsule, consisting of a green glass bottle filled with old coins into a hole drilled into the cornerstone of the Northgate casino.

... *"There must have been a hundred people gathered around the spot - two neatly dressed young ladies and some respectable-looking men & the rest rabble..."*

Ann Walker gave a speech directed at the main contractor. She said her friend Miss Lister had asked her to lay the first stone, and she said that *"we"* felt interested in the prosperity of Halifax. Anne Lister spoke and said... *"My friend Miss Walker has done us a great honour...I earnestly hope that the work we are beginning will do credit to us all."*...

The inscription written onto lead sheet was also put into the bottom of the foundation said that the first stone of the casino had been laid... *"by Miss Ann Walker the younger, of Cliff Hill, Yorkshire, in the name & at the request of her particular friend, Miss Anne Lister of Shibden Hall, Yorkshire, owner of the property."* ...

In recognition of this significant occasion Anne Lister gave Ann Walker a silver trowel with the Lister coat of arms engraved upon it and the inscription, *"To Miss Ann Walker the younger, of Cliff Hill, Yorkshire, for laying the first stone of the Casino, to be annexed to the Northgate Hotel, at Halifax. 26 September 1835."*

The fact that they had officiated together at a public ceremony to lay the foundations of a public building was brave, it was an attempt to try to illustrate a respectable couple going about their business, doing their duty not in any way hiding the fact that they had joint enterprises, joint interests, or that they lived and travelled together. They refused to hide away from society in both their private and public rituals as they believed that it would arouse even more speculation, but it was unlikely that their togetherness could have been interpreted as anything other than a romantic connection. Perhaps they hoped that familiarity would result in acceptance of their situation.

DIVISION OF PROPERTY

Lister made sure to mention at the beginning of most subsequent relationships that she would provide for whoever lived with her and that she was willing to leave a life interest in the Shibden Hall estate to that same woman. She expected financial disclosures and support in return.

She exchanged financial information in almost all her sexual relationships with a view to how much money a woman could provide for her immediate use if they committed to each other. Lister had herself attached terms to Walker's inheritance. If Walker subsequently married her claim to the estate would... *"henceforth cease ... as if the said Anne Walker should have then departed this life"* ...

The division of the Cliff Hill estate between the two Walker sisters occupied a good amount of Anne Lister's attention in 1835. Both Lister and Walker were astonished to learn that Mrs. Elizabeth Sutherland had in her marriage settlement, transferred most of her inheritance to her husband in direct contradiction to the clause of her late fathers Will, in which he had specified that... *"his daughter's inheritance was for her sole and separate use, not to be transferred to any person or persons with who she may intermarry"* ... Most of her property went to her husband, George Mackay Sutherland, against the express will of her trustees. Later Elizabeth was persuaded to sign all her remaining property rights over to Captain Sutherland.

Ann Walker told her aunt Ann that her sister had done this, and she and her aunt had a long discussion about Wills, each sharing with the other the details of their own legal testament regarding their assets. Aunt Ann had wrongly suspected that her niece had Willed everything to Anne Lister, Anne wrote...

"The long & short of it is she thought Ann had left all she had to me & so she, Mrs. Ann Walker, had the next thing to cut her out for it... Ann pleased by saying she had left all to Sackville. [Her sister's son. *"Nothing yet settled about me but if Ann did not marry should probably stay with me & we should mutually give each other a life estate in all we could"...*

In another long talk between Ann Walker and her aunt, the latter told her, *"furniture, plate, linen, and china first left to Ann now to her sister but as Ann has not given all she has to me her aunt may change back again in her favor"...*

Once they had set up a joint household at Shibden Hall, Lister and Walker kept up the social round as far as possible, although there was some coolness among the local community towards Lister. Her involvement as a diehard Tory in the campaign to re-elect the Hon. James Wortley Montagu, and her increasing interference (as it was seen through the eyes of Ann's relatives) in Anne Walker's business, and estate dealings, brought her into conflict with Walker's relatives and local Whig merchants (who in many cases were the same), which culminated in two public expressions of open hostility towards their relationship.

Heterosexual marriage in this class gave the wife security in the event of their partner's death, but in the case of a companion or partnership co-existence, the same concept of inheritance was not legal.

Ann Walker sometimes regretted that her property was willed to the Sutherlands, who were having babies, who would in the future be beneficiaries of all the family fortune rather than any offspring that Ann herself might have had. Ann once told Anne Lister that she wished for children of her own, primarily so that her property could be passed to them. Lister recorded herself as replying..."*You shall never find me any obstacle to anything you have much at heart,*" and with much concern *"How can I think of permanence with Ann?"...* Sometimes Ann Walker seemed... *"queer about money. This will never do. We shall never stick together. I will labour at my accounts and set myself straight & prepare to do without her in case of need."* ...

Nevertheless, the admixture of the business of the two estates continued.

In April 1835: The two ladies went to see Mr. Gray Anne's solicitor in York concerning Ann Walker's property...

"A- explained the matter of the division of the joint property- what she had written to Mrs. Sutherland & What Mrs. Sutherland had replied- & put the affair regularly into Mr. J. Gray's hands. He thinks the coming over in July a mere put-off......I then asked J.G.- to draw me up conditions of lettering by ticket my coal & stone in Upper Place Land- he is to call at 11 am tomorrow" ...

"Mr. Gray came at 11 ½ brought me Bythewood's Conveyancing. Thought I had better look this over to see what conditions would have advisable & left me a volume to this (end). Read us the copy what he will write by tonight's post to Captain Sutherland, merely saying he is employed by A- in the matter of the division of the joint property & asking with whom he shall correspond as Captain S's solicitor on the subject" ....

The following day the solicitor returned to bring Ann a codicil to her Will authorising & desiring Anne Lister as her trustee to proceed with the division of the joint property, if it should not be completed on her death, using Eugenie and Joseph Booth to witness it.

Although the two ladies felt happy with what was being undertaken with the division of Ann's property, in Scotland Sutherland was less than pleased. He was furious at the suggestion that he had behaved improperly and one factor that he was particularly unhappy about was his younger children's inheritance.

Udale 18th April 1835

My dear Ann

By today's post I am in receipt of a letter by your Instructions from Messrs Gray Solicitors York, and I have also perused your letter to Elizabeth. When I say that the natural inference deductible from both pains me in extreme, I but feebly indeed express what I feel. In your letter you state that in Consequence of the Settlement Elizabeth made in February 1831 she has relinquished all control over her Property and it therefore seems to you that no progress can be made in the Division [of the joint property] by any further correspondence with her.

From similar considerations which prompted my Wife to make the Settlement you allude to in 1831, I assure you we have long been anxious for a Division of the Property, situated as the Estates at present are. We could make no definite, or at all events satisfactory, settlement on our Younger children while half the property on which it was secured belongs to you......Since your return [from Scotland], you have never expressed the remotest dissatisfaction, or hinted at a wish to have the property divided-until December when you intimated it for the first time....

It did occur to me, and I will entertain the same opinion, that in a matter so very important I ought to satisfy myself about Matters embracing Interests so complicated and serious, that...someone might seem [appear] to me which he [Washington] had overlooked....Elizabeth is naturally anxious to see you and has long expressed a wish to see her Aunt and numerous other Friends in Yorkshire- from her being nursing, she could not properly go south before

July....I of course must go South, and it occurs to me that her presence also will be requisite. Could you not therefore postpone the Division, until the period most convenient and desired by her?

I won't write to Messrs Gray until I hear from you. I shall have no objections in the remotest degree to that firm or any other person you may appoint to act for you- but I certainly will not appoint a Solicitor to act for me (in a Matter regarding which there is no dispute) independent of the necessary Deeds. They would charge several hundred pounds for merely looking over what S. Washington has already done...I am aware all Trade must live, but the Law is the last I would feel inclined to Patronise.

Elizabeth is quite well as also the children, with the exception of John, who is suffering severely from the poor effects of Teething for some days back. We feel more anxious as the Smallpox and scarlet fever is in our immediate Neighbourhood, even least the three eldest, send their love, in which Elizabeth joins me, and with best compliments to all at Shibden Hall.

Believe I am My dear Ann

Yours Most Sincerely

G. Mackay Southerland.

MARRIED LIFE

Anne Lister was partially dependent financially upon Ann Walker for the alterations to Shibden and her business ventures, but continually schemed to make sure she was independent in case their relationship should end. This was a constant concern due to her partner's mental health problems making her at times, difficult to live with. There were no laws against lesbian divorce. Despite their ever more frequent rows, Anne Lister struggled to maintain her temper, writing on one such occasion...

"We owe two great duties to society, to be useful, and to be agreeable. And we more especially owe these duties to those upon whom our welfare more immediately depends."

Sometimes Ann Walker expressed her anxiety over the sheer number of estate projects Anne Lister had committed herself to and was increasingly distressed at what she saw as a huge financial drain... *"having so much upon [her] hands. Did not suit her [Ann Walker]. Had always said she would not marry a man in trade"* ...

Lister tried to reassure her. Between them, they tried to devise ways of living comfortably together and distributing their income... *"Could not bear the anxiety. In tears. I tried to convince her all would go well at last."* Anne Lister told Mariana that she had *"many jobs in hand, draining, walling, wood-felling, planting, drift-driving"* ...

Much of Lister and Walker's leisure time was spent together. They enjoyed the evenings talking, they played cards or backgammon or some other board game, shopped in town together, and they particularly enjoyed brief excursions, especially picturesque locations such as Wharfedale, North Yorkshire, like the time they went to Bolton Abbey at Easter so Ann Walker could sketch. Often Anne Lister would walk by Ann Walker's side when she rode on horseback to Cliff Hill or visit relatives.

244

Anne Lister purchased two chestnut horses, one slightly shorter at 14-1/2 hands for her partner to ride as opposed to the one for herself at 15. Occasionally when in York they rode their ponies together out to Sheriff Hutton and back. Sometimes Anne Lister would read in the evening while Ann Walker wrote letters or sketched. Sometimes Anne Lister read things like Burton's Lectures on Ecclesiastical History or J.B. Bernard's Theory of the Constitution aloud to Ann Walker.

They often discussed family matters. They both visited and expressed regard for the other's aunts even though Ann Walker senior was on occasion brusque and cool to Anne Lister, making it obvious that she did not approve of their association. When Lister's Aunt Anne died, both women went into mourning for a year. Anne Lister showed a great deal of tenderness towards Ann, frequently rubbing her partner's back... *"with spirit of wine and camphor, for 15-20 minutes in the evening to relieve discomfort"* ... On another occasion, she rubbed Ann Walker's foot with brandy after she had slipped.

Ann Walker had an undying sense of duty towards her aunt and on occasions she would stay over-night at Cliff Hill to keep her company. Sometimes Lister would send Walker notes if the latter happened to stay at Cliff Hill overnight. On one of these occasions, Lister commented...
"Poor dear Ann - how different all is without her!"

One of the most regular private rituals of their partnership was the Sunday morning gathering of the inhabitants of Shibden Hall in the south parlour for prayers. In this case, the activity itself took place in a gendered and even patriarchal context. Had Anne Lister's father still been alive, it would have been he who led the household in Sunday prayers. Her typical entry on these occasions ran...
"Then Ann and I....read prayers to my aunt & Oddy & Eugenie & George [the servants] in 35 minutes...."

The language of the journal on these occasions is always... *"Ann & I."*... It was the most family-type occasion of the week. They both attended church together on Sundays, usually in Lightcliffe, and both contributed money towards the building of churches.

The constant repetition of these acts simultaneously reinforced both their respectability and their respective gender roles. Of their more public joint rituals, visiting was of paramount importance. Visits were an occasion on which Anne Lister could either emphasize the fact that she was carrying out a respectable feminine duty, or they could be opportunities for emphasizing her masculinity.

The two women usually called on other ladies in the Halifax area, though occasionally went visiting in York as well. When in York they called on the Balcombe's together, as well as on the Norcliffe's at Langton. On a single afternoon in the summer of 1837, they both went off in their yellow carriage to make calls in the local Halifax neighbourhood, speaking or leaving cards with Miss Briggs, Miss Ralph, Mrs. Dyson, Miss Dyson, Mrs. Henry Priestly, Mrs. William Henry Rawson, Miss Wilkinson and Mrs. Veitch.

Certainly, such extensive visiting was something women usually did and was quite in keeping with usual feminine roles for women of the gentry. The local gentry had been aware of Lister's gender differences for many years ... Whether they associated Lister's masculine traits with sexual practise is a matter of conjecture...

"Called at the vicarage. Mrs. Musgrave not at home. Ann left her card & I wrote my name on it in pencil. Then to Wellhead. Saw Mrs. Waterhouse (nee Rawson) *[&] her son John"* ... John was an astronomer and member of the Royal Astronomical Society. Amongst many other achievements he was a Fellow of the Geological Society, President of the Halifax Mechanics' Institute, Fellow of the Royal Society, and a violinist. Their house had an observatory and a garden where Mr John Waterhouse grew exotic plants and seeds which he gathered on his travels around the world... *"Mrs & Mr. Musgrave came for a minute and a Mr. Inglish? came in & was introduced to us. We found Miss Bramley there on our arrival. Mr. John Waterhouse the only one with her. Introduced her to me. My stately freezing bow forbade all advances... Mrs. Waterhouse hoped Ann would not learn to walk*

and be like me. One Miss Lister quite enough. Could not do with two. One quite enough to move in such an excentric [sic] orbit" ...

From the very beginning both women held a gender roll in their marriage. There are numerous examples of how Lister perceived the operation of separate gender spheres.

It was Ann Walker's business to deal with providing shirts for poor people in Hipperholme, and any expression of philanthropy mainly fell to her. Ann Walker had to be consulted when Anne Lister and her sister Marian were determining who should pay household expenses, including servants' wages... "for all the indoors trouble would fall on her Ann quite against having anything to do with housekeeping."

Anne Lister represents herself in the journal as responding to some social calls in the way in which gentlemen of the gentry might have responded. When the two unmarried Rawson daughters, Catherine, and Delia, visited them at Shibden Hall, Anne Lister sat with them about half an hour... "then left them to Ann"... while she worked on her correspondence.

When Mr. & Mrs. Stansfield Rawson paid the two of them a visit at Shibden Hall Anne Lister left Ann Walker and Mrs. Rawson together and took Mr. Rawson out to the Trough of Bowland Forest, the western spur of the Pennines once described as the... "Switzerland of England"... to show him the new approach road, asking his opinion about a lodge. Mrs. Rawson got a tour of the rooms of the house. This strongly suggests gender differentiation.

When Ann Walker's sister and her husband came for a business visit, Anne Lister directed most of her talk to Captain Sutherland, allowing the two sisters to discuss the Sutherland children and other family matters. Lister's record of the scene reflects the social interactions of two married couples. Ann Walker showed her sister the kitchen, bedroom, and blue room, while Anne Lister took Captain Sutherland and showed him the north chamber and discussed her alterations to the Hall. These types of visits always involved precise and repeated social rituals, indicating not only that the two women's partnership was accepted for its asexual public face, but also that such visits allowed gender differentiation between the two women.

Lister had the power of her class to help her surmount any social difficulties which a lesbian marriage might entail. Because of this, if she was hidden and reticent about her sexual practice, she was particularly bold about her relationship and its gendered aspects. While some local women who had known Anne Lister for many years might have surmised that there was a sexual element in the relationship, this was not discussed openly. Anne Lister usually left her partner at Whiteley's bookshop while she went to her solicitor's office. Walker's main participation in Anne Lister's business life seemed to be when she occasionally copied business letters for her, though Anne Lister was apparently in the habit of telling Ann Walker what business concerns currently occupied her.

Anne Lister dictated or wrote the first draft of most if not all of Ann Walker's most important business correspondence. This fact was almost always hidden in code... "Then till nine & a quarter writing for Ann copy of what she should write to her sister about the coal account. Wrote for her this morning what she should write about Patterson's cond[uct]."...

When Ann Walker woke Lister to tell her that she thought she heard someone in the house, it was expected that Anne Lister was the one who should get up out of bed to confront the situation... "with a pistol in one hand and a candle in the other."...

Ann Walker sometimes repaired Lister's clothing or made things for her partner, such as knitted handkerchiefs. In the evenings Lister and Walker sat upstairs occupying their leisure time by Walker knitted or sewing. She made a blanket for Aunt Anne Lister, also knitted a pair of slippers for Mariana Lawton. Anne would relax by reading the London papers.

Anne Lister never recorded herself doing any of the usual womanly pursuits. Ann Walker was a competent and regular artist, always drawing or sending drawings to her drawing master, Mr. Brown, in York. Anne Lister rarely attempted drawing anything, though it was considered one of the necessary accomplishments for a

248

gentlewoman, who were also expected to achieve acceptable skills in music, singing, dancing, and modern languages, Lister certainly possessed accomplished skills in music and dance, and few would dispute her abilities in languages.

Ann Walker stayed at home or rode her pony to visit her aunt at Cliff Hill, received visits, sketched, looked over old manuscripts, worked on her estate accounts, spoke with her tenants (usually with Anne Lister in the room for advice or support), and arranged for some estate improvements of her own. Anne Lister sometimes supervised these for her.

In 1835 Elizabeth Wilkes Cordingley her long-standing housekeeper left Anne's employment, so sister Marian took over as Housekeeper controlling the day to day running of the house. "went to Marian.... What A-& I pay is perhaps not quite enough to cover the additional expense-said we would pay whatever more might be required-offered to take the whole establishment (?) upon myself if Marian herself had no objection-but my father must be consulted. Well said I, & so must Adney, [Ann Walker] for all the indoors trouble would fall on her. Said I was glad Cordingley was really going or gone" ...

Elizabeth Cordingley's departure from Shibden and Anne's employment drew a cursory acknowledgement in Anne's journal. Elizabeth had been a loyal servant for many years, first as her ladies maid, then as housekeeper and cook. A replacement was therefore necessary as Ann was strongly against having anything to do with housekeeping.

Anne realizing that her partner needed to be occupied for her health's sake, she tried to make a daily schedule for Walker. There were times throughout the 1830's that Anne found it necessary to consult Dr Henry Stephen Belcombe on Ann's health, and sometimes sent her to his private asylum in York. To the doctors, Lister would sometimes remark that Walker was feeling much better when her bowels were right and when out travelling.

Anne Lister was outside for most of the day, every day supervising her workmen in the various projects which she undertook. Ann

Walker was quite involved in initiating and supporting a Sunday School at Lightcliffe, and though both were involved in interviewing potential schoolteachers, Anne Lister left the final decision to Ann Walker, who often vacillated between candidates.... "[Mr.] West is the best," wrote Lister, ".... mais crest egal – But it is equal, - Ann must decide." ... Within the context of a lesbian "marriage" in the early nineteenth century, with gendered differences between the two partners, Lister imposed her idea of appropriate gender roles onto the relationship. There are many examples of when Lister took the controlling role, particularly in business and general household decision making... Ann Walker was seen by Lister as the more emotional, more indecisive partner, resigned to a more submissive position. During their courtship, Lister had told Walker she would begin to make decisions for her, which Walker appears to have wholeheartedly welcomed, but as her confidence grew in later years, Walker began to be less submissive with a stronger will, which resulted in cross words and general disagreements. This was not their main point of contention, however.

Like most other couples be they heterosexual or gay, money, rank, and sex seemed to be the main areas of tension in their relationship almost throughout its existence. Rows occur in many if not most close, intimate relationships and they were certainly a regular part of Lister and Walker's. Ann Walker's emotional expressions led Anne Lister to complain of the latter's temper and vow to *'manage'* her more feminine' partner better...

"Ann rather queer with me this evening because I said her four mahogany hall chairs would not look well in the blue room. Her temper is certainly odd but perhaps I shall manage it. At any rate, I hope I am sure of my own temper & all its patience will probably be required" ...

Almost every time they had a row (only once in the first six months of 1835) Anne Lister vowed to herself that she would... *"manage her partner's temper better in future"* ... This idea of "managing" a more 'feminine' partner certainly has gendered power implications. On one occasion she wrote... *"What a temper Ann has. But I will master it someway or other or give up altogether"*... and on another... *" while she is with me, I must hold the rein tighter"*...

After a fight about carriages, Anne Lister commented privately... *"I see there will be a struggle for the upper hand. I shall not give way come what may."* And again, *" see I must not give up to her too much"* ...

In August 1835 they began having more serious arguments. Understandably Ann Walker was upset because Anne Lister had been unwilling to introduce her to her aristocratic female friends. "Ann Walker cried and *said the sooner we parted the better" ...."* I *took all well but thinking to myself, there is danger in the first mention, the first thought that it is possible for us to part. Time will shew. [sic] I shall try to be prepared for whatever may happen"* ... Anne Lister's friends among the aristocracy in London were occasions of great stress within their relationship because Anne Lister did not introduce Walker, a woman of lower rank. Lister and Walker may have considered their partnership to be a kind of marriage, but it was not recognized as such by Lister's aristocratic friends. The relationship had no social status which was a huge embarrassment in Lister's eyes and one that she was uncomfortable within the presence of her friends.

When Anne and Ann went to London, Anne Lister alone visited the Stuarts, much to Ann Walker's annoyance. In a heterosexual marriage, the wife's rank changed to that of her husband, therefore the wife would have been given the privilege to entre these select circles. This, of course, was not the case within Anne Lister's partnership.

Mixing in the upper circles of society was an important privilege for Anne Lister, without the important contacts Anne herself would not have had the power to mix with the highest echelons in aristocratic society. Ann Walker a relatively unknown Halifax heiress, though exceptionally rich, remained excluded. Anne Lister's former lover Mariana Lawton though having gained wealth and some status through her marriage to Charles had failed to reach the dizzy heights of nobility and therefore was also excluded, she could not have socialized comfortably with, as Anne termed it, "the great ones of the land."

Vere [Hobart] Cameron, on the other hand, held a position within the uppermost ranks of social hierarchy. Vere functioned almost as Anne's patron in aristocratic society, introducing her to women she might not otherwise have had any contact with.

Lady Vere [Hobart] Cameron did not expect to lose or gain any status through her association with Anne Lister and neither did Lady Gordon. Lister, on the other hand, did expect her status to rise because of her association with them. Her rank within the hierarchy, however, remained that of an unmarried minor gentry-woman, socialising with the aristocracy on sufferance as it were, because of her social and scholarly talents. She was welcomed to the upper circles as a special case. Had she attempted to introduce formally her lower-ranking partner Ann Walker; her own position would have been jeopardized. Rules were rules. Anne Lister was able to continue her contact with the Stuarts because she was obsessively careful to observe prevailing social etiquette.

One evening at Shibden Hall Ann Walker read over one of Anne Lister's letters to Lady Harriet de Hagemann and burst into tears. Upon further inquiry Anne discovered that the mention she had made of her in the letter was, to Ann Walker, not complimentary enough, or perhaps did not allude to the precise circumstances of their relationship. Anne Lister retorted it was the same kind of mention she would have made of Lady Vere Cameron and this seemed to comfort her temporarily. However, she asked Anne to eliminate the passage entirely before sending the letter, and this Anne agreed to do.

They had another argument about contact with the upper echelons of the women's network once when they were in London together. Anne Lister went off to spend the day at Richmond Park with Lady Stuart and left Ann Walker to visit with her respectable friend, Mrs. Plowes. Ann Walker made it clear she was not pleased about the arrangement. Anne Lister responded by saying that if she were in her place, she would not care to be taken just to be looked at, she would think it bad taste.

Lister invariably referred to Walker in the diminutive whenever she referred to her at all in her letters to these friends. When Lister told

Lady Vere Cameron about her travel plans, she wrote... *"I shall have the pleasure of presenting my little quiet amiable friend, and we will spend 2 or 3 days...with you en passant...*

When the two ladies travelled to visit the Norcliffe's at Langton staying overnight before travelling to York, found that although their hosts were pleasant and welcoming, Anne quickly sensed that her friends would have preferred her to have visited alone without Ann...

"A little play last night, but not even amounting to a grubble- yet she was rather excited and complained of being knocked up.... A- went upstairs to bed at 9 ¼ & I sat downstairs talking till 11 ¾. Isabella Norcliffe then came & sat with me while I undressed till 11 50 all very kind & civil- she wanted to joke about my warming A- in bed but I put off all talk of this kind. All very kind & acquitted herself very well. But I see they don't want me unless they can have me alone" ...

Anne Lister often thought of being *"au large again"* but aside from her visit with Mariana in December 1834, she was faithful to Ann Walker from their engagement in 1834 until her death in 1840. Anne Lister recorded one row they had because Ann Walker was upset at having to go to church in the yellow carriage... *"I do not know why this was upsetting"* ... Lister said she would order it differently immediately, but, disillusioned and tired of Ann Walker's moods, and the worry that Ann's feelings for her had faded; she at once began fantasizing of being companion with someone else.

At one point, Lister wrote... *"I feel now at last resigned to my fate and take it very quietly. She has no mind for me. I shall not meet with one that has in this world. Let me be thankful for all the mercies, the blessings I have, rather than sigh for more"* ... After another row, Lister commented... *"she has a queer temper & as she gradually begins to have a will of her own her queerness, her requiring much attention, her emptiness as a companion strike me more & more. Her Leaving rue shall be her own doing, but I hope I shall be ready when the time shall come & not fret myself to death about I"* ...

Not entirely happy with Walker, even though she accepts that her own feelings are still strong for Ann, Lister constantly planned how to manage financially without her, while at the same time becoming more dependent on Walker's income. At one point, Ann Walker wrote a note to Lister saying that she was leaving. Walker even made plans for buying furniture and taking it to Scotland and wrote to her sister to that effect. In the ensuing row, Lister told her that she...

"should have no trouble with me. She had only to do as she liked. She began crying. I changed my manner. Said all this was ridiculous. She wanted a good whipping & I got her right I told her I must buy a rod & in truth I must not indulge her too much. Said I should take her by Hull to Rotterdam the end of next month & she made no objection" ...

DIARIES OF 1836

It was in March 1836 that work to make their Wills began, Mr. Gray visited Shibden to take their instructions for giving Ann a life estate in all of Anne Lister's property real and personal appointing her joint trustee with Mr. Gray, and instructing that John Lister junior and his sister would inherit everything after Ann Walker's death...

"On mentioning that my aunt was not in a state to manage the affairs herself and that she was sufficiently provided for out of the estate by my uncle's will, Mr Gray represented that if she had a life estate in property, Marian and her intended husband might claim and get the management of everything during the remainder of my aunt's life. I on account thought it best not to give my aunt a life-estate, but to mention that I put A-in possession immediately on my death, in assurance that she would take care of my aunt and live principally at Shibden and do all that I should have done myself if I had lived" ...

There was also a question of if Ann were to become ill and unable to manage her affairs how they could ensure that Anne Lister could manage them for her and how Captain Sutherland could be prevented from taking over the management. This was an important and necessary requirement to be included in Ann Walker's Will.

Wednesday 23 March... *"No Kiss. A-very low, till I told her I had no fear, nor had Doctor Belcombe, of her going really wrong (in her mind) – she then cheered up & seemed better"*
The event, which occurred in March 1836 in the wake of serious property disputes between Lister (acting on behalf of Walker) and the Rawson's. Anne picks up on details of an earlier attack, but in a

manner altogether more atavistic, archetypal. Lister described it laconically in her diary...

" Mr. Rawson set the people on & treated the[m] to rum-tea-drinking ... & the people burnt A- & me in effigy, he thinks it was last Tuesday. Strange piece of business on the part of Mr. Rawson" ...

Rawson was a longstanding thorn in Anne Lister's side, with suspicions about her sexual orientation; he used his cruel sense of humour to make brutal aspersions to push his rivalry with Anne. Christopher Rawson was determined to bully her out of sinking her coal pit, wishing to rent the rights to mine her coal himself to make the most profit but he failed to outsmart her on this venture.

Lister and Walker in the attempt to prevent the trespass and use of a well on the Walker property, which was claimed a source of drinking water for the whole community, had poisoned the water with tar. The actions of the two women, instigated by Lister, had antagonised the neighbourhood. Revenge was initiated and influenced by Christopher Rawson, fuelled by strong drink bought by Rawson, in what must have been a most devastating action by the town's locals, as prejudices were evident in the burning of two effigies. Effigy-burning was not uncommon it was generally used as a method of political protest, but in this event had more startling associations. The fact that it was a double burning alluded to the 'marriage' or 'connection' between Lister and Walker that had already been pilloried in the recent newspaper announcement.

The practice of parading two straw-stuffed effigies representing an adulterous or scandalous couple through the streets of their hometown, and burning them, preferably before the windows of the offending pair, was still current in nineteenth-century Yorkshire. Known as 'Riding the Stang', it is described in Halliwell's 1889 Dictionary as 'a custom well known throughout the North'. Indeed, the practice was common to many parts of England and Wales.

The passing of Jeremy, Anne's father on 3 April 1836 at 4 ¾ hours was a sad period in the Lister household. Jeremy had lingered for some time...

"death could not have come more gently, more easily – though at the bedside, I scarce knew that the last breath had passed away... read prayers to A- as I have done both night and morning since our return from York" ...

Aunt Anne lingered in her room now weak and bedridden but said how thankful she was that there had been no suffering on Jeremy's passing. Anne & Ann were both suffering from chesty flu that robbed them both of their energy and made them feel wretched, almost unable to cope, particularly so because of the sad situation they found themselves; and on top of that, Ann was very low and deeply depressed.

"A – Low on coming in entreated her to bear up if possible, for my sake she took 2 of Doctor Belcombe's pills last night and hope will be all better for them. Where I to give way, what would become of us! God be thankful for all his mercies! I feel in some sort the feverishness of mental harass, but yet I feel as if I could think of everything. A heavy responsibility presses on me for A- and for us all-but I hope that I shall be enable to do that which is right....A- and I read prayers (Lesson, Psalm and Collect and Epistle and Gospel and 2 or 3 prayers) to my aunt in 20 minutes; A- read half the service for I could not read except with difficulty – I have had cold on my chest.... My aunt wished me my health and many happy returns of my birthday...a melancholy birthday today! A- so low and in tears and her breath(ing) so bad, for she would take no luncheon- fancies she takes too much (food) – that sleeping with her is not very good for me. Really, I know not how it will end. At this rate I must give (her) up – she is getting worse and I cannot go on long without some amendment" ...

Marian would be the sole beneficiary and executrix of Jeremy's Will, but it was Anne, not Marian who managed Jeremy's formal funeral arrangements as she had done for her uncle James. Marian had insisted that Mr. Duncan be called as undertaker. The bearers were eight of the Lister's most prominent tenants, with sixteen further tenants joining the formal procession. The streets were full of people standing to watch and to show their respects. It appears Jeremy had been a well-liked and respected gentleman. As the mourners left the church one woman was heard to say...

"there is not many tears"... "*No thought I, I have not shed one - nor did I shed one when my father was with me over my mother's grave, nor over my uncle's there may be grief without tears"* ...

With the passing of their father, there was nothing to bind the two sisters together, Marian was to depart Shibden for Market Weighton and be replaced as Housekeeper by Mrs. Briggs widow of the late James, who had been steward of Lister Estate. It was 8 ½ on the 10 May when Marian finally left Shibden for the last time for Market Weighton her future home.

One of the saddest if not the most devastating events in Anne's life was the death of her dear and beloved Aunt Anne...

Monday 10 October 1836... "*Went to my aunt at 8 20. The house maid had sat up till 4 a.m. & Oddy had had no sleep. My aunt had been restless all the night & had been up 3 times since I had left her... Still restless & would be got up 3 times from my going to her at 8 20 to my going down to breakfast at 9 10. I had lifted her into bed again the 1ˢᵗ of the 3 times without her seeming incommoded. The 2ⁿᵈ & 3ʳᵈ times Oddy thought it best for one to lift her shoulders while the other raised her legs. After the 3ʳᵈ time of getting up she seemed so exhausted I thought she was gone but she rallied before I went to breakfast"* ...

For the last week, Aunt Anne seemed not to have as much pain and so her suffering seemed to decrease along with her strength. John Booth was sent at nine for Mr Abraham Jubb medical practitioner and he came about 10 or 10 10...

"My aunt had been up while I was at breakfast and was getting up again as I went back into the room at 9 ½, but Oddy & I lifted her gently back into bed & she soon became more settled. By 10 she seemed quiet and composed & Mr Jubb as he sat by her bedside said (at 10 20) that her pulse was gone. Her feet were getting cold. I told him she was warm all over an hour before. She never attempted to get out of bed after 10. Mr Jubb sat by her ¼ hour or 20 minutes. Tried to give her brandy & water but she could not swallow it. He said if we could keep her mouth moist it would be a relief to her but what could we do? The last thing she took & that with difficulty was a [jelly?] about noon just" ...

"At 10 50 Oddy called me (Matty had been with my aunt ever since 9 ½ a.m.). She & Matty thought my aunt going. Mr Jubb went up with me & stayed till 10 55 when I said that if he could do no good, I would not detain him. He thought my poor aunt could not continue very long. She breathed again & continued breathing rather short but [illegible] & not very loud" ...

"A- came for me and I was just in time to see my poor aunt in her last moment of life in the world. the increasing difficulty of breathing as I think [ ]. Matty was at dinner & only Oddy & I present. Her countenance was tranquil when the vital spark was gone" ...

"I remembered my feelings on the loss of my uncle, & that of my father is quite recent, but my aunt is the last of the last generation. She was always good and kind to me. None will ever think so highly of me. None was more interested in my interest None" ...

THE ASCENT OF VIGNEMALE

A relatively unknown yet no less an important landmark in the history of mountaineering is Anne Lister's ascent of Vignemale on August 7, 1838 from what was previously thought inaccessible French side off the mountain. Anne completed the first "official" ascent of the Vignemale, at 3,298 metres, Vignemale is the highest of the French Pyreneans. This required a 10-hour hike to reach the summit, and another 7 to descend.

Mountaineering in the Pyrenees had become a challenge for Anne Lister; in 1830 when she was the first woman to ascend Mount Perdu. This achievement was then crowned by the even more difficult feat of completing this climb in 1838 by being not only the first woman but also the first recorded person, (amateur) to do so.

In the early 19th century, the Pyrenees attracted fewer tourists when compared with the number of visitors to the French and Swiss Alps. It was the ancient health resorts built around the therapeutic springs thermal and mineral water spas found in the Alps that attracted visitors rather than the opportunity to climb mountains. Only later when the conquering of this mighty peak was known that it become a challenge to climbing enthusiasts from around the world.

It was a guide from Gedre, in south-western France, named Henri Cazaux accompanied by his brother-in-law Bernard Guillembet, who found the accessible route to the summit of Vignemale in 1837 via the Ossoue Glacier on the northern slope of the Spanish boarder.
On their assent they fell in a large crevasse, found their way across a glacier for a free-form descent into the Rio Ara side of the mountain. This circuitous southern route was used by Anne Lister to make the first ascent by a visiting amateur climber.

Anne Lister as we have discovered from her journals was an adventurer and keen amateur mountaineer, who took advantage of the two guides knowledge, to make her own attempt at conquering the highest mountain in the Pyrenees. It was not until the early 20th century that the facts relating to this outstanding achievement was made common knowledge after the discovery of Anne Lister's journals. Miss Lister's ascent, the first made by an amateur climber, were found in her manuscript journals among the Archives of Halifax Corporation.

Anne Lister with Ann Walker arrived at St Sauveur on July 9, 1838, for a six-week stay, arranged primarily for the benefit of Ann Walker's health.

Miss Lister was keen to engage Jean Pierre Charles, her guide from 1830; his friend, Jean-Pierre Sanjou was asked to attend Ann Walker during Miss Lister's attempt at the climb, as such dangerous and physical endurance was not something Ann Walker intended to take part in.

Each guide was to have five francs a day for himself and three for his horse; saddles were hired separately on a month to month basis. Jean Pierre Charles had been a guide to Vincent de Chausenque, whose book, Les Pyrenees ou Voyages Pedestres dans toutes les regions de ces montagnes depuis l'Ocean jusqu' a la Mediterranee, published in 1834, (*The Pyrenees, or Pedestrian journeys in all the regions of these mountains from the Ocean to the Mediterranean, Paris, Lecointe and Pougin)* which Anne was reading.

Her Journal records... *"Read him Chausenque's observations: Vignemale inaccessible du cote de France. Charles says a man from Gedre has discovered the way to the top"* ...

Anne, keen to attempt the unexplored peak of this majestic mountain instructed Charles to make enquiries to retain Cazaux, for the venture. The same afternoon Miss Lister procured a thick cape and cloak from Charles to use on the expedition. On July 23, Charles having reported that the guide's wife had assured him there would be no difficulty in acquiring her husband's services, both Anne's and their guides rode up to Gedre to spend the night.

The intention was to climb the Pimene on the east side of the Gave de Pau on the 24th and descend to Qavarnie, where Ann**e** Walker would remain. Anne Lister would continue up the west side of the valley towards Vignemale, spend the night in a hut, and be ready for the ascent early on the 25th; thereafter they would continue into Spain for a few days' explorations.

In the event, the Pimene expedition proved far more strenuous than expected; the weather was not in their favour turning cloudy and the Vignemale attempt was temporarily abandoned. Nevertheless, on the Pimene they had encountered Cazaux, the Vignemale guide, who asked for twenty francs for his services which they accepted, and he was engaged for the climb.

On Sunday, August 5, miss Lister keen to begin decided to try again, but once more the weather turned misty, and a message was sent to Cazaux to say that "*if tomorrow not favourable I* should be at the cabane the first favourable day afterwards". "Brouillard (Fog) low on the mountains again. F.69! at 9·...

The following day she recorded the first hint of competition ... "The chasseurs-guides say that Cazaux, the Gedre Vignemale guide has been engaged by Prince of Moscowe" ...Joseph Napoleon Ney, known as the 2nd Prince de La Moskowa and the eldest son of Napoleon's trusted military general Marshal Michel Ney. The Prince had secured Cazaux to lead them to the top of Vignemale on Thursday. The title, 'Prince of Moscowa' was created by Napoleon Emperor of France, after the battle of Borodino, to Marshal Ney, he also won the title Duke of Elchingen in 1808 after the battle of Elchingen both were victory titles. The guides also told Anne that the Prince is to sleep at Gavarnie on Wednesday night, be the weather fine or not. The knowledge that he, too, was anxious to climb Vignemale may well have spurred on Miss Lister to set out as speedily as possible.

The guides much to Anne's relief said that they expected the weather to improve, at 3·35 that afternoon Miss Lister's party were finally off on horseback from St. Sauveur. It is incredible to our 21st century minds to expect success on such a venture knowing the extent of Anne's climbing apparel; the profusion of petticoats, capes, shawls, and cloaks, her skirts ready to be tied up above her knees by a complication of loops and tapes, her pockets stuffed with necessary items for her personal use, and included 100 francs secreted in the toe of a thick grey woollen stocking. The crampons used on Mont Perdu were also taken and Charles thoughtfully provided a baton ferre (Alpine pickaxe)". Yet,' she concluded, 'I was lightly equipped, and my heart was light" ...

With the party all mounted and accompanied by Charles's brother-in-law to bring back the horses, Miss Lister rode by Gavarnie to the cabane des Saoussats Dabats, and arriving at 8. 5 p.m. was pleased to find Cazaux and his brother-in-law waiting for them. Together with five shepherds, the party spent a brief night lying head to foot close together to retain as much body heat as possible.

The Journal entry for August 7 records...

"Off at 2. Sent back the horses at 4·55· ... Breakfast at 4·55 and off at 5.20 on foot. At the first degree at 6.40. Climbed the chimney. Rest at 7·7· for I2 minutes... At the second degree, that is at the neige (snow peak) at the Cirque, (an amphitheatre-like valley formed by glacial erosion). At 8.5. Put on crampons and off again at 8. I8. On the snow without quitting it till 9.8., then rested on a little grassy knoll till 9.20" ...

The thick cloak Anne had borrowed was a welcome protection from the night-time cold.

... "Took off crampons at 10.10. Rested on top of second crete at I I. I lay down a little; "put on my cloak and did not feel the air cold. Thick clear all the morning, except about sunrise and for about an hour... Off again at I I, Sick just before. At the top at I then descended for 1 hour to. See the Rochers a Pie and glacier and Col" ...

At last, they reached the summit, conquering this majestic and mighty prominence. The list of names in Anne's party of climbers was recorded and placed into a bottle to be a permanent record and undisputable proof of her accomplishment. They then descended jubilantly, Anne recording the time as 2. Io... *"At the bottom of the first snow at 2.38. At snow again, where we ~ad left our crampons and put them on again at 3. Io... Over the whole and took off crampons at 4" ...*

The evening was fine and sunny the air fresh and clean. The party once again began their downward journey after taking a welcome snack and continuing at 4.Io... *"I tried a little bit of bread with my weak brandy and water... Back at the cabane of Saoussats Dabats at 8. 5. Tired, but would have pushed on to Gavarnie, but Charles said it would be dangerous to attempt such a road in the dark" ...*

The group took a rest at the cabin until 1.30 when presumably moonlight gave enough light to allow them to return to Gavarnie in safety. They were back there by 1, 1. 5 a.m. and Anne Walker arrived at 9 the next morning August 8th to meet her partner.

Cazaux left them to go to Gedre, where, it will be recalled, he was due to meet the Prince of Moscowa on that day. It was not until August 13 that the two ladies were back at St. Sauveur, having spent the intervening days trekking over the Spanish border as far as Jaca, a city of north-eastern Spain in the province of Huesca, on the border with France, and returning by Cauterets.

During an afternoon ride towards Gedre on the 14th... *"Charles told us how Cazaux had deceived the Prince de la Moscowa...* The guide let the Prince think he was the first amateur climber to reach the top. When Anne discovered the guide's deception, she refused to pay him until he rectified the matter... *"Had told him I had not gone to the top, was sick on the glacier, and could not get further than the little Pie, but the guides had gone to the top, that Charles himself was sick"...*

Charles was immediately sent to meet the Prince and returned to report that Cazaux had written to the Prince saying that Miss Lister had only reached the lower Pie... *'Cazaux lui avait donne le laurier, ce qui est fait, est fait,"...* The Prince had told him that Cazaux claimed that there had been no bottle at the summit, he also claimed that the pile of stones that Charles and Pierre had placed around the bottle was done by himself and his brother-in-law on their original assent in 1837.

The quarrel became serious; diplomacy failed to work either with Cazaux or the Prince... "Poor Charles... The Prince set his word quite at nought ... and Cazaux the one to be believed against the three.". [Anne, Charles, and Pierre.] On August 16th Miss Lister, taking Charles with her went down the valley to Lourdes to consult a lawyer, M. Latapis, who sympathised with Anne's firm stand, and wrote out a certificate which Cazaux must be persuaded to sign; if he refused, then action would be taken against him, the lawyer considered that withholding payment for the climb would be sufficient inducement to compel its acknowledgment.

The next day came the grand denouement. Miss Lister and Charles rode up to Gedre in the afternoon, arriving at 4pm...
"Cazaux at home. Sent for him, as also for the aubergiste ... and for his brother-in-law with him. I ordered bread and wine and cheese for them all ... went down to the kitchen and stayed with them all the whole time. Cazaux came in perhaps ten minutes or 1 hour and then joined heartily in talking the story over, in everything agreeing with and confirming the statement of Charles and myself" ... The certificate was read... "Cazaux made not the least objection to sign it; declared fully and openly that all I and Charles had said was true, and that I had got up to the top and got up very well too. Cazaux then signed and Charles, and the aubergiste, saying he was Maire and could not sign these things, his brother-in-law signed as a witness" ...

The date, August 17ᵗʰ, 1838, is written in Anne Lister's writing. Cazaux was then paid, given an extra five francs, and two more to look after the bottle on the summit and ensure that no-one raised a higher stone column than Miss Lister. She then ordered more wine for the company and everyone relaxed.
Anne later wrote in her diary... *"I thought not of certificate, nor cared more for mounting Vignemale than Mont Perdu, the ascent of which last mountain nobody believes. What matters it to me? I have made each ascent for my pleasure, not for eclat. What is eclat to me?"* ...
Another interesting entry in her diary Anne writes...

"In about two hours hardish climbing up the rock, we ...got to the first glacier, so steep that in spite of iron cramps strapped round our feet and long iron pointed sticks in our hands to hold by, it was with some difficulty we got up it. In the next glacier, still worse than the other, one of the Guides with an axe cut little steps for himself and the rest of us, that we could just stick our toes into, and one after another we all got safe over......Getting to the bottom did not give me much trouble – my foot slipped, I found myself sitting instead of standing, and in this way, glided down so nicely that all thought I had done it on purposes – well there was no crevasse near where I was"...

THE LAST ADVENTURE

Anne Lister did pressure Walker many times about being included in Walker's will. Before leaving for their last trip abroad to Russia they seemed to have agreed on the principle and subject of their wills. Walker did eventually connect her accounts to Lister's accounts. They had lawyers in London to help them with this.

Anne's last and greatest trip began in June 1839. The trip appears to be as much for Ann Walker's health as an adventure. In her diary Anne records that... *"Ann Walker dreads the journey"* ... Lister also remarks... *"But what does she fear? death?"* ... Ann had been deeply depressed for several months, there was a concern that her family might ask her sister Elizabeth to place her under the protection of Chancery. Lister would under their relationship circumstances have no say in the matter. It was therefore imperative that they get away as soon as possible... *"A-[Ann] terribly helpless and low – she is like a baby that wants looking after and keeping employed had I any time to myself I could get on three times as fast"* ...

It seems that Ann required constant attention, on occasion she could not bring herself to face tenants or visitors or deal with day to day running of her estate business. It was necessary for Anne to take control on these occasions... *"then with A-[Ann] walked with her 1/4 hour in front of the house till about 12 1/2 - then took her in to luncheon and sat with her while she took a glass of Madeira and a little cold beef - then seeing her seem poorly advised her lying down for a little while - sat by her 10 minutes and then went down for 5 minutes and then stayed with her while she got up about 1 1/4 when Messers Whiteley of the village of Stainland and James Harper Walker of the district of Stainland called to see A-[Ann] - she sat in my room (blue room) and I went down to them"*...

Anne's sister Marian came to visit and willingly took over Ann's care whilst Anne attended to the estate business and organisation of their upcoming trip abroad... *"A-[Ann] sat with Marian for 1/2*

hour - A-[Ann] so low this morning did not let her be out of my sight knowing she would do nothing but say her prayers and cry"
...

On the morning of their departure... *"then sat down A-[Ann] and I to tea - enjoyed it - took our time - just before setting off, on my saying we past the possibility of arriving at Manchester for the 6 1/2 a.m. mail train and we might as well go to bed at M-[Manchester] till afternoon A-[Ann] said she never much liked going by the rail road - will you said I, post it? We can do it very well - a moment sufficed to alter our plan - Told William to drive to Wakefield instead of Rochdale and we would take the four horses all the way - and 4 horses forward from there to Doncaster - Robert Mann and George Thomas were waiting to see us off - fine morning - fine dawn of day - wished good bye to Robert and bade him do his best to make all things answer - A-[Ann] and I stepped into the carriage and full of baggage drove off at 2 50/"*

Leaving Shibden Hall the two ladies accompanied by two servants, travelled in their carriage, the first place that they had to visit was London to leave their last Wills with their lawyers. On through France, then Belgium, Holland, Germany, Denmark, Sweden, Norway, (part of the kingdom of Sweden) Finland (part of czarist Russia) arriving in St Petersburg Russia in September and on to Moscow in October. Ann Walker hated the cold and wanted to return to warmer climes, but Anne persuaded her to continue their travels fitting them both out with men's knee-length leather boots and fur coats.

In January 1840 Anne and Ann Walker had been in Russia for several months. Lister was eager to be off from Moscow and to begin their long journey into unknown territory. Due to the seasonal weather conditions they had to wait until February before leaving Mrs Howard's clean and comfortable Hotel. ... *"There is one, however, of which we heard while we were there, kept by an Englishwoman, Mrs. Howard, which we were told was far superior to any of the others in comfort and cleanliness"* ... (Venables 1839, page 263). Lister & Walker travelled in a Kibitka (a Russian sleigh or sledge vehicle pulled by horses). The servants, a married couple Mr. Gross & Mrs. Grotza, also accompanied them in a second Kibitka.

Their destination was the Caucasus, a hot and humid mountainous region between the Black and Caspian seas. In the summer of 1840, they reached the city of Kutaisi.

However, the extreme cold on the journey was not to Ann Walker's liking, she found little pleasure in travelling around in such freezing conditions and occasionally resorted to completely submerging herself beneath blankets to keep warm, hiding from the freezing cold. The inclement weather had less effect on her companion who enthusiastically absorbed the Russian landscape, architecture, history, and customs as she was able.

They travelled south, along the frozen Volga River, to the Caucasus. Few Western Europeans had visited this area, certainly not lone West European women. They visited Kazan where they sampled a Tatar breakfast, and invited to see a Tatar Haram and *"attended the divine worship in the great mosque"* built in the traditional Tatar medieval design of architecture, combined with provincial baroque style,
(Lister, Anne, and Muriel M. Green. *Miss Lister of Shibden Hall: Selected Letters (1800-1840).* Lewes: Book Guild, 1992.)

In some areas unrest amongst the local population against the Tsarist regime' required them to have a military escort, so there was a great deal of danger in this their last trip together.

The two women were a source of great curiosity to the local people they visited. As Anne noted in her diary... *"The people coming in to look at us as if we were some strange animals such as they had not seen the like before"* ...

They relied upon the kindness of strangers to accommodate them in their homes as there were no hotels in which to stay, but this gave them a chance of meeting local people along their journey.

Anne's very last diary entry dated 11th August 1840 was written when she was in the Caucasus Mountains of Georgia. It is possible she kept private notes and proposed to write them into the diary later – but if they did exist, they have not survived. The writing is poor and not easily read, possibly written on the move whilst traveling in the kibitka.

"Awakened last night between 1 & 2, cats at my cheese & children squalling enough to distract the old gent himself. A- awoke me before 6 anxious to be off. She ordered the horses. She out of sorts. Terrible! Did a good job. So many [women?] & people knew not whom to give to. Gave nothing. The cottages so hid amid the trees & vines & 8 ft high maise hardly visible except when close to them. Off at 6 50. The children especially & the men & women look pale & yellow & unhealthy in this moist, hot [bottom?] ...

At 7 35 Eugom[?]. *"Fine river nearish left, ascend highish (left bank) above it & go upwards along its broad boulder bedded islandy streamy course. Forever through lanes of alder & hazel, every now & then in [our eyes?]. Bits of deep mud every now and then.*

At 8 ¼ at village of Dujani ie orchards, vine-covered trees, alders [?] [?] etc. The woods [chi...?] beach & next in quantity oak. At 8 20 close up the Eugom, then ascend again on higher ground always in the village of Dujani. No houses to be seen – all hid. Fine view viewing downwards amid lower green woodland [illegible], beautiful hills & upwards amid higher such hills. Beautiful valley. At 8 55 at the large beautiful [qua..?] green opposite village. In style of [Zujdich?] with several [picturesque?] goodish [galleried?] [sacks?] scattered around. Alight at one opposite (empty)".*

Their journey took them through some very inhospitable terrain, most of the roads they travelled were simply mud and sand flats, all elements that interfere with smooth, problem free travel. They spent fourteen days struggling across boggy ground in ferocious winds. The Volga at that time had no clearly defined shoreline, and prone to flooding up to twelve miles during the spring thaw. It was impossible to detect in places whether they were travelling on ice or frozen land. On one occasion whilst dosing in their kibitka they were awakened from their slumbers by the plunging of the horse as the ice cracked and one horse plunged through almost over its head. It must have been a heart stopping episode with the threat of catastrophe almost upon them. Luckily, they were near enough to the shoreline and so escaped deeper water and assured death. Often the party encountered swamp-like places with all the elements that this terrain brings, biting flies, mosquitoes etc. For parts of the way they had the company of fleas, making it necessary to de-louse at regular intervals.

At 9 to breakfast. *"The [whi..?] [kupost?] [cast...?] on wooded ridge of the hill almost hid among the wood. Close [over?] the river (left bank). Wrote so far till now 11 10 & of very nearly 21°. [Breakfast?] from 11 ¼ to 12 50 including a [tolerably?] [comfortable?] wash in the [back?]".*

"Off at 1 ¾. At 2 50 out of our narrow lanes through tall bracken in the [bottom?] & passed this wood ([buck?] & Spanish chestnut & alder & walnut) & up steepish [mount?]. Good aspect & then fine view over rich [illegible] wooded plain & the old town of [pr..ce?] [Appakidzi?]. At the village of Satchina close left. Stop 5 mins under [illegible] lime tree for the men to get Off again from Satchina at 2 55. Steepish [illegible] descent [illegible] wood again from [illegible], then up the hill & down & forded little stream & 2 or 3 [illegible] cottages".

"At 3 ½ still, the village of Satchina & [illegible] came 9 or 10 feet high. A village Sapeli & is a little district. At 3 35 ford good broadish stream the Inseeral & at 3 42 ford the Isleeah an equally good stream. Beautiful little green [c..y?] [valley?] among the rounded wooded hills & here & there [illegible] & [forest?] on the low hills. At 3 47 found the Isleeah again. Several more scattered cottages, still the village of Satchina".

"At 4. 10 the village of Nardoogee [illegible] at a little [illegible] left. At 4 18 in the bottom [of the cart?] & ford little stream & ascend after. At 4 40 pul on mackintosh cloak. The rain was not heavy but likely to continue. At 4 55 stop at wicker [herji?] [against?] [illegible] of [illegible] [illegible] said to be & village of Djkali though I see no [illegible] at all. The old [illegible] of Djeyali ([prince?] Martchar Dadian) [he?] lives at some [illegible] village. Cart deserted & empty? A beautiful group of valleys & rounded

hills. *Mingulia very beautiful & fine race of men eg our David &
son others whom we have seen. All of my 3 men have left us to seek
some food or some [illegible]. [Adam?] came back in ½ hour. A-
had had an egg beaten up & I had the [illegible] off my horse &
done up my mackintosh. David does not know the road. Got a man
to go with us to the village. He now says it is 6 instead of 3 hours
from here to [word missing] & 6 days from here to [Muni?].
Terrible! An hour lost here".*

*"Off to the village, Djkali at 6 5 & arrived at 6 ¾. 2 [sacks?].
Arrange ourselves in the [illegible] corn barn. A little wicker place
perhaps 4 ¼ x 3 yards. Spread our [buscas?] on straw & now 8.
25 I have [just] in it the last 9 lines".*

*"High hills [illegible] & [illegible] ridges of wooded hills rising
every now & then into little wooded conical summits. The sides of
the hill [surrounded?] and little conical summits on the [ridges?]
of the [illegible]. Tea & coffee at 8. 25".*

THE DEATH OF ANNE LISTER

Six weeks later - on 22nd September 1840 at the age of 49 years Anne Lister died. She died from a fever believed to have developed after being bitten by a tick at Koutais (now Kutaisi in Georgia). Ann Walker was stranded 4,500 miles from home, faced with the decision of either allowing Anne Lister to be buried in the land where she died, or returning her body home to be re-united with her ancestors. Perhaps it was not a decision that she made alone, Ann would have realized that Anne's last wish would have been to be laid to rest with her beloved Aunt Anne, Uncle James, her father, and her ancestors in Halifax in the Parish Church. Perhaps when both ladies became aware of the deteriorating condition of Lister's fever, they would surely have spoken about Anne's desired last place of rest.

It has long been a romantic notion that Ann Walker accompanied Lister's body to Moscow for the embalming, and then travelled with the casket through northern Europe before the voyage home. Recent research by Steve Crabtree and Diane Halford, Calderdale Researchers, have made several discoveries that make the presupposition that Walker travelled with the coffin back home a legend, an assumption grown up out of previous lack of evidence to the contrary. A recently discovered letter in the Calderdale Archives, in which Ann Walker writes to David Booth, asking him to make certain arrangements, reveal that it was sent from Moscow on December 17th, 1841. On the 19th of February 1841, a letter arrived at Parker & Adam's law firm from a Reverend James Gratrix, Vicar of St James Halifax mentioning that Ann Walker is "recently returned", This letter indicated that he would like to purchase some land from her at Northgate.

York Solicitor William Gray, executor of Anne Lister's Will and co-trustee of the Shibden Estate, wrote to Ann Walker at Shibden Hall on the 5th of March 1841. Gray expresses his concern over the lack of news regarding the ship – 'Levant Packet'. This almost certainly was the vessel which was transporting Anne Lister's coffin home. The letter asking for news was also dated before Anne Lister's body arrived back in England, and the subsequent invoice for the transportation of the coffin also discovered recently, indicate that after Lister died, Ann Walker returned home alone. The Calderdale Researchers also found evidence that a ship bearing the name 'Levant Packet' makes shore at Gravesend, London, on or around the 9th of April. Following the arrival of 'Levant Packet', Anne Lister's Will is proved on 17th April in London, her coffin arrived in Halifax on 24th April, and she was finally laid to rest on the 29th April. It took six months for Lister's embalmed body to reach home. In the newspaper obituary, Walker was described as Anne Lister's friend and companion. Ann went to a great deal of expense to give Anne Lister the grand funeral that her status demanded in one last act of love for the woman she had admired and loved for most of her life.

Some Lister scholars have described Anne and Ann's union as not a happy relationship, accusing Lister of wanting Walker purely for financial benefits. Anne did use Walker's wealth to finance many projects, but she was working within what were the excepted principles in heterosexual relationships. Anne did show a great deal of patience and loving concern towards her partner, who often suffered bouts of melancholia, reduced appetite and seems unsure throughout their union of Walker's commitment to her. Lister often remarked on how tired she is of Ann's behaviour, yet Lister suffered and tolerated Walker's heavy mood-swings and mental health problems throughout their relationship and did her best to seek treatment for the wellbeing of her partner.

From Anne Lister's journal, we get the impression that as time passed, Ann Walker began to develop a mind of her own and was not so easily swayed. On occasion she acted wilfully with temper tantrums. On these occasions Anne showed tolerance and restraint which would have been impossible if she had not cared for Ann. The pressure that they endured from family, friends, and society in general, would have added to their difficulties.

Lister had taken it upon herself to manage both household work and estate business. Yet another obstacle was Anne Lister's masculine thinking, which failed to understand the need to consult her partner on many matters both in business and social events, which resulted in Ann feeling incompetent and resentful and therefore to some extent this must have put pressure on their relationship. Lister also wrote many times about being... *"hurted by Ann's harsh language"* ... Anne writes about Ann's *"queertemper"* in letters translated in, *"Miss Lister of Shibden Hall, Selected Letters"* by Anne Lister (Author), Edited by Muriel Green, published in 1992 by The Book Guild, who reveals many unhappy situations with Lister almost in despair and suggests that their relationship was at times at breaking point.

Since the revelations about Anne Lister and her diaries surfaced, there has been a great deal of interest about Ann Walker, and her thoughts on the relationship with Anne Lister. Anne Lister had been involved with countless women throughout her life, Anne's overwhelming desire to have a loving, lasting relationship meant that she was continuously seeking out a permanent partner to share her life. Mariana Lawton was the truest love of Anne's life, the only one that we can say with certainty that she truly loved. Anne's relationship with Ann Walker was for the most sufficient, though never intense. It is evident from the beginning of their relationship that Anne lacked the same passion she felt for Mariana *'If she was fond of me and manageable, I think I could be comfortable enough with her.'*

It has always been believed that little if anything of Walker's account has survived. Though she too wrote a diary it was surmised that it may have been destroyed, possibly by one of her relations to hide the events surrounding her sexual relationship with another woman. Exciting revelations have recently been discovered. In October 2020, The Yorkshire Post's leading headline was, 'Amateur Historian Sensationally Discovers 'Gentleman Jack' Anne Lister's wife Ann Walker's secret diaries hidden in plain sight'.

It was Diane Halford, a member of a research group called 'In Search of Ann Walker', who made the exciting find when examining papers collected by the Rawson family, now kept at the West Yorkshire Archive Service's Halifax. The papers included travel journals from 1835 that had been previously attributed to Anne Lister. Researchers found that a reference by the author to the death of 'my poor brother John five years earlier'. This could not have been written by Anne Lister, her brother John died in 1810 so the passage must have been written by Ann Walker whose brother died in Naples, Italy in January 1830.

The documents were first catalogued around 10 years ago, this is only one of many items. Walker does not use code as her partner did, but she does use an abbreviation to refer to Lister - 'Dr t' for 'dearest'. The group's find has now been verified by archivists, and although this Walker diary only covers a year, it includes accounts of their domestic life together at Shibden Hall, and their travels in Europe during their 'honeymoon'.

Anne Lister was buried in the parish church in Halifax, West Yorkshire, on 29th April 1841. The earliest remaining Lister tombstones date from the 1750s and are in the south aisle; these include that of Anne's grandfather Jeremiah, who died in 1788. Later Listers were buried not too far away. At the time of her Uncle James Lister's funeral on 3rd February 1826, Anne mentions in her Diary... *"Our burying place is in the south chapel, at the west end, next to the constable's pew."*

From this, it may be deduced that the Lister Family vault was then at the west end of the Holdsworth Chapel, adjacent to the screen. From records at Wakefield, the Constable's pew in Halifax Parish Church was then to the rear of the pews on the south of the south aisle of the nave. There is no sign of a vault today; the area is covered with floorboards, which date from 1879. And sadly, there are no memorial inscriptions to Anne's uncle and aunt, her father, and their generation; nor to her two young brothers who lie there also.

Further information about the family vault in the Chapel may be gleaned from an entry in Anne's diary. At the time of her Aunt's burial in October 1836, Anne records... *"I stood over the grave the whole time, saw the coffin lowered.... It was the same vault in which my father & I had seen my uncle laid in 1826. I saw no trace of my uncle's coffin, yet my aunts seemed to sink deep down, deeper than I expected tho' I had ordered it to be laid as deep as possible..."*

In 1840, it took five weeks for news of Anne's death in Georgia to reach Halifax; it was announced in the Halifax Guardian on 31st October.

The announcement includes these words: *"...We are informed that the remains of this distinguished lady have been embalmed and that her friend and companion, Miss Walker, is bringing them home by way of Constantinople, for interment in the family vault."*

On 1st May 1841, the same newspaper reports the burial *"...The remains of this lady (who, our readers will remember, died at Koutais, in Imerethi, on 22 September last), arrived at Shibden Hall late on Saturday night and were interred in the parish church on Thursday morning"* ...

Information regarding the family vault may be gleaned from two other entries in Anne's Diaries. At the time of her father, Captain Jeremy Lister's, funeral on April 11, 1836, Anne records *"Mr. Musgrave (vicar] did the duty very well... The grave took up the whole breadth of the aisle – deep enough for 2 coffins above my father's – let down steadily – plenty of room.*

Again, from Anne's 1836 diary entry, it seems fair to conclude that there remained space in the Lister vault after the burial of Anne's Aunt later in that year. Surely this was where she would have wished to be buried, and the scheme mentioned in the newspaper report of October 1840 would have been carried out when Anne's burial took place on 29th April 1841.

For some reason this did not happen; The theory is that the large lead shell coffin in which Anne's body would have been placed after her embalming, was encased in a larger wooden coffin. This could have resulted in the casket being far too big to be placed in the remaining space in the small family vault. Therefore, it is presumed a new grave was dug, at a completely new location in the church.

When the Millennium restoration of the Parish Church in March 2000 was in progress, Anne's tombstone once lost, was rediscovered. Having been covered by wooden flooring in 1879, it was found near the north-west corner of the church. The broken incomplete pieces of Anne's tombstone were adjacent to its recorded location in the early 1870s.

Today, what survives is only about a sixth of the stone. Its original width may be gauged by the known missing words, and presumably, it was originally some six feet long. When you view the remains, you will find the deceased's name has been chiselled out, and the stone shattered. Was this a deliberate act of vandalism? James Lister of Shibden Hall (1847 – 1933) recorded that, in his youth, Anne's stone was... "in the north aisle"...

ANNE LISTER'S LAST WILL AND TESTAMENT

This is the last Will and Testament of one Anne Lister of Shibden Hall in the Township of Southowram in the Parish of Halifax in the County of York Spinster made the ninth day of May in the year of our Lord one thousand eight hundred and thirty-six I give and devise all my estate called Shibden Hall and all and singular the messuages farmlands tenements and real estate whatsoever and wheresoever which I am in any wise seized of or entitled to or have power to dispose of unto my friend Miss Ann Walker who is now living with me at Shibden Hall... aforesaid...I declare my said estates shall be In trust for John Lister Esquire the only son of the late John Lister of Swansea....Provided lastly and I do hereby declare that in case of the marriage of the said Ann Walker all and singular the trust estates monies and premises...hereinbefore given to or respond in her shall thenceforth cease and determine in the same manner to all intents constructions and purposes as if the said Ann Walker should have then departed this life... Signed sealed and published and declared by the said Ann Walker the testatrix as and for her last will and testament.

SCOPE AND ARRANGEMENT
· Last will and testament of Anne Lister: 9th May 1836: (MISC 4150a): including three codicils; ink on 5 folded sheets of parchment, along with printed probate form, filled out in ink.
· Surrender document relating to James Lister of Shibden Hall: 30 Nov 1764: (MISC 4150b): also mentioning a Samuel Lister; ink on folded sheet of parchment.
· Document relating to Jeremy Lister and land at Hipperholme: 27 Feb 1767: (MISC 4150c): ink on folded sheet of parchment; encloses itemized bill, signed "Marshall," to "Jeremiah Lister," for legal fees.
· Lease indenture between John Carr and Anne Lister: 6 Jul 1826: (MISC 4050d): ink on folded sheet of parchment.

· Conveyance of property in Northowram from John Carr and others to Anne Lister: 7 Jul 1826: (MISC 4050e): property comprises three closes and a road; ink on three folded sheets of parchment.
· Deed of covenants from Hannah Hammerton and others to Anne Lister: 2 Jan 1835: (MISC 4050f): to surrender and for the title of a copyhold estate in Northowram; on 8 folded sheets of parchment.
· Admittance, from Hannah Hammerton to Anne Lister: 13 Feb 1835: (MISC 4050g): ink on folded sheet of parchment.
· Admittance, from Anne Lister to Jane and Ann Preston: 12 May 1837: (MISC 4050h): ink on folded sheet of parchment.
· Copy of affidavit of Samuel Washington: 18 Dec 1849: (MISC 4050i): in support of facts "in the matter of Ann Walker spinster of unsound mind" under the Lunacy Acts; ink on sewn paper fascicle, 3 leaves.
· Conveyance of the estates of Anne Lister to new trustees: 5 Jun 1854: (MISC 4050j): to William Gray, Robert Parker, and John Rawson; ink on folded sheet of parchment.
· Court paper regarding the administration of Ann Walker's estate under the Lunacy Acts: 3 Oct 1855: (MISC 4050k): ink on sewn paper fascicle, 7 leaves.
· Mortgage for securing £3000 of land at Southowram by John Lister: 1 Aug 1877: (MISC 4050L): ink on two folded sheets of parchment.
· Reconveyance of Oak End Farm and other land at Southowram to John Lister: 3 Oct 1886: (MISC 4050m): ink on folded sheet of parchment, with very large red wax seal.

Lister of Shibden Hall, Family and Estate Records
This record is held by West Yorkshire Archive Service, Calderdale.

SURROUNDED BY VULTURES

The two women lived together as a couple until Lister's death when Walker inherited Shibden Hall estate. Her brother-in-law George Mackay Sutherland endorsed by her sister Elizabeth and Lister's Welsh relations had other ideas however, each felt that they had a right to take over Shibden Hall now Anne Lister was no longer around, and Ann's health unsurprisingly had once again begun to fail.

Ann Walker, without doubt had gained a great deal of confidence and self-belief through living with and loving Anne Lister. Without her partner, she did try to emulate Anne's business abilities, but the undertaking would prove to be too much, not having Lister's intellect, experience, and knowhow she made some poor business judgements, and when extreme pressure was applied by her family and business dealings, she made critical errors in her judgements. It appears that she tried to operate without taking the advice of those more qualified to fully understand all aspects of the undertakings she was pursuing.

Soon after Anne Lister's funeral, Ann Walker bought up several properties surrounding the Walker estate. Ann added Smith House and Hoyle House Farm and land in 1842 at a cost of £3,750. The previous year she had bought Green House and land between Wakefield Road and Cliff House from Joseph Armitage for £3,150. (source; Lightcliffe and District History Society). The 1851 Halifax Rate book reveals that Walker already owned 89 properties in her own right. These varied in type from predominantly commercial to domestic, bring an annual rental revenue of approximately £500,000 today. Walker's investment in the Halifax area was only a small part of a much larger investment portfolio that she had inherited or accumulated herself through investment or purchased.

Ann also added to her own Will by giving a £300 annuity to Anne Lister's sister Marian with a clause of 'as long as she continued unmarried' and left the rest of her own estate to her sister's eldest son, George Sackville Sutherland. Poor George died in 1843 at the age of 12 years.

Things began to go wrong for Ann after this initial entrepreneurial flurry. Ann's relatives must have realized that she was finding it difficult, if not impossible to manage her affairs thus giving them an opportunity to acquire even more wealth than they already enjoyed. Ann's neglect of herself and her home made her position perilous. It is also possible that she was suffering from the onset of tuberculosis, a fact borne out by the handkerchiefs spotted with blood found in her bedroom after she left.

However, she wrote coherent and logical personal memoranda and business letters to Parker and her architect in at least in January, July, and December of 1842 and continued to push through the conversion work on Shibden Hall that Anne Lister had begun. On 11th June 1842 Ann Walker signed an agreement with the Manchester & Leeds Railway for them to purchase some land in Halifax, which they needed for the new train station. The Walker estates were compensated for the new line that would run from the 'Travellers Rest' (originally Traveller's Inn) through Hipperholme and Lightcliffe almost to Pickle Bridge station beyond Norwood Green. Land for Lightcliffe railway station and sidings would also have been sold. The line past across land owned by the Lister estate, Sunderland & Howarth. In a solicitor's undated letter, the railway paid 'damages' of £9,300 covering both the Lister & Walker estates. £2,200 of this was the Walker property. The balance of £7,100 was apportioned to Ann Walker who was at that time in possession of Shibden Hall. Ann had sold land at Shaw Syke in Halifax for the line near where the first station was built for just over £1,000 and at Water Lane for £1087.

Meanwhile, surveyors that were planning the new line of the railway, which was to emerge from a tunnel and run directly through the middle of the Shibden Hall estate, some 76 yards from the house itself. No doubt this would have horrified Anne Lister had she been alive to witness this proposal. Ann Walker with several of her employees and tenants confronted the Ordnance Survey surveyors, who were escorted by soldiers commanded by a Capt. Durnsford. As the intruders entered the property, Ann and her supporters challenged them, fearing disruption to the gardens. For this act of defiance, she was prosecuted through the courts. Her fine was £2, 8s, 6d for obstruction and hindering Corporal Bernard M'Guchin, of the Sappers and Miners, and others employed in the Ordnance Survey team. A new law allowed the surveyors the legal right to enter any estate and conduct a survey, and if necessary, dig up ground, affix markers and carry out other tasks such as repairing boundary posts. There was also another ongoing piece of business, which was to become incredibly significant to the committal process.

On the 27th of September 1842, her long-time steward signed a purchase agreement on her behalf with a man named Charles Horncastle for the purchase of a neighbouring property. The agreement Washington signed stipulated that Ann was to pay £3,750 for the land and the purchase had to be finalized within 2 months from the date of the agreement. Should a 2-month period expire past the designated time scale, and the purchase be incomplete, then Ann was liable for 4% interest (per month) for the duration of the delay. It appears that a William Towne Radcliffe, a descendant (son) of the original owner, Mr. Charles Radcliffe had been given a life interest in the estate and was entitled to live at Smith House until his death. The property would then pass to any of his descendants. In the absences of descendants, the property would only then pass to Horncastle, a first cousin. It could not be passed onto Horncastle while Mr. William Radcliffe still lived. Yet another disturbing problem was that Mr. William Towne Radcliffe had been declared a lunatic. Therefore, it was necessary for a lunatic to have a Committee who would manage his affairs and estate. Even though Mr. William Radcliffe was unlikely to produce an heir, Horncastle would still need to gain the approval of the Committee to gain his inheritance.

This meant that the land was not Horncastle's to sell at that point in time and these facts appear not to have been revealed at the time that the purchase agreement was signed. Ann correctly predicted that the tenant would live another twenty years. In fact, William died at Smith House on the 6th of September 1862 at the age of 73 years. Ann points out that under the contract, maintenance of the property would be at all her expense, probably indicates yet another reason for her resistance.

Samuel Washington obtained a copy of the Will of Mr. Charles Radcliffe, deceased, stating that he did not agree with stipulations that Horncastle wanted in the Purchase Agreement. Washington insisted that the solicitors should write a fresh agreement that was in accordance with Mr. Charles Radcliffe's Will. Washington had grave concerns that, in the unlikely event that Mr. William Towne Radcliffe were to produce a lawful heir, Ann would lose all the purchase money.

Under the circumstances with the obvious risk involved with this sale, Ann felt that the purchase price was too high, Ann stated that the clause concerning the interest, which was at the rate of 4% monthly should be instead 4% per annum. Horncastle's solicitors were adamant that she had agreed the price and that she had got a good investment for the future, particularly as the land in question was adjoining her own property. She never paid Horncastle the money, even though Horncastle made a huge fuss, adamant that she had agreed to pay.

On the 24th of June 1843 Ann wrote to Horncastle. In her letter she claimed only to have seen the Deed of Purchase a few days prior and therefore she wished to insert additional demands to the clauses and that these clauses should be inserted in the Deed, which under the circumstances appear perfectly plausible.

The demands were as follows: -

1)That the buildings upon the Estate shall be left in proper tenantable repair, by the Trustee to the Will of the late Mr. Radcliffe, during the life of his son Mr. Radcliffe; and afterwards by Mr. Horncastle, until he gives up possession of the Estate to the purchaser, Miss Walker, or in case of her death, to her Heirs or Executors.

2)Ban the cutting down of any more Wood upon the Estates, and to secure the proper preservation of all the Wood upon the Estate at the time the purchase Agreement was made.

3)Clause Stating the Terms of the original agreement on Stamps, given to Miss Walker, in which the conditions of the purchase are, that if the Principal is not paid on the Execution of the Deed, she is bound to pay 4% per annum on the Principal Purchase money.

Ann added that with such a Purchase Agreement on Stamp Mr. Horncastle will find that it is not in his power to demand money so long as the Interest upon it is duly paid; and that it really is not correct to claim the payment of the Purchase money for an estate, until he has it in his power to yield to her.

On 1st July 1843 Horncastle sent another demand letter. On 17th July 1843 someone, possibly one of the solicitors Grey or Parker, sent a letter to Ann's sister Elizabeth Sutherland in Scotland. Their concern regarding Ann's mental stability, and the deterioration of her situation, prompted them to suggest that Elizabeth's signature, and the opinion of two medical men would be needed to declare Ann Walker a person of unsound mind. The incomplete document finishes abruptly... *"The Smith House & Railway contracts will have to be completed. Very many accounts with....to be settled... Should she recover there might be an attempt"* ... [Incomplete manuscript.]

On 23rd July of 1843, Ann Walker wrote a letter to Horncastle's London solicitors protesting about the papers that were served on her by Mr. Jones from the Law Office of Messer's Fenton and Jones in Huddersfield and asking the reason for such proceedings. She stated that Mr. Horncastle will receive his payment when the property is his to sell, that is, after Mr. William Radcliffe is deceased. Protocol demands that the letters which Ann wrote to both Hardcastle and his solicitors should have been undertaken by her solicitor and not herself, but it appears that she had lost faith in her solicitors Grey, Parker & Adam.

Horncastle's solicitors began sending threatening demand letters and acquired a subpoena in Chancery. Solicitors, Grey, in York, and Parker & Adam in Halifax, exchanged a flurry of letters that show they were aware of the situation, which was quickly deteriorating. Grey suggested that Parker should write to Captain and Elizabeth Sutherland with news of what was happening. Ann Walker, Grey wrote, was paying no attention to Horncastle's letters. The potential for public exposure horrified Walker's family. There was another embarrassing factor - Ann Walker had been stating in public her opposition to the railway in letters to the newspapers.

The Sutherlands considered Ann to be incapable of managing her estates and her vulnerability and their greed would make a coup-de-grace an easy matter. Ann fought them for three years until the strain became too much, she became a melancholy recluse in Anne Lister's manor house.

Elizabeth Sutherland wrote to Parker to confirm that she approved of his selection of Dr Belcombe as the medical man to commit her sister. In another, undated letter, probably written around the same time, Elizabeth Sutherland again expresses her approval of the committal process and remarks of her sister... " *what if she should sally forth with a number of Men and again send-off Captain Dunnsford's party! to think of her having six Men living in the house & only Thomas Pearson's little Girl!*"... Ann Walker must have felt she was under siege and that would explain the persons in the house at that time. Those persons were Mr. Short, Surgeon of York, Arthur Hedges, the Groom, John Jennings the Constable of Southowram, a little girl, the daughter of Thomas Pearson, and a daughter of Robert Mann. George Thomas and Samuel Booth were in the Courtyard.

Above all the Sutherlands wanted to avoid the embarrassment of Ann Walker's arrest for failure to pay the Horncastle purchase agreement, and a possible prison sentence that would reflect badly not only on Ann herself but also on their family. They asked Parker & Adam if they would pay the amount in the interim, to avoid the risk of further public humiliation, and this they did. On the 8th of September 1843, Dr Belcombe made plans with Parker for Ann Walker to be removed from Shibden and taken to a place of safety.

His preference was Terrace House, a private Asylum run by a Mrs Tose in Osbaldwick on the outskirts of York ... *"I have been balancing in my mind lodgings and Osbaldwick I am decided in my preference of the latter, and I also believe that if a case can be effected, it is more likely I'd be wrought there, than in temporary lodgings"* ...

When confronted, it is believed that Ann locked up many of the rooms and boxes in Shibden, they probably contained deeds and other legal documents and perhaps fond mementos of her late partner; the keys she took with her when she left. Was it perhaps Ann who hid Anne Lister's diaries behind the wall panel and thus preventing their availability to prying eyes? She was then escorted to the waiting carriage on the morning of the 9th and taken to the asylum near York.

Preceding letters and Robert Parker's memorandum make it clear that Ann Walker left the Hall of her own volition, as she could not lawfully be forcibly removed, as she had not at that time been formally declared a lunatic. She was obviously coerced into leaving by reassurance that it was in her best interest. Perhaps she was resigned to the surrender of her home, Shibden Hall, knowing that she was incapable of continuing alone.

Waiting on the perimeter was Captain and Mrs Sutherland who were staying at Crow Nest. After hearing all particulars of Miss Walker's departure from Shibden Hall, Mrs Sutherland and the Captain proceeded to Miss Walker's Red Room at Shibden, which they found locked. Unable to find the key to enter the room they directed Jennings the Constable to open it, which he did by taking the door off its hinges.

Parker made a private memorandum that afternoon of what he found at Shibden when he entered; he described Ann Walker's room as filthy. The shutters were closed. There was a pair of loaded pistols on one side of the bed. (these probably were the same pistols once owned by Anne Lister). There was a dirty candlestick covered in wax... *"as if the Candle had melted away on it... Papers were strewn about incomplete confusion [there] were many handkerchiefs spotted all over with Blood"*... It is known that Ann was in the process of researching the Walker family history and would have used many old documents in her research. If that is so, then the discarded papers were an accountable explanation for their legitimate presence within the room.

She had been threatened with arrest for failing to pay money which she claimed had never personally signed for or to know anything about until much later in the sale, and the fact that the property in question did not belong to Hardcastle at the time of the sale and therefore a monthly interest rate of 4% was totally ludicrous and unacceptable. She had publicly resisted the railway line through the Shibden Hall estate. Captain Sutherland expressed his opinion that she must have been insane for years and that... *"some people might be mistaken enough to think, indeed say that I had pressed matters to an extremity when there was no necessity, but merely to obtain her Property for my children"* ...

The Lunacy Commission was held in November 1843 when Ann Walker was declared a person of unsound mind as from 15th October 1841, though how and why they decided on that date is not recorded. The Lunacy Committee of Ann Walker's person included Captain Sutherland, and, at one stage, John Rawson, who in this capacity attempted (unsuccessfully) to use Lister's coal shafts, and Parker who apparently had some control over those railway shares connected with the Shibden Hall estate and was the recipient of several letters from potential share buyers in 1845.

There were at least two lawsuits arising from the Walker drama. One involved an attempt by Dr John Lister to have the expenses of the Russian journeys paid for out of the Walker, rather than the Lister estate. In this he was apparently unsuccessful. The eventual Walker heir, Evan Charles Sutherland Walker of Skibo Castle, was still trying in 1879 to obtain the proceeds of the 1842 sale of land for the Halifax train station. Some of Ann Walker's funds were still tied up until at least 1884, which is the last year for which a record exists of William Grey's accountancy as executor of her will.

It appears that the Walker family and in particularly George Mackay Sutherland worked tirelessly after Anne Lister's death to acquire both the Lister properties and those belonging to Ann Walker. He contacted Dr John Lister to declare that he believed that Anne Lister had deceived his sister-in-law, duping her into participating in the construction of their present situation...

"From your long and frequent intercourse with Miss Walker I doubt not you are as sensible as I am of how perfectly simple a matter it was for any designing or unprincipled person to deceive and dupe her; and I unhesitatingly say that Mrs Lister did so to an enormous extent. Step by step, I have traced the proceedings. She first instils into Miss Walker's Mind a Mistrust and hatred of her closest relatives; when this is accomplished, she prevails on Miss Walker to leave her estate, and, as if this was not sufficient injustice to her family, she persuades her to direct that the proceeds of her Estate should be placed to her (Mrs Lister's) credit during their absence abroad. Whether Miss Lister intended that Miss Walker should ever return. God only knows!!...The injury Mrs Lister has done me, my wife and [son?] I sincerely feel and who would not?".

Source: Records held at the National Archives, including C 106/60, Chancery Masters Exhibits:

(The letter refers to Anne Lister as 'Mrs', The title of 'Mrs' was once used to indicate all adult women of higher social status, whether married or not.)

At the time of the 1841 census, the Sutherland family were in Scotland. Both surviving sons were buried in Scotland. A year after young George Sackville's death Ann's sister Elizabeth Sutherland after moving back to England, died of tuberculosis at Abbey Lodge, Merton, Surrey on 28th December 1844. Elizabeth aged 43 is buried in the churchyard of St Mary's, Wimbledon.

As recorded in Anne Lister's diaries the Sutherland family did have stays in Lightcliffe. But after Anne Lister's death and Ann Walker's removal from Shibden Hall to a York asylum, Shibden Hall became the residence of the Sutherland family. It was here on 16th June 1845 that the eldest daughter 15-year-old Mary Sutherland died. She was buried in St Matthew's churchyard with a note that she was the granddaughter of John and Mary Walker and niece of Ann Walker. After his wife Elizabeth's death in 1844, George MacKay Sutherland then living in Shibden Hall, married Mary Elizabeth Haigh, the daughter of John Haigh of Savile Hall, Halifax on 5th May 1846.

Their daughter Mary Elizabeth Sutherland was born on 17th March 1847 and baptised on 12th April 1847 in St. John's Church, Halifax. The baptism was just ten days before her father, George MacKay Sutherland died on 22nd April 1847. He made his will two days before his passing. Forty-eight-year-old Sutherland was buried in St. Matthew's churchyard on 28th April 1847.
The newspaper 'Leeds Intelligencer' of 1st May 1847 included two separate insertions appertaining to George Mackay Sutherland:

Deaths. ... April 22nd, at Shibden Hall, near Halifax, Captain Geo. Mackay Sutherland, of Aberarder, Inverness-shire, North Britain.

The second inclusion reported on a burglary at Shibden Hall.

BURGLARY. – On Sunday night, some shameless villains affected an entrance into the cellars of Shibden Hall and succeeded in carrying off the provisions contained in the well-stocked larder. At the time of the robbery, the corpse of the late lamented tenant of this ancient mansion, Captain Sutherland, who died on Thursday week, was lying in the house. The same cellars have been similarly cleared on four different occasions, and the last time was during the wedding night of the late gallant Captain about a twelve month ago.

We can see by the 1851 census that Ann Walker did return to her family home, Cliffe Hill at Lightcliffe, even though she was a much mentally scared woman.

1851 census
Ann Walker Head 48 Landed Proprietor
Lydia Fenton Widow 55 Housekeeper
Johanna O'Brien Servant 31 Attendant on Ann Walker
Ann Downham Servant 36
Edna Hargreaves Servant 21
Harriet Fawcet Servant 22

John Kelly Servant 44 Coachman
John H Greenwood 25 Servant
Address Cliffe Hill, Lightcliffe

One of her Rawson cousins (Catherin?) arranged care for Ann by appointing Mrs Lydia Fenton, daughter of Rev Robert Wilkinson, curate of Lightcliffe, a friend from Ann's youth as housekeeper. Lydia remained with Ann until Ann's death in 1854 when she returned to live with her sisters in Savile Row, Halifax. Lydia died on 24th March 1865 aged 69 and is buried in the Wilkinson family tomb in Lightcliffe Church, close by the last resting place of Ann Walker.

Miss Johanna O'Brien was also appointed as carer to Ann. We can only imagine the mental pain and suffering Ann had endured throughout her life and in particularly in the last fourteen years. It would be comforting to know that she did have at least eight years of happiness knowing and loving Anne Lister.

During the rest of her life, Ann Walker did receive the rents from Shibden estate as promised in Anne Lister's will.

Ann Walker died at Cliffe Hill in February 25th 1854. The cause of death is recorded as 'congestion of the brain; at the age of 50 years. Ann was buried under the pulpit in Old St Matthew's Church at Lightcliffe on the 3rd March 1854 with a plaque on the wall alongside. The brass memorial plaque was rescued from the old church before it was demolished. The plaque needs restoration, the writing is difficult to decipher and is stored high up inside the tower, the only remaining structure from the old church. The 'Friends of Friendless Churches' financed the repair and restoration of the tower.

The plaque reads:

In memory of Ann Walker
of Cliffe Hill
who was born May 20th, 1803 and died February 25th 1854
and is buried underneath the pulpit in this church.

The plaque also remembers some of Ann Walker's younger relatives, namely a niece and two nephews, the children of her sister, Elizabeth Sutherland nee Walker, her niece Mary who died June 6th, 1845 who was buried in this churchyard and of her nephews George Sackville who died in 1843 aged 12 and John Walker who died in 1836 aged 1 year who are buried in Kirkmichael Rosshire.

Ann Walker's Will was listed on the Prerogative & Exchequer Courts of York Probate Index in May 1854. Her nephew, Evan Charles Sutherland the only surviving son of Elizabeth and George Sutherland had already inherited his father's Scottish estate, inherited all Ann Walker's Lightcliffe estates on the condition that he and his family take the surname, Sutherland Walker.

Evan Charles Sutherland-Walker married Alice Sophia Tudor of Portland Place, London on 3rd February 1859. The Sutherland-Walkers baptised two of their eight children at St. Matthew's Church, a son Alic born 20th September 1863 and a daughter Alice born 2nd April 1865.

The catalogue of April's 1867 Walker sale for The Crow Nest Estates listed the items for sale, included the mansions and parks of Crow Nest and Cliffe Hill, with gardens, conservatories, vineries, stabling and carriage houses. Lidgate House, New House and Smith House were described as excellent residencies and several superior dwelling houses are highlighted. The sale included 10 farms including Laverack Hall, Southedge, Langley's, Mann's, Townend's, Knowl Top and numerous cottages. Four public houses 'The Traveller's', 'The Hare and Hounds', 'The Sun Inn' and 'The Horseshoes', villas and other residential or manufacturing opportunities. Other lots included a tannery (Lees), a surgery, a blacksmith's workshop, 2 joiners' shops, a malt kiln, and a gasworks. Some of the more important lots came with pews or half pews at Coley & Lightcliffe churches. Nearly 700 acres were listed for sale including land for farming, stone extraction and coal mining. The sale took place over 4 days and comprising 280 lots in total. The sale was held in the New Assembly Rooms on Harrison Road starting on Tuesday 2nd April 1867.

Ann Walker's final home Cliffe Hill was purchased by Johnston Jonas Foster and Crow Nest to Sir Titus Salt for £28,000. Evan Charles Sutherland then moved to Skibo Castle in Scotland a millionaire several times over. In 1887, by deed poll, he and his son William Tudor Sutherland-Walker dropped the name Walker, thus ending the Walker Lightcliffe connection. (source Lightcliffe and District Local History Society)

The Shibden estate passed back to the Lister family upon Ann Walker's death as per the instructions in Anne Lister's Will. Around 1855, Dr John Lister and his family moved between Sandown, Isle of Wight and Shibden Hall. After Dr John's death in 1867, the hall passed to his son, John. He lived at Shibden with his sister, Anne, until his deaths in 1934.

Shibden Hall was handed over to Halifax Borough and it was opened as a museum in June 1934.

ANNE'S LEGACY

Lister's journals represent some of the earliest and certainly the most thorough documentation of upper-class lesbian lives available to historians.

It is this combination of the orderliness and the ordinariness of her daily life, with her most intimate, romantic, and sexual feelings which make the diaries unique, and cause them to be recognised as a 'pivotal' document in British history by the United Nations and included on UNESCO's UK Memory of the world register in 2011.

In 2018 the York Civic Trust unveiled a plaque commemorating Anne Lister as a "gender non-conforming entrepreneur"; the plaque adorned the Holy Trinity Church in York, where Lister and Ann Walker took communion together to secretly partake of the sacrament to symbolize their marital union. Outrage ensued at the omission of the word "lesbian," and thousands signed a petition requesting a revision. In 2019, the pressure succeeded, and the plaque now commemorates

"Anne Lister, lesbian, and diarist."

At least two literary images are thought to allude to Anne Lister. Both Charlotte Bronte's Shirley (1849) and Rosa Kettle's Mistress of Langdale Hall: A Romance of the West Riding, (1872). It is assumed that they contain images partly pieced together from stories of Anne Lister of Shibden Hall.

Perhaps a more convincing likeness to our heiress's character is Bronte's 'Shirley', a male name at the time, as well as the sense one gets of a powerful, gentlemanly, unmarried heiress of a former manor house rather interested in traveling with younger female companions.

Scholars now know that Emily Bronte taught at Law Hill, an establishment within walking distance of Shibden Hall, from at least October 1838 until March 1839. Bronte scholars believe Shibden Hall was the model for Thrushcross Grange in 'Wuthering Heights'. Miss Patchett, for whom Emily worked as a schoolmistress, rented a pew from Anne Lister. Miss Patchett and Anne Lister spoke to each other on at least two occasions.

REFERENCE INDEX

Abbott, John

Son of Robert Abbott became a JP. He attended Heath Grammar School (1817). His father left him Spring Mill, Wainstalls – which he leased to J & J Calvert [1861] – and Hole Bottom Mill, Wainstalls. Abbott made his fortune in the woollen industry, his title, a Wool stapler, (Woolsorter, Riddler,and Wooldriver). A single fleece comprised many different staples and grades of wool. The staples of wool were sorted according to quality, colour, length, and fineness. From a young age he was involved in carpet production with his father. He manufactured carpets at his home in Union Street, Halifax.

Abbott retired long before his death on 13th May 1870 aged 70. He owned property in Australia and New Zealand. He was one of the founders of the Halifax Joint Stock Banking Company and one of the Trustees appointed under the Halifax Improvement Act 1823. He was one of the town's first magistrates.

He was engaged to Marian Lister in 1834. In 1844, he bought property in Cheapside from William Emmett. John never married. He lived at Union Street, Halifax at the time of his death. He was buried at Holy Trinity Church Halifax (20th May 1870).

Newspaper reports of the funeral said:

From his home in Union Street to the Church, the streets were lined with thousands of spectators. The cortège included Superintendent Pearson and a body of police, about 300 children from Crossley Orphanage, the teachers of the Parish Church School, members of the Halifax Auxiliary of the Bible Society, directors of the Halifax Joint Stock Bank, directors of the Halifax Permanent Building Society, and members of the Mechanics' Institute.

Probate records show that he left effects valued at under £140,000. The will was proved by Henry Wright, John Whiteley Ward, Louis John Crossley, Thomas Richard Farrar, and Samuel Taylor Rigge. He left his estate and money for charitable purposes, including:-

£60,000 to establish John Abbott Ladies' Homes

£10,000 for the Crossley Orphanage

£10,000 to establish the Abbott Scholarships at Oxford and/or Cambridge
£3,000 to the Bible Society
£2,000 to the Halifax Infirmary
£1,000 to the Halifax Tradesman's Benevolent Society
£1,000 each to the Bradford and Huddersfield Infirmaries, and various sums to nearly all the Sunday Schools in Halifax
John Abbott was one of the subscribers to John Horner's book 'Buildings in the Town & Parish of Halifax' (1835).

Ainsworth, Reverend Thomas
Had shown an interest in Ann Walker, he was Clerk of Northwich, Cheshire. He was born on October 1795 in Manchester, Lancashire, England. Thomas Ainsworth was licensed as a perpetual curate of Hartford, near Northwich, in 1825 and held the cure until his death. He was a Cambridge graduate and lived at Hartford Hall where he died on 15th May 1847. At the time of his appointment to St John's in Hartford it was a chapelry of Northwich and did not become a parish until 1863. In 1820 a public meeting had been called when it was resolved that a new church should be built in Hartford and this was completed and consecrated in 1824. This would have been the church or chapel that Thomas Ainsworth knew, although it subsequently proved to be too small for the growing population and was demolished and replaced with a bigger building, consecrated in 1875. (These details are taken from the clergy of the Church of England database). He married Ann Ainsworth daughter of James & Elizabeth Ainsworth on 26th September 1837 at St John's Manchester. Thomas died 15th May 1847 at Hartford, Cheshire England. His wife Ann died 15 days later, on the 30th May 1847 also of Hartford, Cheshire.

Belcombe, Henry Stephen Dr
(ca. 1790-1856) son of Dr William Belcombe was in practice [or living] at Fieldhead, Newcastle, Staffordshire (1816), Clifton, near York (1817), Petergate, York (1822), and Heworth Grange, York (1834) Eliza Raine was in his care in 1817, at Clifton. In 1832 and 1834, he was consulted by Anne Lister about Ann Walker's mental state. In 1843, he had a private sanatorium – a lunatic asylum at Clifton.

Boyve, Mmm de
Had a flirtation with Anne Lister. The proprietor of Paris pension at 24 Place Vendome where Anne Lister stayed 1824-5.

Cameron, Lady Vere Louisa Hobart
Born in 1803 in the West Indies. Died on the 15th November 1888. Lady Vere Catherine Louisa Hobart was the daughter of Hon. George Vere Hobert and Janet Maclean. She married Donald Cameron of Lochiel 23rd Chief of Clan Cameron, who fought with distinction at the Battle of Waterloo as part of the Grenadier Guards in 1815. He retired from the military in 1832. son of Donald Cameron of Lochiel, 22nd Chief of Clan Cameron and Hon. Anne Abercromby. Vere and Donald married on 31st July 1832. On 9th September 1832 she was granted the rank of an earl's daughter. The Cameron's had 6 children.

Coverture
It was established in the common law of England for several centuries and throughout most of the 19th century, influencing some other common law jurisdictions. It was a legal doctrine whereby, upon marriage, a woman's legal rights and obligations were subsumed by those of her husband, in accordance with the wife's legal status of feme covert. An unmarried woman, a feme sole, had the right to own property and make contracts in her own name. After the rise of the women's rights movement in the mid-19th century, coverture came under increasing criticism as oppressive towards women, hindering them from exercising ordinary property rights and entering professions. Coverture was first substantially modified by late 19th century Married Woman's Property Acts passed in various common-law legal jurisdictions and was weakened and eventually eliminated by subsequent reforms.

Crompton, Henrietta Matilda

(b. 1793 - 1881), friend and a flirtation of Anne Lister. Henrietta was a prolific watercolourist and traveller. Daughter of a wealthy banker, Joshua Crompton, who also owned a country house at Esholt, twelve miles from Shibden Hall. The Compton's were a wealthy banking family at Esholt Hall, Yorkshire, and upon the death of their father, Henrietta Matilda and her eight siblings each inherited the considerable sum of £11,000, the equivalent of £1,264,714.85 today. Henrietta never married and spent a comfortable life making excursions to picturesque locations in the Yorkshire coastal resorts, and occasionally taking longer trips to various continents to capture memorable images.

Gordon, Lady Caroline Duff: nee Cornewell
(1789 - 1875). Friend of Lady Stuart de Rothesay, a friend of the daughter-in-law of Lady Louisa Stuart. Married to the British ambassador to Paris. had a flirtation with Anne Lister in the late 1820s. She married Sir William Duff Gordon in 1810 and was widowed in 1823, the couple had two sons, Alexander, and Cosmo. Cosmo and his wife Lucie were survivors of the Titanic. Lady Gordon told Anne that if they lived together, she would naturally "take the woman's part." Lady Gordon died in 1875 and was buried at Hendon, London.

Greenwood, Caroline
Daughter of Mrs. Greenwood had a flirtation with Anne Lister, Anne mentioned her in sexual fantasies in her diary.

Halifax Guillotine
Halifax was notorious for its gibbet, an early form of guillotine used to execute criminals last used in 1650. A replica has been erected on the original site in Gibbet Street. Its original blade is on display at Bankfield Museum. Punishment in Halifax was notoriously harsh, as remembered in the 'Beggar's Litany ' by John Taylor (1580–1654).

Horner, John
(1784-1867) Born in Halifax (23rd March 1784). was a landscape artist / a drawing master (1851) / an art teacher at Heath Grammar School and painted in his spare time. He had his studio and a drawing school in Bond Street. In the 1820s, he painted Marian's View, a view of Shibden valley for Anne Lister now hanging in Shibden Hall.

Horner, Joshua
(1812-1881) Son of John Horner Halifax-born artist and portrait-painter. He painted the portrait of Anne Lister which hangs in Shibden Hall.

Horses owned by Anne
Caradoc - a black horse acquired in August 1823
Hotspur - a 3-year-old bay colt bought in May 1822. Anne sent him to the army barracks at York for breaking in. His name relates to Sir Henry Percy (1364-1403), who was known as Harry Hotspur. He was the son of Henry Percy, 1st Earl of Northumberland, a famous northern warrior, Hotspur was immortalised in Shakespeare's *Henry IV, Part I.*
Vienne - a mare bought in May 1822 Vienne, so named because it was the birthplace of her married lover, Mariana in 1790.
Percy – after Mariana, whose full name was Mariana Percy Lawton. In 1822 the Lister's old mare 'Diamond' had to be put down on the 22nd January... *'One of the Mr Taylors (the young man) came at 7 this morning to destroy the old mare. He stabbed her thro' the heart & she was dead in less than 5 minutes'...*

Industrial Revolution
The Industrial Revolution influenced every aspect of daily life. Average income and population began to exhibit unprecedented, sustained growth. The major effect of the Industrial Revolution was that the standard of living for the general population in the western world began to increase consistently for the first time in history.

The main features involved in the Industrial Revolution were technological, socioeconomic, and cultural. The changes that took place are considered the most monumental achievements in technological advancement that had ever been realized. Changes included the following: the use of new basic materials, chiefly iron and steel, the use of new energy sources, such as coal, the internal combustion engine, the steam engine, steam locomotive, steamship, the invention of new machines, such as the Spinning Jenny and the power loom that permitted increased production with a smaller expenditure of human energy, a new organization of work known as the factory system, which entailed increased division of labour and specialization of function. Textiles were the dominant industry of the Industrial Revolution in terms of employment, value of output and capital invested. The textile industry was also the first to use modern production methods.

There were also many new developments in agricultural, economic changes that resulted in a wider distribution of wealth, the decline of land as a source of wealth in the face of rising industrial production, and increased international trade, political changes reflecting the shift in economic power, as well as new state policies corresponding to the needs of an industrialized society.

The common working man witnessed the wealth of the ruling classes rise as production methods were overtaken by machines imposed by the aggressive new class of manufacturers that drove the Industrial Revolution. On 9th October 1779, a group of English textile workers in Manchester rebelled against the introduction of machinery which threatened their skilled craft and reduced opportunities for paid employment for the masses. This was the first of many Luddite riots to take place. The word 'Luddites' refers to British weavers and textile workers who objected to the introduction of mechanised looms and knitting frames. Their rebellion was followed by workers in Nottinghamshire, Yorkshire.

The Luddites were a secret oath-based organization but were not, as has often been portrayed, against the concept of progress and industrialisation as such, but feared for their livelihood and survival. The group went about destroying weaving machines and other tools as a form of protest what they believed to be a deceitful method of circumventing the labour practices of the day.

Despite considerable overlapping with the "old," there was mounting evidence for a "new" Industrial Revolution in the late 19th and 20th centuries. In terms of basic materials, modern industry began to exploit many natural and synthetic resources not hitherto utilized: electricity, petroleum, lighter metals, new alloys, and synthetic products such as plastics, as well as new energy sources. Combined with these were developments in machines, tools, and computers that gave rise to the automatic factory. in transportation and communication, the automobile, airplane, telegraph, and radio, and the increasing application of science to industry. These technological changes made possible a tremendously increased use of natural resources and the mass production of manufactured goods.

Although some segments of industry were almost completely mechanized in the early to mid-19th century, automatic operation, as distinct from the assembly line, first achieved major significance in the second half of the 20th century.
Sweeping social changes, including the growth of cities, the development of working-class movements, and the emergence of new patterns of authority, and cultural transformations of a broad order. Workers acquired new and distinctive skills, and their relation to their tasks shifted; instead of being craftsmen working with hand-tools, they became machine operators. Ownership of the means of production also underwent changes. The oligarchical ownership of the means of production that characterized the Industrial Revolution in the early to mid-19th century gave way to a wider distribution of ownership through purchase of common stocks by individuals and by institutions such as insurance companies.

Lister, Rev John
(1703-1759) Eldest son of James Lister. In 1729, he inherited Shibden Hall. In 1749, he erected a weathervane on Shibden Barn. He was headmaster of Bury Grammar School, Lancashire (1730-1749).

Lister, John
(1771-1836) Son of William Lister who lived in Swansea where the family had settled after returning from Virginia. He married Anne Morris (1780-1870) and they had a son John. Around 1833, Anne Lister bequeathed the Shibden Hall estate to him and his son Dr John Lister who practiced as a Surgeon.

Lister, Dr John
(1802 – 1867) a doctor of Swansea was the great grandson of Thomas Lister of Virginia. Around 1855, and after the death of Ann Walker, Dr John Lister and his family moved between Sandown, Isle of Wight and Shibden Hall which they inherited from Anne Lister. He lived with his wife Louisa Ann (née Grant) Lister and

three children. He had two boys, John and Charles and a daughter, Anne. Before John inherited Shibden, the family had Lived at Brading, Isle of Wight, but had been a practising doctor in Sandown on the Isle of Wight; after they moved, they continued to visit the Island regularly. In 1856, he sold the Northgate Hotel, Halifax (part of his inheritance) to George Watkinson and Mr. T Parker. It was in 1835 a licence had been granted to Anne Lister to convert the building into the Northgate Hotel and Anne also had a casino built at the premises. The official laying of the foundation stone was arranged. Anne wrote in her diary on Saturday, September 26th1835... *"Ann and I are off at 10-45 in my own carriage (with our two men behind) to Northgate Hotel. They were not quite ready for us. Began looking over the drawings at Northgate and by mistake kept the people waiting and did not begin the ceremony until about 11-45, which lasted about a quarter of an hour. Ann did her part very well"*. Dr John Lister died at Aberystwyth 06/08/1867, effects under £14,000

After Dr John's death in 1867, the hall passed to his son, John. He lived at Shibden with his sister, Anne, until their deaths.

Lister, John
(March 1847-October 1933) Born in Marylebone Middlesex, Lister was a philanthropist and politician, last member of the Lister family to reside at Shibden Hall. He stood as a Liberal Councillor in Yorkshire and was a founder member and treasurer of the Independent Labour Party. In 1893, he stood as the first Labour candidate for Halifax in the parliamentary by-election, polling over 3000 votes. Lister grew up in Sandown on the Isle of Wight and Halifax in the West Riding of Yorkshire. He attended Winchester College, then Brasenose College at the University of Oxford and finally Inner Temple, where he qualified as a barrister. He was a keen historian and made President of the Halifax Antiquarian Society He was a founder of the Industrial School for errant children and was a governor of Hipperholme Grammar School for 47 years. He converted to Catholicism midway through life and there are many letters relating to this amongst his papers.

By 1923, John was in a desperate financial position and the bank called in his mortgages. Most of his money had been spent in charitable works and the upkeep of Shibden Hall.

Mr. A S McCrea, Lister's friend, and a Halifax Councillor came to his rescue by purchasing 90 acres of parkland, which he presented to the people of Halifax as a public park. The Prince of Wales opened this in 1926. McCrea also bought the reversion of Shibden Hall, which allowed John and his sister Anne to live out their lives there. Anne died in 1929 and John in 1933. Shibden Hall was handed over to Halifax Borough and it was opened as a museum in June 1934.

Norcliffe Family
Mary Wray inherited the Langton Hall Estate a Grade 11 listed Georgian country house and parkland, built in about 1770 by Leonard Smelt and altered in the 1960s to its present state by the present owner's father. Mary Wray was succeeded by her nephew, Thomas Dalton, Esq., born 31st Dec 1756 in St. Helen's, Yorkshire, the eldest son of John Dalton, Esq., and Isabella, the second daughter of Sir John Wray. Mr. Dalton inherited the estate in 1807 according to the terms of the will, assumed the surname and arms of Norcliffe. He was Captain of the 11th, Dragoons, and was afterward lieutenant-colonel of the York Volunteers. He married Ann Wilson on the 13th of December 1784. Ann (b.13th December 1784 in Belfreys, York, she died 25th September 1835), was the only daughter and heiress of William Wilson, Esq., of Allerton Gledhow. The Norcliffe's had three sons and four daughters. The two younger sons died in youth, and three of the daughters died unmarried, Emily (d 1817), Charlotte (d 1844) Isabella (d 1846) who was Anne Lister's lover. Mary, the fourth daughter, married Charles Best, M.D., of York. Mary Ellen was married at the church of Saint Michael-Le-Belfry in York on 11th June 1807 aged 17 years, her white muslin wedding dress, influenced by the styles of ancient Rome and Greece, known as the Empire line, typical of the Georgian period is on display at the V&A (Victoria & Albert Museum) in London.

Until recently Langton Hall served as an independent preparatory school, but historical records note that the earliest part of the Hall dates from 1738 when the village was the seat of the Norcliffe family, whose descendants still own the property today. The property has evolved and grown over its nearly 300-year history, the main hall dating from around 1820 captured in several watercolours by Mary

Ellen Best in 1833, who herself was a member of the Norcliffe family. The gardens and grounds extend to some 6.5 acres around the buildings; magnificent trees lining the entrance driveway and boundaries, the main lawned gardens being to the south and east. Beyond these are some fabulous views across the neighbouring parkland, melting into unspoiled farmland and the lower slopes of the Yorkshire Wolds.

Northgate House Halifax

Built between 1735-1742 for Richard Clapham. It was a part of the estate of the Lister family and the home of Joseph Lister. On the death of Joseph's widow Mary in February 1822, the property became vacant and passed to James Lister of Shibden Hall.
From 1822, Marian and Jeremy Lister lived there as James's tenants. On James's death in 1826, the property passed to Anne Lister. In the 1830s Anne Lister decided to convert this house into a hotel and annexe in the form of an assembly hall – which she termed a 'casino', though it had no connection with gambling – at a cost of about £10,000.

Obscene Publications Act
The 1959 is an Act of Parliament of the United Kingdom that significantly reformed the law related to obscenity in England and Wales. The Act created a new offence for publishing obscene material, repealing the common law offence of obscene libel which was previously used, and allows Justices of the Peace to issue warrants allowing the police to seize such materials.
The first noted prosecution under the Obscene Publications Act was of Penguin Books Ltd (1960) for publishing Lady Chatterley's Lover.

Paley, Elizabeth
(17?? – 1856) Daughter of Dr William Paley (1743-1805) Of Lightcliffe. He was a theologian, archdeacon of Carlisle, Subdean of Lincoln, rector of Bishopwearmouth- a proponent for the abolition of the slave trade.
Elizabeth was born in Dalston, Cumberland. Together with her sister Ann were close friends and confidantes of Anne Lister. In

1808, Elizabeth married William Priestley at St Mary's Church, Carlisle. Ann married her cousin Dr Robert Paley.

Parliamentary Elections - Voting in the 19th century

Today, the right to fair and free elections is almost taken for granted. However, many of the rights we have today as voters - including the right to a secret ballot and for elections to be duly supervised - were not commonplace until the late 19th century. Until this point, elections results were often open to corruption through practices including bribery and treating of electors, and intimidation and threatening of voters.

In early-19th-century Britain very few people had the right to vote. A survey conducted in 1780 revealed that the electorate in England and Wales consisted of just 214,000 people - less than 3% of the total population of approximately 8 million. In Scotland, the electorate was even smaller: in 1831 a mere 4,500 men, out of a population of more than 2.6 million people, were entitled to vote in parliamentary elections.

Large industrial cities like Leeds, Birmingham, and Manchester did not have a single MP between them, whereas 'rotten boroughs' such as Dunwich in Suffolk (which had a population of 32 in 1831) were still sending two MPs to Westminster.

During August 1819, at one gathering in St Peter's Field, Manchester, when working class people from towns and villages around the area, gathered to demand political representation at a time when only wealthy landowners could vote, developed into a bloody episode, a blot on the British establishment's reputation, to be remembered for generations to come. An army numbering 600 Hussars, several hundred infantrymen; an artillery unit with two six-pounder guns, 400 men of the Cheshire cavalry and 400 special constables, paid for by the affluent locals and mill owners waited to attack. The first fatality was a child, his young mother carrying him in her arms was knocked down, her baby son fell from her arms to be trampled to death under the horse's hooves. Manchester magistrates ordered the Hussars on horseback, armed with sabres and clubs to storm the crowd. An estimated 18 people died including four women and a child from sabre cuts and trampling and more than 650 were seriously injured. The crowd of peaceful

306

protesters, many wearing their Sunday best clothes, who had gathered to hear speeches were attacked by the troops, who instantly dashed at full gallop amongst the people, hacking their way up to the hustings, slashing and trampling down women and children under thundering hooves. After the 'Peterloo Massacre', as this shameful, infamous incident became known, the government passed a series of repressive measures, and parliamentary reform still seemed a distant prospect.

Voters based their choice of MP on personal or local issues. Many were bribed and others were afraid to vote against the wishes of the local landowner.
• There were no organised political parties in the modern sense. There were parties called 'Whigs' and 'Tories', but MPs tended to group and regroup into Whigs or Tories according to the issues being debated.
• Voting was not secret. Voters called out the name of the person they were voting for, and this was entered in a Poll Book.
• MPs were not paid a salary. They had to own property worth at least £300 a year so they could afford to work as an MP for free. Parliamentary Elections who could vote:
• All men owning or renting property worth at least £10 a year could vote which excluded six adult males out of seven from the voting process.
• In the counties, men could vote if they owned property worth more than 40 shillings a year or rented land worth £50 a year.

Anne Lister was deeply involved with political matters though being a woman she could not vote herself. Her relentless support of the Tory candidates caused her a great deal of trouble in a volatile period in history. It was during this period that the anti-tory lampooning of Anne Lister in connection with her obvious masculinity came to a head with an invitation to an all-male dinner and coincided with the violence and intimidation taking place throughout England and Wales.
Before the Great Reform Act of 1832, one in every ten men had the vote After the Act one in every five.

For men, land ownership did not only confer status; the landowner was also proprietor, employer, landlord and client. In a constitution, where the franchise was based on land and property, the more substantial landowners assumed their place as the natural leaders of the community.

Both the Conservative and Liberal parties put an equal emphasis on the importance of office holding; but the Conservative candidates were weighted in favour of land-owning and military service, whilst the Liberals had a bias in favour of industry. These descriptors of the two parliamentary parties continued until the 1870s. lack of empathy for the conditions of the working classes in the industrial towns of the West Riding, appears almost to be a Whig electioneering tactic. The rights of the manufacturers and merchants were emphasised the legitimate claims of the unenfranchised were belittled.

The three parliamentary reform Acts introduced in 19th-century Britain (in 1832, 1867 and 1884 respectively) satisfied moderate reformers rather than radicals. The Prime Minister, Lord Grey, supported reform to 'prevent the necessity of revolution' and was responsible for the first (or 'Great') Reform Act of 1832.
The Tory politician Lord Derby described the second Reform Act (1867) as 'a leap in the dark'. And yet only two in every five Englishmen had the vote in 1870. Even the third Reform Act (1884) - which enfranchised all male house owners in both urban and rural areas and added 6 million people to the voting registers - fell some way short of introducing universal manhood suffrage.

Treating, bribery, influencing and intimidating were commonplace practices well into the late 19th century, with candidates often attempting to influence voters through gifts of alcohol, food, indirect payments and employment arrangements. Due to the lack of a secret ballot, voters could be dismissed from employment or evicted from housing if they were known to have voted the wrong way.

The Exclusion of Woman Voters:
Women, despite the symbolic ending of their notional right to vote, were enthused rather than discouraged by the Reform Act and discovered methods by which they could participate in politics. In theory, women could vote in parliamentary elections before 1832 as county and many borough franchises were based on property ownership.

The change brought by the 1832 Reform Act was the formal exclusion of women from voting in Parliamentary elections, specified for the first time, that the right to vote was restricted to 'male persons. In 1835 the Municipal Corporations Act also excluded women, disenfranchising many who had previously voted for town councils. The focus on these two significant pieces of legislation has led many to conclude that the early to mid-nineteenth century witnessed a masculinisation of the public sphere.

In the early 20th century, there were two main groups active in the campaign for women's suffrage, a term used to describe the right to vote. These two groups were the 'suffragists' who campaigned using peaceful methods such as lobbying, and the 'suffragettes' who were determined to win the right to vote for women by any means. Their militant campaigning sometimes included unlawful and violent acts which attracted much publicity.

Women who owned property gained the right to vote in the Isle of Man in 1881, and in 1893, women in the then British colony of New Zealand were granted the right to vote. Most major Western powers extended voting rights to women in the interwar period, including Canada (1917), Britain and Germany (1918), Austria and the Netherlands (1919) and the United States (1920). Notable exceptions in Europe were France, where women could not vote until 1944, Greece (1952), and Switzerland (1971).

Pickford, Frances

Friend of Anne Lister who was born at Royton Hall in 1778, third daughter of Joseph Pickford. Little is known about her childhood. In 1796 Joseph Pickford inherited Marsden and Milnsbridge estates and the surname of his maternal uncle, William Radcliff. The Listers became friends and in-laws bringing Anne into contact with Frances who by the 1830's was living in Bath at a house named 'Tylehurst' in Sion Hill. Frances owned a great deal of property and ran a money lending enterprise and building speculator in Bath and Bristol. At the grade old age of 83 she died in Bath, her last request that her estate be left to her surviving sister Mary. Frances had requested that she should be buried "without ostentation and with as little expense as may be consistent with my station in life".

Priestley, William
(1779-1860) Son of John Priestley and cousin of Ann Walker. Born in Sowerby (8th October 1779). Baptised at St Peter's Church, Sowerby (24th November 1779). He was a friend of Anne Lister, and his wife Elizabeth (Paley) became a close confidante.
He was Deputy Lieutenant / a wool clothier, an eminent local musician, antiquary & literary figure / an enthusiastic music-collector.
He held musical evenings at his home until 1817.
In 1817, he founded the Halifax Quarterly Choral Society. He presented a manuscript score of Mozart's arrangement of Judas Maccabaeus to the Society. He had acquired to manuscript from a Moravian settlement north-east of Dresden.
They lived at New House, Lightcliffe and Wray Wood House. Around 1835, William & Eliza moved to Thorp Arch, where they both died. His collection of choral works, music, and books were bequeathed to Halifax Parish Church and the Halifax Literary & Philosophical Society.

Radicals
A political group that took a stance for the right to vote, freedom of the press and many other issues. Radical wanted largescale, rapid change in society.
Nineteenth-century Britain was governed by an aristocratic, propertied elite, another political world existed in which large numbers of people, mainly but not exclusively drawn from the middling ranks of society, were able to influence the decisions taken

by the ruling elite and were often able to act independently of them. A century of political, social, and economic changes had combined to create a growing body of opinion critical of the power and the policies of the aristocratic elite. A century of commercial expansion and population growth created towns in which moderately prosperous men had learned to exercise increasing control over their own lives. Urban growth produced an expanding middle class whose davening wealth and improved education inspired demands for greater social status and increased political influence. Political weakness had economic consequences as the burden of taxation was steadily shifted from the shoulders of the great landowners onto those who produced, sold, used, or purchased many items of popular consumption.

Raine, William

Eliza Raine's father was appointed an Assistant Surgeon on 23rd February 1764. He became Head Surgeon, after the death of Thomas Davis, on 30th April 1788, and two years later became the third member of the Medical Board, when Mr. Duffin was reduced from that position. On 14th February 1794, Alexander Anderson, one of the Presidency Surgeons at Madras, brought against Raine certain grave charges of neglect of duty. Raine requested a trial by Court-martial, and on 21st February was placed under arrest. I have not seen any record of the result, but, as he was not removed from his position, presumably he was acquitted. In 1796 Raine lost his seat at the Medical Board, when it was reduced to two members, but continued to be Head Surgeon of the General Hospital. He again succeeded to the Medical Board in the following year when Lucas died. He went on furlough in 1800, and died on board the 'Asia', on his passage home, on 7th July 1800.
Taken from the Indian Medical Gazette P397

Rawson, Christopher

(1777-1849) was the eldest son of John Rawson. His father disinherited him when he rejected the family's banking business and ran away to sea. In 1805, he distinguished himself whilst serving as Chief Officer on the East India Company's ship the 'Exeter' fighting the French in the China Seas. He returned to become an important and one of the most powerful men in Halifax.

He became a magistrate and banker in charge of the Huddersfield branch of Rawson's Bank. Deputy Lieutenant for the West Riding, a member of a Committee supporting those affected by the Luddites (1813) he was a landowner and industrialist, with an impatient temper and no scruples when it comes to abusing his influence. He married Mary Anne, daughter of Thomas Brooks of Great George Street, Westminster. They resided at Stoney Royd, Halifax. Hope Hall, Halifax. They did not have children. Died 6 May 1849 in Halifax, Yorkshire, England. Buried at Holy Trinity Church, Halifax.

In 1810, when a man forged a £250 bill in the name of Rawson's bank, Christopher apprehended the man single-handedly, and the culprit was subsequently executed. Christopher was offered a knighthood by George 111, but declined on the basis that he felt he was not wealthy enough to live up to the title. In 1811, he became a partner in Rawson's Bank and was the first Chairman, he remained in that position until 1843 when the Bank became the Halifax & Huddersfield Union Banking Company. He had interests in several local coal mines, and this made him a business rival of Anne Lister who claimed that he raided her coal mines.
Siblings:
Rawson Stansfield born 1778 in Halifax.
Rawson Grace Elizabeth (Waterhouse) (1780-1849), married 3 Jun 1817 in Walkington, Yorkshire, England,
William Henry Rawson (1781-1865) A landowner and woollen manufacturer at Triangle. He was involved in the family banking business and was Chairman of the Halifax and Huddersfield Union Banking Company 1856-1864. In 1813, he was a member of a committee supporting those affected by the Luddites.
Rawson John JP
Rawson, Mary Ann born 26 Jul 1785 in Halifax.
Rawson Jeremiah (1787-18390 He had a copperas (shale, coal substitute) production business at Cinder Hill and Exley. Around 1836, he became a cloth manufacturer at Old Lane Mill, Halifax. He subscribers to John Horner's book Building in the Town & Parish of Halifax [1835],
Rawson Ellen (Empson) (1791-1884) She was an acquaintance of Anne Lister

Rawson Thomas Samuel (1793-1860) He was a merchant, and he was also involved in mining, with interests in mining and anthracite in South America and Australia, and
Rawson Emma (Saltmarsh) (1796-1834) friend of Anne Lister, although Anne considered her "*vulgar*".
Rawson Catherine *(1803-1885)* daughter of Stansfield Rawson. Married Thomas Worsley on 20 June 1842 - Close friend of Ann Walker. She died in 1885 at Downing Lodge, Cambridge. Thomas was born in 1797. He was the son of Rev. George Worsley and Anne Cayley. He studied at the University of Cambridge, England and became a clergyman. He returned to Cambridge University where he was appointed Vice-Chancellor and Master of Downing College. He also died in 1885.

Retreat, The
The Retreat in York led the world in the humane treatment of the mentally ill. It was founded by William Tuke and the Society of Friends (Quakers) in 1792 and opened in 1796. After seeing the appalling conditions and treatment of patients. Incompetent financial management the institution was struggling and conditions for the patients were poor.   Close examination of the steward's books made it clear that deaths had been concealed.   Ill-treatment of patients was widely accepted in the asylums of the time. Many believed that 'lunatics' were insensitive to hot and cold, sub-human, like animals.   Beatings and confinement were accepted practice, as was underfeeding patients.
An innovation was 'The Appendage', a half-way house 'for those needing least supervision'. This radical approach began a series of reforms and a greater understanding of mental health in the nineteenth century and psychiatry textbooks today still refer to the Retreat.

St Anne in the Grove
The present church building, in the vicinity of the older chapel, was consecrated in October 1819 and designed by Thomas Taylor (also the architect of St Mary the Virgin, Luddenden) in a restrained Gothic Revival style. The church is known as St Anne's-in-the-Grove and is said to have inspired Emily Bronte in her writings. Spinster Marian Lister moved to the estate she inherited at Skelfler, Market Weighton in 1836. Marian died on the 6th of August 1882

aged 84. Burial 9th August at St Anne in the Grove Churchyard Southoram, Calderdale, West Yorkshire.

Stump Cross Inn
The Stump Cross Inn is located at Stump Cross in Shibden Valley, close to Anne's home Shibden Hall and part of her Estate. Anne bought the Masons who completed her gatehouse, she drank there in Summer of 1837.

Sutcliffe Wood farm
Owned by the Lister's and had a tenant, the Rev Sutcliffe Snowden who officiated at Charlotte Bronte's wedding.

Vallance, Mary
The twenty-five-year-old daughter of a Kent brewing family was a regular visitor at the Norcliffe home Langton Hall. Miss Vallance became an interest of Anne Lister's who wrote in her journal of March 8th, 1821 *"I care not about my connection with Miss V. She gave me licence enough"*.

Walker, Aunt Ann
Elderly Aunt Ann Walker, 'Miss Cliff Hill', was still living at Cliffe Hill in 1841. She would die there on 29th October 1847 aged 90 and buried, as all the Lightcliffe Walkers were in St Matthew's churchyard.

Washington, Samuel
Land agent to the Walker family of Crow Nest and land agent / steward for Anne Lister at nearby Shibden Hall. He was also recorded as having been a "schoolmaster and land surveyor" in 1822. He lived in Lightcliffe most of his life. The previous steward to the Lister family of Shibden Hall had been James Briggs. But he became seriously ill in the summer of 1832 as recorded in Anne Lister's diary. Samuel Washington was the youngest son of James Washington and his wife Esther Mann. Samuel's wife Hannah Washington 'of Lidgate' died in July 1852 and her husband Samuel Washington died in November 1857. Both he and Hannah were buried in St Matthew's Churchyard.

SHIBDEN HALL RECORDS

The Shibden Hall manuscripts are divided into seven main classes comprising: -

Estate records relating to individual Lister properties: Broadgates and Bairstow in Skircoat; Butterworth End in Norland; Dove House, Little Ireland Farm, Sougholme and Upper and Lower Place in Southowram; Highroyd, Lower Brea, Over Brea, Scout Hall, Shibden Mill and Will Royd in Northowram; Hill Top, Mytholm, Southedges and Roydlands, Spouthouse, Sutcliffe Wood, Wood Top and Yew Trees in Hipperholme cum Brighouse; Northgate House in Halifax; and Shibden Hall (including accounts), 1362-1925.

Records relating to the whole estate, including Shibden Hall estate accounts, rentals, leases, valuations and bonds for properties in Halifax, Crow Nest, Hipperholme, Lightcliffe, Northowram and Southowram; estate maps, plans of proposed alterations to Shibden Hall, photographs and drawings of the family and estate; coal mining agreements, leases and accounts of coal mined and sold from the Shibden Hall and Listerwick Collieries; accounts of clay and brickworks, accounts and agreements relating to stone quarries, 1629-1933

Family papers, including personal papers, legal papers, funeral notes, sermons, accounts, household, bills, notebooks and receipts, and plans relating to the Calder and Hebble Navigation, 1366-1933

Local deeds relating to non-Lister properties in Hipperholme, Halifax (including election cartoons) Lightcliffe, Northowram, Ovenden, Skircoat, Southowram, Sowerby, Bradford, Embsay and Warley c1318-1892

Non-Yorkshire deeds relating to properties acquired by the Listers through marriage in Buckinghamshire, Cambridge, Essex, Kent,

Lancashire, Lincolnshire, London, Nottinghamshire, Suffolk, and Surrey, 1473-1880

Abstracts and transcripts from local deeds, rentals and surveys, Wakefield manor court rolls, papers of the Pilgrimage of Grace, pleadings and depositions in the Duchy of Lancaster, Star Chamber and Exchequer Court, records relating to the woollen trade, ulnagers' subsidies, wills and inventories, [1250-c1800] 19th century.

Correspondence, including letters relating to the Wakefield and Halifax turnpike road; letters of the Revd John Lister, 1717-1759; General Sir William Fawcett, 1725-1806; Dr David Hartley, 1735-1756; Francis Fawkes, 1738-1759; Joah Aked, 1757-1812; Captain Jeremy Lister, 1770-1828; Anne Lister (correspondence with friends and family, account books, journals partly in a letter by letter code, travel notes and passport), 1800-1840; Dr John Lister, 1827-1884; John Lister MA 1860-1933

In all cases, papers relating to the same subject are arranged together. For example, wills are not placed together as one class but are classified with the property to which they refer; accounts relating to coal mines are not with the other accounts but constitute a sub-section of the Coal Mining section.

ACKNOWLEDGEMENTS

I would like to say how much I have enjoyed my journey through history as I researched the life of this fascinating, bold spirited woman. Writing about a real person, especially one so pivotal in the history of woman's identities has been a real pleasure and awakened me to many intriguing facts that I previously knew nothing about.

After watching Sally Wainwrights' marvellous adaptation, and the magnificent portrayal of the central character by Suranne Jones I was spellbound and eager to learn more of a life lived 220 years ago. Whilst writing my first addition my perception of Anne Lister's character continually changed, but the emerging new findings have given me a new understanding. There have been more surprises after several newly research documents were revealed in 2020. My acknowledgement of her achievements and dedicated persistence to live her life as she wanted to live it, is evident I feel.

At each revelation I was drawn into her story and rich lifestyle. Thank you to all the people who worked painstakingly and tirelessly on the original journal documents. Work on the diaries and letters continues, and new information reveals more fascinating facts to add to the life and times of Anne Lister.

A special thank you to Helena Whitbread for her dedication in deciphering the fascinating account of one remarkable woman's life and the way in which she selflessly shares the knowledge and intense passion for the subject matter, and all her help she so generously gave me.

To Sally Wainwright for her dramatization to bring this unique character to the attention of the populous. In my opinion, no one could have done it better; and to those who worked alongside her to make that visual dramatization so enthralling; and to the actors who gave such wonderful performances bringing the characters to life, and for making them so fascinating and real, which in turn gave me the enthusiasm to learn more about Anne Lister and write this book.

Special thanks to West Yorkshire Archive Service Calderdale, Central Library and Archives, Square Road, Halifax, for their help and information I received.

I would like to thank Simon my publisher who gave me such great advice and guidance and for undertaking this venture. To Elaine for all her work editing and producing the book ready for printing and her moral support. To Joe, my grandson who was enthusiastic for me continue with this project.

Printed in Great Britain
by Amazon